BY HONOR
BOUND

BY HONOR BOUND

TWO NAVY SEALS, THE MEDAL OF HONOR,
AND A STORY OF EXTRAORDINARY COURAGE

TOM NORRIS AND MIKE THORNTON

WITH DICK COUCH

WITH A FOREWORD BY SENATOR BOB KERREY

ST. MARTIN'S PRESS ⚏ NEW YORK

BY HONOR BOUND. Copyright © 2016 by Tom Norris, Mike Thornton, and Dick Couch. Foreword copyright © 2016 by Bob Kerrey. Preface copyright © 2016 by Drew Dix. Introduction copyright © 2016 by Dick Couch. All rights reserved. Printed in the United States of America. For information, address St. Martin's Press, 175 Fifth Avenue, New York, N.Y. 10010.

www.stmartins.com

Designed by Omar Chapa

Maps courtesy of W. Robert Singleton Jr.

Library of Congress Cataloging-in-Publication Data

Names: Norris, Tom (Thomas R.), 1944– author. | Thornton, Mike (Michael E.), 1949– author. | Couch, Dick, 1943– author.
Title: By honor bound : two Navy SEALs, the Medal of Honor, and a story of extraordinary courage / Tom Norris and Mike Thornton, with Dick Couch; with a forward by Senator Bob Kerrey.
Description: New York : St. Martin's Press, 2016. | Includes index.
Identifiers: LCCN 2016001120 | ISBN 978-1-250-07059-3 (hardcover) | ISBN 978-1-4668-8073-3 (e-book)
Subjects: LCSH: Norris, Tom (Thomas R.), 1944– | Thornton, Mike (Michael E.), 1949– | Vietnam War, 1961–1975—Personal narratives, American. | Vietnam War, 1961–1975—Biography. | United States. Navy. SEALs—Biography. | Medal of Honor—Biography.
Classification: LCC DS557.5 .N67 2016 | DDC 959.704/345092273—dc23
LC record available at http://lccn.loc.gov/2016001120

Our books may be purchased in bulk for promotional, educational, or business use. Please contact your local bookseller or the Macmillan Corporate and Premium Sales Department at 1-800-221-7945, extension 5442, or by e-mail at MacmillanSpecial Markets@macmillan.com.

First Edition: May 2016

10 9 8 7 6 5 4 3 2 1

In Memory of a Great American
My Daddy
Edwin G. Thornton
A Husband, Father, Grandfather, Mentor
My Hero

MIKE THORNTON

Dedicated to the families and loved ones of those brave men who
gave their lives in the rescue of Bat 21.
They were the true heroes.

And to all those who serve today to keep us free.

TOMMY NORRIS

CONTENTS

AUTHORS' NOTE

This is a true story, though some names and details have been changed.

ACKNOWLEDGMENTS

A book like this, with some of the seminal events taking place close to a half century ago, does not get done without the help of a great many people—former teammates, shipmates, platoon mates, training cadre, colleagues, and friends. The authors and their narrator would like to thank the following individuals for their help with this book. Your input, support, recollections, and above all, your humor, are sincerely appreciated. In no particular order:

Craig Dorman, Charles "Sandy" Prouty, Mike Jukoski, Nguyen Kiet, General Louis Wagner, Terry Moy, Dick Flanagan, Bill Woodruff, Ryan McCombie, Hal Kuykendall, Ed Moore, Chuck Zedner, Dr. Wally Grand, Gary Stubblefield, Dick Marcinko, Norm Carley, Mark Falkey, Wayne Manis, Cecil Moses, Bob Sligh, Rear Admiral Gary Bonelli, Ron Rand, Chris Seger, Carol Fleisher, and Darrel Whitcomb.

And a special note of thanks to our brother special operators Bob Kerrey and Drew Dix. Your kind words set the tone for this effort and are much appreciated.

And finally, we would be remiss if we failed to mention our teammates at St. Martin's Press, to include Charles Spicer and April Osborn, who have stood solidly with us on this literary combat deployment.

FOREWORD

Tom Norris, Mike Thornton, Dick Couch, and I are all friends. We are about the same age. We all served in the United States Navy, volunteered for Underwater Demolition Training, and were selected to be Navy SEALs. We all came of age in Vietnam. Other than having comparable respiratory, digestive, and central nervous systems, we have little in common. By that I mean, they conducted multiple SEAL combat operations. I managed to get wounded after only a few weeks in Vietnam, so my time in that war was relatively short.

I left the University of Nebraska School of Pharmacy in June 1965 and went to work. I finished the six hours remaining to earn my degree through a correspondence program and a course on the Bible at a small college on the Iowa side of the Missouri River. This prompted the federal government to change my draft status, give me a free physical exam, and inform me I would soon be offered an opportunity to serve in the United States Army. To be drafted into the Army was ticket to a year of duty in Vietnam—sometimes a one-way ticket.

I had just finished reading Herman Wouk's World War II clas-sic, *The Caine Mutiny*. I fell in love with the idea of commanding a destroyer at sea and volunteered for service in the fleet reserve of the United States Navy. At Officer Candidate School I was introduced to Underwater Demolition Teams and volunteered immediately, mostly for the challenge and the possibility that my stock would rise with women my age. I was naive about a lot of things, including the notion that women would be attracted to a Navy frogman.

All of this is to say I became a Navy SEAL by accident, not by intent. And were it not for the rapid escalation of the Vietnam War and a growing demand for SEAL team platoons that coincided with my completion of Underwater Demolition Training, it is un-likely I would have seen duty with SEAL Team One. That I would later be selected to receive the Congressional Medal of Honor was a confluence of the fortunes of war, a combat operation that did not go as planned, and the need to recognize the contributions of Navy SEALs in Vietnam. I was the first SEAL to be so honored.

My time in the war was measured in weeks before I was wounded and sent to the Philadelphia Naval Hospital. What I know about war I learned recovering from those injuries; my teach-ers were men like John Zier, Jim Crotty, and Lewis Puller Jr. They taught me a great deal about courage, resilience, and the tragedy that is war. Along the way I became an expert on pain management and rehabilitation. It was a much longer and more difficult journey than becoming a Navy SEAL. Past that, I will leave the war stories to men like Dick Couch, Mike Thornton, and Tommy Norris.

Thanks to Dick, we have two great stories from that ill-fated war. Two stories, two heroes—and the actions for which these two SEALs went above and beyond in their service to their nation and to their brothers in the close fight. And their gallant service came in the waning moments of a war that was all but lost. In war, the moment of retreat can sometimes be more dangerous than during an attack. And in 1972, when these two stories took place, America was in full retreat in Vietnam.

Tommy Norris's heroism is remarkable to me because his actions were taken to save lives. He didn't suddenly rush across a field to save a friend; mortal danger was not unexpectedly thrust on him. He planned and executed three exceptionally risky operations knowing that the odds were not in his favor and knowing that if he succeeded, it was unlikely the story would ever be told. These were dangerous missions, excursions behind enemy lines that called for a courageous volunteer. Having succeeded in saving one downed airman, he could have elected not to return; he could have said it was too dangerous, too risky. But he went back again—and again a third time. He did much, much more than duty required. And he preferred the secrecy that kept most from knowing what he had done.

Tommy Norris doesn't tell his story as if the war were only about Americans. He correctly places a higher value on the sacrifice and heavy burden borne by our South Vietnamese allies. He says about them that "they'd known nothing but war for their entire life, and this mission, difficult as it might be, was just another day for them."

Mike Thornton's extraordinary bravery is more muscular, and like Mike himself, bigger than life. He saved Tommy's life and the lives of two Vietnamese frogmen who were also wounded during a reconnaissance of the naval base on the mouth of a river that was the legal boundary that separated North and South Vietnam. I know of no other individual who could have or would have done what Mike did that day. As Mike's story unfolded, I kept asking myself, "Holy shit, how did he do that?" Mike, Tommy, and those Vietnamese frogmen should all be dead today. They aren't, because Mike Thornton did the impossible. Whenever I read or hear the phrase "a man among men," I think of Mike Thornton.

This book, their stories, has caused me to reflect back on my war and the men I was privileged to call my SEAL brothers. I went off to war and came home very quickly. Dick Couch completed his SEAL deployment and left the Navy. In 1972, while I was still in rehab and Dick was a young case officer at the CIA, Tommy and Mike were still fighting—Tommy on his second rotation, Mike on his third. Had the war lasted several more years, they would have gone back again and again. Like their South Vietnamese allies, they were committed for the duration. Only war's end or their combat wounds could keep them from returning to the fight. In the words of James Michener from *The Bridges at Toko-Ri*, "Where do we get such men?" They are indeed true warriors.

Both Tommy and Mike received the Congressional Medal of Honor. Both richly deserved it. But there was something about Mike's mission that caught my attention beyond the details of his heroism and the gallant fight that he and Tommy waged that terrible day. They got into serious trouble because they were lost. Of course, these were the days before GPS and satellite phones and smart bombs. But they were in the wrong place at the wrong time, and had limited ability to call for help. This caused me to wonder if this one battle wasn't a pretty good metaphor for the entire war.

—*Bob Kerrey*
Medal of Honor recipient
Former governor and senator from Nebraska

PREFACE

I'm honored and proud to call Tommy and Mike my brothers. The term "brother" is used often by those of us who serve in the special operations community. "Brother" in the special operations world has a singular meaning because only those who've answered that calling can know and understand the sacrifices made by special operators and our families on a routine basis. Much like our blood brothers and sisters who know us well, such as our vulnerabilities and weaknesses, battle buddies also know our strengths and weaknesses. Those of us in the Medal of Honor Society often refer to each other as brothers, because no one else can imagine what it's like to wear the Medal of Honor or, more to the point, the burden of wearing it. We share the knowledge of the strengths and weaknesses of our fellow recipients. Tommy and Mike can certainly call themselves brothers—brother SEALs and brother MoH recipients. Yet they have a third qualifier. They shared the danger and mixed their blood on the battlefield; they faced death and came through it together, as brothers should.

I met Mike in the early 1970s soon after he received the Medal of Honor from President Richard Nixon. Mike was not just the latest recipient from the Vietnam War; he was one of the youngest. Since I had received the Medal more than two years before and was at the ripe old age of twenty-eight, I thought I should help him become acquainted with the ways of the Medal of Honor Society. In those days the SEAL community probably consisted of fewer than four hundred in only two teams—SEAL Team One on the West Coast and SEAL Team Two on the East Coast. Because I knew so many of the older SEALs and operated with them in Vietnam and elsewhere, I thought I would lend a special welcome to Mike. We became good friends, or should I say brothers, because we shared the same experiences in the special operations community. Now we were brother recipients and members of the greatest and closest-knit organization in the country, or perhaps in the world—the Medal of Honor Society.

A very unique characteristic of the society is that except for the few older recipients whose World War II stories were in movies and had become part of our upbringing, not many of us were aware of the actions for which other recipients had received their Medal. At society events, we seldom sit around and tell stories, at least not about ourselves. Only when Tommy finally recovered from his extensive head wounds and was able to come to the Medal of Honor convention in Houston did I learn his and Mike's story—that Mike had received his Medal for saving Tommy's life on that ill-fated mission along the Demilitarized Zone in Vietnam. At the time of the Houston event, Tommy had been approved for the Medal of Honor, but it was not yet public knowledge. Tommy, though he was and is shy and reserved, fit right in.

What became immediately apparent to me in Houston was that the term "brother," when Mike and Tommy use it in referring to each other, went much deeper. For the first time in modern history, the Medal of Honor was awarded to a recipient for saving the life of another recipient. These two men were brothers by having served together in high-risk combat; now they share the honor, and the burden, of wearing the Medal of Honor. This unique distinction alone makes their story compelling and, after close to a half decade, well worth the read. And what each of them did on the battlefield was simply incredible.

Now for the first time in print, we can learn about the incredible lives of these two exceptional men. Like true siblings in any family, they are so very different. They don't need to live near each other to be close. Each has gone his own way; each has lived on his own terms. Yet their lives are connected like those of true blood brothers. Each has experienced life's ups and downs and met its challenges head-on. Each knows the other's weaknesses and strengths. And, as brothers, between them there is trust and love.

I never served with either Mike or Tommy in combat, even though I would have been honored to have operated with these two Navy SEAL warriors. I have been around them enough over the years to know that to go on an operation with either of them would be one hell of a fight. And I'd be honored to fight alongside them. But that was another time, back in the day.

No matter what we accomplished in our distant past, the measure of a true hero is what you do with your life after you receive recognition. Tommy and Mike are true heroes, not just for what they did so many years ago but for what they are doing for the men and women who are serving us today. They gave of themselves in close combat, and they continue to give of themselves today.

I'm proud to call them my brothers.

—Drew Dix
Medal of Honor recipient

Drew Dix is one of my personal heroes. During the Tet Offensive of 1968, then Staff Sergeant Dix rallied the defenders of the provincial capital of Chu Phu in defense of the city. He repeatedly led South Vietnamese forces and an element of Navy SEALs to rescue civilians trapped in the city. In close to three days of intensive fighting, he saved a great many lives and helped to drive the enemy from this provincial capital. His actions during the defense of Chu Phu led to his Medal of Honor, the first enlisted Special Soldier to be so recognized. Drew is the author of *The Rescue of River City* and cofounder of the Center for American Values in Pueblo, Colorado. He continues to serve his nation. For more, see DrewDix.com.

—Dick Couch

INTRODUCTION

MY ROLE

On the cover of this book it says "with Dick Couch," and this is an apt description of my relationship with Tommy Norris and Mike Thornton. I was with them as SEAL teammates going back to the late 1960s—back when few people had even heard of Navy SEALs. I have been with them over the intervening years and as aging warriors we have periodically met to relive the battles of our youth in that long-forgotten war. But what these two American heroes did should never be forgotten. Their individual acts of courage are timeless, and they continue to serve as role models for today's operational SEALs. Therefore it is with no small sense of purpose that I am privileged to serve as narrator and help them tell their story. It's the story of two selfless American warriors who went back.

GOING BACK

It is deeply ingrained in our military culture that we leave no one behind. At great risk and against all odds, we will do anything and everything to save a fallen buddy or a captured comrade. Within the Navy SEAL teams, it is a sacred covenant. From day one in Basic Underwater Demolition/SEAL training, those aspiring to join this elite band of warriors are taught that you never, but never, leave a man behind. In a training regime that is demanding in the extreme, SEAL cadre instructors reserve their harshest punishments for a man who becomes separated from his swim buddy. In the SEAL teams, and indeed all special-operations components, it is axiomatic that a brother warrior is never abandoned.

The Congressional Medal of Honor is our nation's highest military decoration—reserved for those who at great personal risk go above and beyond the call of duty. It is no wonder that a great many of those who receive the Medal of Honor have earned this distinction because they went to the aid of another in peril. They went back.

This is the incredible story of two Navy SEALs who went back. One for a buddy, the other for a brother warrior he had never met. The actions of both represent the pinnacle of courage and selfless service.

THE MEN

In 1974 I was living in Northern Virginia just south of Old Town Alexandria. At the time I was a young case officer at the Central Intelligence Agency, risking my life daily—not spying for my country but commuting up the George Washington Parkway to CIA headquarters in Langley on my motorcycle. My wife and I had just bought an old home that needed a lot of work. For most of that first year I had a boarder who lived in the spare bedroom and helped me with the renovations in exchange for a place to live. He was only with us periodically, as he was in and out of Bethesda

Naval Hospital for cranial reconstructive surgery. His name was Tom Norris.

Tom and I first met in the fall of 1968 when we were two officer trainees enrolled in Basic Underwater Demolition/SEAL training. He had come from naval flight training, and I had come from duty aboard a Navy destroyer. We were both junior grade lieutenants, or "JGs." Following training, he went to SEAL Team Two, and I, after a short tour at Underwater Demolition Team 22, joined SEAL Team One. I got through Vietnam without a scratch. Tom was not so lucky. In the course of a running firefight along the so-called Demilitarized Zone that at the time separated North and South Vietnam, Tom was shot in the head. The round went through the orbit of his left eye and took out a good chunk of the left side of his skull. A mortal wound for sure, had it not been for a SEAL petty officer named Mike Thornton, who fought his way back to Tom's side and spirited him to safety. Mike and I were teammates at SEAL Team One.

One evening I asked Tom about the events of that day. We were both combat SEALs and for us, this was shop talk. Still, the details of a running firefight are difficult to recall, even without a serious head wound.

"We were being hard pressed by a large North Vietnamese Army force—probably a battalion. We'd been fighting for an hour or more among a series of sand dunes along the coast. I'd been on the radio trying to get some naval gunfire support, but I wasn't having much luck. I had one LAAW [light antiarmor weapon] rocket left and was getting ready to fire it. Then things went dark. The next thing I knew, Mike was by my side, kneeling over me.

" 'Can you run?' he said to me.

" 'I can run,' I told him, 'but I can't see.'

" 'Then let's go. We can't stay here.' "

Through a hail of enemy fire, Mike managed to get Tom off that beach, into the relative safety of the South China Sea, and into history.

While Tom was in and out of the hospital, and helping me to rebuild my house, Mike was awarded the Medal of Honor for his rescue of Tom. When Tom was later awarded the Medal of Honor for his previous rescue of two American airmen shot down behind enemy lines, these two gallant but separate combat actions became unprecedented. Never in the modern history of American combat arms and the storied lore of the Medal of Honor had a soldier, sailor, airman, or marine received the Medal for saving the life of another recipient.

Tom and I were classmates and suffered through the rite of passage that is Basic Underwater Demolition/SEAL training. Mike was a teammate. I remember Mike as a second class petty officer who worked in the team parachute loft and had a solid reputation as a SEAL operator. He also had a reputation as a guy who liked to raise hell and have a good time. So I knew these men before they entered the elite status that our nation reserves for its most distinguished warriors. Navy SEALs come in all shapes, sizes, and temperaments. Regarding those characteristics, I don't know of two more physically dissimilar "team guys" than Tom Norris and Mike Thornton. Yet there is something special, a no-quit grit, that makes them brothers—as young Navy SEALs during the close fight and to this day as aging brothers-in-arms. And the Medal of Honor has joined them at the hip. *By Honor Bound* is the story, in their own words, of these two unusual and remarkable American heroes. I was privileged to call them teammates back in the day. Today, they are friends. Now I'm honored to help them tell their story.

THE MEDAL

Before Tom and Mike begin to share their journey with you, it might help to learn something of this singular award, a medallion suspended by a star-spangled sky blue ribbon that these two men now wear only on formal occasions. It not only binds them to each other, but to the historical procession of our nation's greatest heroes.

The Medal of Honor has a curious history. The fledgling military of our new nation wanted to not be like its European counterparts, turned out in epaulettes, sashes, and decorations. For almost a century there were no decorations or medals awarded American soldiers, sailors, or marines. In the throes of the Civil War, Congress authorized a single medal to be struck, a medal for conspicuous gallantry—a medal to be awarded (to Union soldiers) for the highest order of courage and heroism. There were no other awards at that time, just this single award then called the Congressional Medal of Honor. Brevet General George Custer, perhaps the most heroic Union figure of the Civil War, never received this decoration. His brother, Tom, received the Medal of Honor—twice. It has been awarded to whole combat units. Over the years, other medals and decorations have become commonplace and worn in order of precedence on the left breasts of our warriors. Yet all are subordinate to the Medal of Honor. Since the First World War, the constraints and conditions for the Medal have become more formatted and elevated. Senator John McCain from Arizona had numerous political differences with Senator Bob Kerrey from Nebraska, but when Senator Kerrey enters a room, Senator McCain always rises to his feet. Bob Kerrey is a Medal of Honor recipient.

Nearly all recipients have been men. Only one woman has received the Medal: Nurse Mary Walker, for her courageous service during the Battle of Bull Run. Four hundred and seventy-one members of the greatest generation were awarded the Medal in World War II; 146 in Korea and 258 in Vietnam. Of those in Vietnam, fifteen were Navymen and three of those were Navy SEALs. As this book goes into print, there are seventy-nine living recipients of the Medal of Honor, with about two-thirds of those from the Vietnam era. Each year this select group becomes smaller. In twenty years, there may be but a handful.

Since the close of the Vietnam War, there have been nineteen recipients—two from the Battle of Mogadishu, four in Iraq, and thirteen in Afghanistan. Nine of the nineteen were posthumous awards. Five of the nineteen were special operators. Master Sergeant Gary Gordon and Sergeant First Class Randall Shughart, both Green Berets, died in Mogadishu in 1993 in a heroic stand of a downed Black Hawk helicopter—*the* Black Hawk Down. They fought to the death defending wounded crewmen trapped inside the crashed helo. SEAL Lieutenant Mike Murphy was leading a small patrol in the mountains of Afghanistan in June 2005 (the Lone Survivor incident) when they engaged an overwhelming Taliban force. He died while repeatedly exposing himself to enemy fire to call for help. In September 2006, SEAL Petty Officer Mike Monsoor perished during the Battle of Ramadi in Iraq. He died smothering an enemy hand grenade to save the lives of those SEALs fighting on either side of him (as portrayed in the film and book *Act of Valor,* and first detailed in the book *The Sheriff of Ramadi*). In a vicious firefight in Afghanistan in May 2008, Ranger Sergeant Leroy Petry had been shot multiple times through both legs. Yet he was able to grasp an incoming enemy grenade and toss it from the midst of his team. Though the exploding grenade cost him his hand and multiple shrapnel wounds, he saved the lives of his Ranger team fighting close by. Of these five special operators, only Leroy Petry survived to receive his Medal of Honor in person. It was awarded to him by President Obama on 12 July 2011.

On 12 November 2015, President Obama presented Army Captain Florent A. "Flo" Groberg with the Medal of Honor for gallantry during a combat action in Afghanistan in August of 2012. Captain Groberg, a French American, is the most recent living Medal of Honor recipient.

THE STORY

Over the last four decades, Tom and Mike have been approached numerous times to have their story told in print and on film. Each of these opportunities was met with obstacles. There have been issues of timing, authenticity, and personal commitments. In May 2014, Tom, Mike, and I found ourselves in Coronado, California, working on a PBS special on the history of the SEAL Teams—*Navy SEALs: Their Untold Story*, which first aired on Veterans Day, 11 November 2014. We talked about the business of getting their story into print—and that none of us was getting any younger. Warming to the subject, we agreed that now was the time. We also agreed that it would be Tom and Mike telling their own story and that I would serve as their narrator. So it is with no small amount of pride that I am honored to help these two authentic American heroes to make public their incredible story.

—Dick Couch
Ketchum, Idaho
March 2016

Valor is a gift.
Those having it never know for sure whether they have it
till the test comes.
And those having it in one test never know for sure
if they will have it when the next test comes.

—CARL SANDBURG

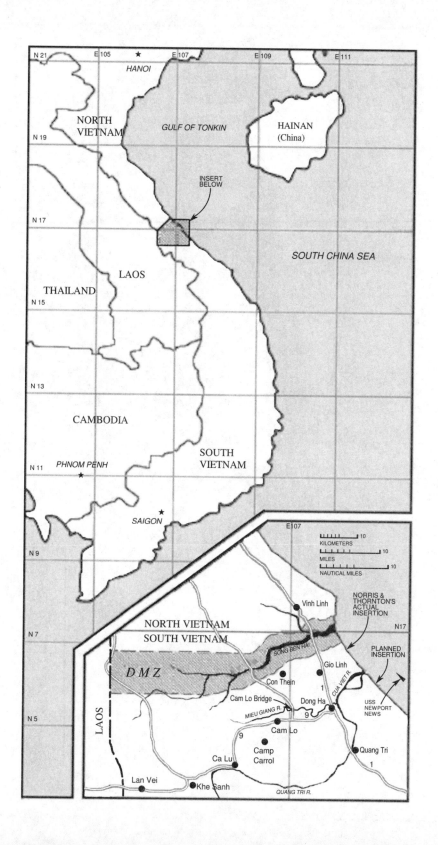

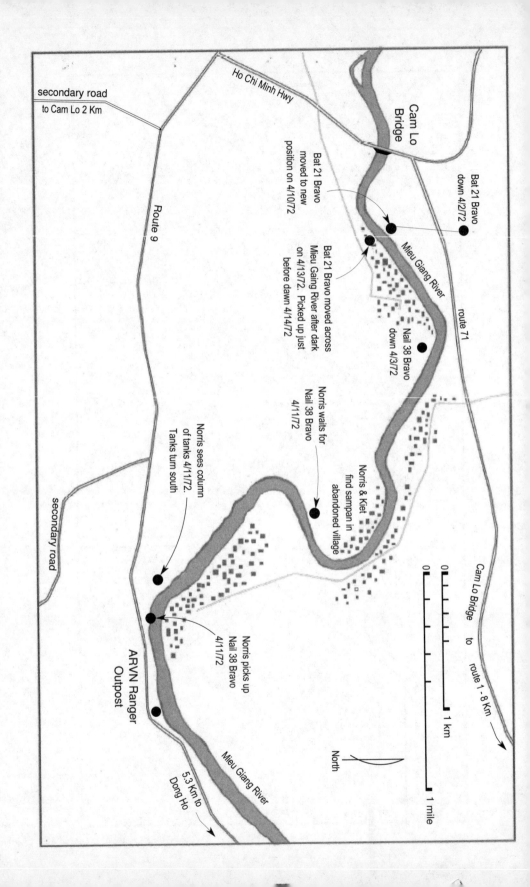

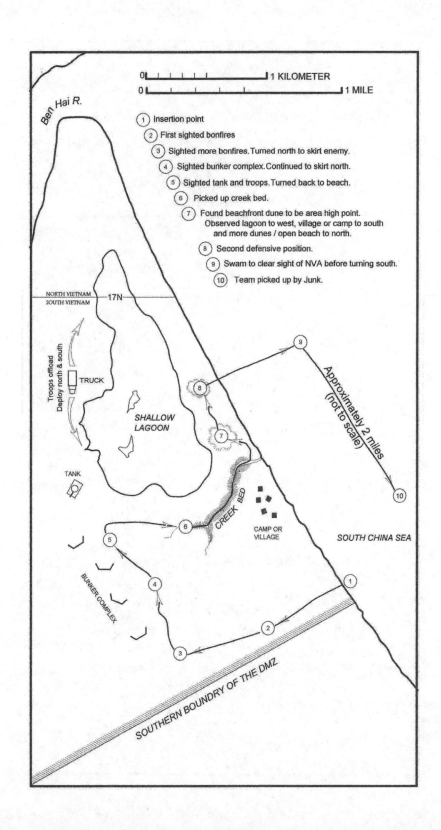

0 |___|___|___|___|___|___| 1 KILOMETER

0 |___|___|___|___| 1 MILE

(1) Insertion point

(2) First sighted bonfires

(3) Sighted more bonfires. Turned north to skirt enemy.

(4) Sighted bunker complex. Continued to skirt north.

(5) Sighted tank and troops. Turned back to beach.

(6) Picked up creek bed.

(7) Found beachfront dune to be area high point.
Observed lagoon to west, village or camp to south
and more dunes / open beach to north.

(8) Second defensive position.

(9) Swam to clear sight of NVA before turning south.

(10) Team picked up by Junk.

Ben Hai R.

NORTH VIETNAM
SOUTH VIETNAM   17N

Troops offload
Deploy north & south

TRUCK

SHALLOW
LAGOON

TANK

Approximately 2 miles
(not to scale)

CREEK BED

CAMP OR
VILLAGE

SOUTH CHINA SEA

BUNKER COMPLEX

SOUTHERN BOUNDRY OF THE DMZ

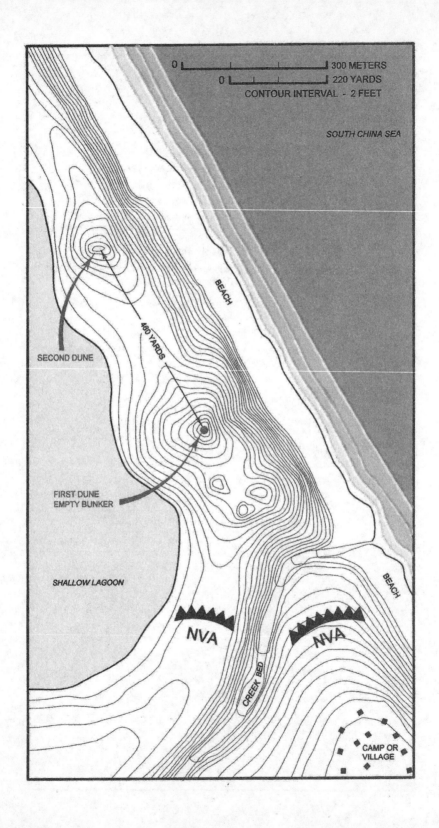

BY HONOR BOUND

PART ONE

BAT 21

MACVSOG

"It was never easy moving from one part of Vietnam to another," Tom Norris said of his time in-country. "You typically go down to the airstrip and see what's flying and where it might be going. If you're lucky, you find a helo or a fixed-wing going somewhere closer to where you want to go than where you are now. Usually, it's a UH-1 Huey helo. There's no schedule and no reservation number to call; it's all done by personal contact. You find the crew chief and see if he's got room for you, and if he says you've got a spot, you've got a spot. That day I was in the lower Mekong Delta checking on two of my Sea Commando teams on my way back to Da Nang and our home base, Camp Fay. But I had to make a stop at our headquarters in Saigon, the Military Assistance Command Vietnam, Studies and Observation Group—MACVSOG or, often, just SOG. This day I was lucky. Coming out of Bien Thuy, I found an Army Huey that was going straight to Tan Son Nhut Airbase in Saigon. The flight north was bouncy and erratic. We thrashed our way across the Rung

Sat Special Zone, trying to stay under the layer of thunderstorms moving in from the South China Sea and above the ground fire. After we set down, I thanked the crew chief, collected my pack and rifle, and set off for the main gate of the big airbase. No one knew when I would be getting in, so there was no car waiting for me. It was late morning on Sunday, April 9, 1972.

"Just outside the gate, I flagged down an open motorized tuk-tuk, one of the smoke-belching three-wheelers that crowd the streets of Saigon. Even on Sunday morning it was crowded as we fought our way through traffic to the MACVSOG compound. I was soaked—from sweat and the 100 percent humidity, and from the occasional rain shower that swept the Saigon area from time to time. At the gate to the compound, I said hello to the Vietnamese sentry who waved me through. Once inside, I headed down the hall to the SOG Maritime Branch.

"'Can I help you?' said an officer seated behind a battered desk.

"'I hope so, sir. I'm Tom Norris and I'm looking for Lieutenant Commander Dorman.'

"'Tom! I wasn't expecting you until tomorrow. Come in—come in.' He reached his hand across the desk. 'I'm Craig Dorman. Glad to finally meet you. Good flight?'

"'A little bumpy, but not bad. Welcome to Vietnam, sir.'

"'Thanks, I think, and it's just Craig. It's good to finally get here.'"

Tom took Dorman's hand, then dumped his pack and AK-47 in the corner of the small office and took a seat. Both men were dressed in rumpled jungle greens, a light, rip-stop cotton poplin uniform that was identical to the operational jungle cammies, but of a solid, olive drab color. Both had their last name stitched on the slanted right pocket of their blouses, "U.S. Navy" on the left. Dorman wore muted gold oak leaves on his collar points; Norris wore no rank.

Lieutenant Commander Craig Dorman had been in Vietnam for less than a week, and unlike the veteran Tom Norris, it was his first tour in-country. He had just taken over as the head of the Maritime Section of the Military Assistance Command, Vietnam, Studies and Observation Group. MACVSOG was a secret organization of U.S. and Vietnamese special operators with a generous sprinkling of CIA personnel. Established in January 1964, its shadowy mission was to conduct strategic reconnaissance, intelligence collection, and unconventional warfare operations in South *and* North Vietnam, Laos, and Cambodia. It was one of the few organizations associated with the U.S. military that was authorized to conduct cross-border operations.

Tom Norris was six months into his second tour in Vietnam. In this role, he was the primary American advisor to the Vietnamese Sea Commandos. His previous Vietnam rotation was as an assistant officer in charge, or OIC, of a SEAL platoon from SEAL Team Two. Now he was on a yearlong tour, having relieved a lieutenant from SEAL Team One named Sandy Prouty, who would later play an important part in Tom's post-Navy career.

During Tom's first combat tour as assistant platoon OIC, then Lieutenant Mike Jukoski was the OIC. "Tom and I were both new to SEAL Team Two," said Mike Jukoski. "I had a tour in the fleet and had been with Underwater Demolition Team 21 for several years before coming to Team Two. Tom was right out of basic SEAL training and, like me, he had been through SEAL Team Two cadre training. Tom had also been through Army Ranger School. We had a good ninety-day workup before we went over, and we had a good deployment. The platoon left for Vietnam in early 1970 and rotated back in August of that year. Since he and I were both on our first combat deployment, we were assigned some terrific enlisted SEAL operators."

"I can't say enough about our enlisted guys," echoed Tom. "Our platoon chief was Chief Cressini, one of my BUD/S instructors, and we had experienced operators like Jim Glasscock and Al Ashton with us. They were invaluable."

"Early on, Tommy developed a reputation for being aggressive in the field," Jukoski said. "But he always listened to his senior enlisted SEALs, and they liked him because he did listen to them. He was never known for going against their recommendations, and that was important. But he was aggressive. All this earned him the nickname of 'Nasty.' And as we all know, his personality is just the opposite of that."

Those of us who knew Tom Norris in SEAL training and in the teams remember him then as a quiet, serious, and unassuming officer. He liked to hang out with the guys, but if he drank at all, it was a single beer. And he never, but never, used foul language. As one SEAL put it, "I can just imagine Tom Norris, in a firefight, saying, 'Oh, heck. Here come those gosh-darn Viet Cong again.'"

During his first combat rotation with SEAL Team Two, Tom Norris established himself as a solid operator and combat leader. He also had his share of close calls on that first combat rotation. On one occasion, a Viet Cong fighter popped out of a spider hole in front of him and engaged him with an automatic weapon. Tom took several rounds through his clothes but amazingly all the bullets missed him. When he tried to return fire, his weapon jammed. The SEAL behind him, armed with a Stoner rifle, stepped to one side and laid down a base of fire, allowing the rest of his team to come on line and overrun the enemy position. For most of us, an event like this would have at least been the source of more than a few sleepless nights. For Tom Norris, it was just another close call. Another time, on a mission to capture an enemy fighter, Tom entered a hut and was jumped by an enemy fighter armed with a knife who was trying to escape through the doorway. The enemy fighter managed to slice him with his knife before Tom could kick him away and take him down with a barrel strike. It was a flesh wound that required only a few stitches, but definitely a combat wound. I knew that Tom had only one "official" Purple Heart, and it was not from this stab wound. I asked him about the incident.

"Heck," he said, "I didn't count that as a real combat wound. And I didn't really want anyone to know that I'd let a bad guy get in close enough to cut me with a knife."

This was vintage Tom Norris. He cared little for medals or recognition. He was all about the mission and getting the job done. And as I learned in talking to more than one Navy SEAL who was with him in combat, he simply did not seem to notice or react to personal danger.

Dorman's posting to the maritime billet at SOG was like receiving a set of orders to serve as a deck officer on the *Titanic*. The war in Vietnam was winding down, and winding down fast. Unit after unit of the U.S. military was being rotated out of the country. The last SEAL platoon had left Vietnam in December 1971. Those American SEALs remaining in Vietnam in the spring of 1972 served as advisors and were primarily engaged in the training of Vietnamese SEALs. Most of those, about a dozen of them, were assigned to the conventional Military Assistance Command, Vietnam (MACV). Only Norris and Dorman were assigned to MACVSOG. Tom's duties involved the training and operational tasking of the Vietnamese Sea Commandos, or Biet Hai. Craig Dorman's assignment as the MACVSOG maritime representative was primarily administrative and dealt with the turnover of maritime assets to the Vietnamese.

The Vietnamese SEALs under MACV were recruited and trained by U.S. Navy SEALs in a program that went by the name of Lien Doi Nguoi Nhai or LDNN. The literal translation: "soldiers who fight under the sea." The mission of the LDNNs was similar to that of the American SEALs, and they were assigned missions in South Vietnam proper. The Sea Commandos were assigned to MACVSOG, and were trained by American SEALs and Reconnaissance Marines. They operated in South Vietnam as well as in Laos, Cambodia, and, on occasion, North Vietnam. The training was similar, but the Sea Commandos could operate cross-border and often did.

MACVSOG itself was downsizing into a smaller, purely advisory unit to be known as the Strategic Technical Direct Assistance Team (STDAT) 158. Much of this wind-down to America's Vietnam adventure was opaque to men like Tom Norris and Craig Dorman. They were focused on day-to-day operations and training their Vietnamese counterparts and, when possible, running operations against the Viet Cong and North Vietnamese Army units that were coming south in increasing numbers. Tom traveled the length of Vietnam, but his home base was the MACVSOG training unit at Da Nang known as Camp Fay. On the SOG organizational chart, those at Camp Fay were listed as the Maritime Studies Group (SOG) 37, but their unclassified title was the Naval Advisory Detachment, Da Nang. Norris was in Saigon at the MACVSOG headquarters to personally brief Craig Dorman on the activities of the Camp Fay detachment. A great deal of the Studies and Observation Group's advisory activity was taking place in the northern part of South Vietnam, and Tom was responsible for Sea Commando/Biet Hai training and operations there.

"This was the first time I'd laid eyes on Craig," Tom said of their meeting, "but the SEAL teams back then were a close fraternity. There were less than four hundred of us and seldom more than a hundred and twenty of us in Vietnam at one time. And that included the platoons as well as the advisors. But in the spring of 1972, there were probably only a dozen or so of us left. And while I'd never met Craig, I knew he was a smart guy, a lot smarter than most of us. And now he was my boss and the senior naval officer at SOG, or what was left of the MACVSOG organization. We were just about to become the Strategic Technical Direct Assistance Team. Things were changing fast. The Americans and American units were disappearing. Every time you turned around, someone was rotating out and no one was coming in to take their place."

"I was the new guy in town, and I'd heard a lot about Tom Norris," Dorman said of his only SEAL subordinate. "I was a West Coast team guy, and Tom was East Coast. But he had a fine reputation both at SEAL Team Two and during his tour at SOG. Sandy Prouty, his predecessor, spoke highly of him. I couldn't wait to meet him."

Both Dorman and Norris were Navy SEALs, but their time in service could not have been more different. Tom Norris was an operational SEAL, and Craig Dorman was an academic. After graduating from Dartmouth, he joined the Navy and graduated with BUD/S Class 32 in 1964. Shortly after he was posted to Underwater Demolition Team 11, he was sent to graduate school at Monterey for his master's degree in oceanography, then on to MIT/Woods Hole Oceanographic

Institute for his Ph.D. Yet like many career-minded officers of that era, he needed a tour in the combat zone, in Vietnam, to improve his chances for promotion. More than that, it was the war of his generation of SEALs, and he, like most SEALs I knew at the time, wanted to be a part of it. Dorman would go on to serve as the commanding officer of Underwater Demolition Team 11 and, ultimately, return to academia. He served as the chief scientist at the Office of Naval Research and would retire with the rank of rear admiral. Following retirement, he would go on to serve as the director of the Woods Hole Oceanographic Institute. But in the spring of 1972, he was the new guy on the MACVSOG staff, trying to get his arms around the complexities of the secret MACVSOG organization and a waning but still vicious war.

The issues relating to East Coast SEALs and West Coast SEALs was still a big thing back then. The training was conducted on each coast to provide men for the Underwater Demolition Teams and SEAL Teams on that coast. Training was equally hard in both places, but different. Unlike today, there was no standardization of operating procedures, equipment, or advanced training. The Team One and Team Two SEALs talked to each other, though, and, being adaptable creatures, learned from each other. They melded well when called upon to work together in the battlespace. And there was mutual respect. Yet from their inception of the SEAL teams in 1962 up through the end of the Vietnam War, SEAL Team One in Coronado, California, and SEAL Team Two in Little Creek, Virginia, were two separate and distinct cultures.

"I had two objectives for my meeting with Tom. I needed to know what he was doing, both training-wise and operationally, and what I could do to support him. I had read his after-action reports, so I had some idea of what he was doing in Da Nang as well as down farther south. But I wanted to hear it from him. My direction was to downsize our presence in Vietnam and to expedite our turnover of assets and responsibilities to the Vietnamese. And in addition to getting Tom what he needed, I wanted his ideas on what we might do to help the South Vietnamese resist the recent NVA push into South Vietnam. Neither of us knew much about what was going on up north, but we knew a major battle in Quang Tri Province just south of the DMZ [Demilitarized Zone] was in progress."

It was called the Easter Offensive. In late March 1972, the North Vietnamese Army, or NVA, had just conducted a surprise push across the Demilitarized Zone into South Vietnam and had taken control of the northern portion of Quang Tri Province—the province just to the south of the DMZ. The South Vietnamese Army had fallen back to a defensive line along the southern banks of the Cam Lo and Cua Viet Rivers, temporarily halting the NVA advance. For this offensive, the North Vietnamese had committed literally their entire Army with a spearhead of some thirty thousand troops backed by large quantities of armor. The Americans did not have the troop strength to counter the offensive, but they did have the air power to make it very costly for the massed NVA troops. General Creighton Abrams ordered the B-52 strikes that effectively blunted the NVA advance, but the battle for Quang Tri and other northern provinces raged throughout the summer and into the fall. Eventually the NVA would capture the provincial capital of Quang Tri City. The city of Hue was threatened, as was Da Nang itself.

"There was not a whole lot I could tell Craig at the time," Tom recalled. "The NVA offensive caught us all by surprise, and it was a conventional push with tanks and massed infantry. We were primarily a reconnaissance force and were used to operating in very diverse, squad-sized units. The NVA came across the DMZ with armor and in division-sized strength. We Americans knew this war was winding down for us—we were going home. Those of us who were left were just advisors. We went out into the field with our Vietnamese, but it was now their show. At the time, I was anxious to get back up to Da Nang and Camp Fay, where most of my South Vietnamese Sea Commandos were at the time."

"Tom and I were the only two SEALs still attached to MACV-SOG," Craig Dorman said. "And Tom was by far the most experienced SEAL officer still operating in Vietnam. He was what we call a pass-down item. I had just relieved a marine major in the SOG maritime billet, and Tom was one of his subordinates. My direction at the time was to get ready to close things down, here in Saigon and at Camp Fay up in Da Nang. Then just as the SOG organization was downsizing, here comes this push from the north. So I was very interested in our operations up there. In addition to Tom's work with the Sea Commandos, we had a small fleet of fast patrol boats that were engaged in the interdiction of North Vietnamese coastal smuggling operations and taking our own agents up into North Vietnam. And on top of that, I was a very green SEAL officer. This was my first trip to Vietnam. Tom was the go-to SEAL at MACVSOG, so I was glad to finally meet him."

ESCAPE AND EVADE

Unknown to both Tom Norris and Craig Dorman, a tragic series of events was unfolding in the air and on the ground south of the DMZ, events that would involve them both. In order to counter the North Vietnamese Easter Offensive, General Abrams authorized B-52 strikes to slow the enemy advance. By this late stage of the war, the North's surface-to-air missile (SAM) capability had improved to a point that our B-52s were vulnerable. To counter this threat, electronic-countermeasures aircraft with radar-jamming capabilities flew sorties against these SAM batteries to protect the big bombers. On the afternoon of 2 April 1972, Easter Sunday, two Air Force EB-66C Destroyer aircraft from the 42nd Tactical Electronic Warfare Squadron sortied from the Korat Royal Thai Airbase. Their call signs were Bat 21 and Bat 22, respectively. The two EB-66s, indistinguishable by a layman from the Navy A-3 Skywarrior, were on a mission to protect three B-52s that were attacking NVA troop concentrations just north of the South Vietnamese city of Cam Lo. Between them, the three big bombers carried a payload of close to a hundred tons of high explosives—a good measure of discouragement for the NVA infantrymen marching south. Unknown to the bombers and the EB-66 crews, the advancing North Vietnamese had brought south with them the very dangerous and capable SA-2 SAM. It was the same surface-to-air missile that protected Hanoi and Haiphong and a forerunner of the SA-11 that brought down Malaysian Flight 17 over eastern Ukraine. It was a SAM ambush of the American aircraft working along the DMZ.

The three B-52s and Bat 22 completed their mission and made it off target unscathed. Bat 21 took a direct hit. The 440-pound warhead destroyed the aircraft and five members of the six-man crew perished; only one man escaped. Lieutenant Colonel Iceal "Gene" Hambleton managed to clear the wreckage and parachute to safety. He was the Bat 21 navigator, and his prearranged call sign was Bat 21 Bravo. Hambleton was fortunate enough to escape the SAM hit and to land unhurt, but there his luck ended. He parachuted into the middle of a major enemy offensive. He was literally surrounded by tens of thousands of North Vietnamese infantrymen. The fifty-three-year-old

Hambleton was just weeks away from the end of his tour and months away from his military retirement. From the perspective of the enemy, he was indeed a prize. From his previous Air Force tours of duty, Hambleton had detailed knowledge of American strategic ballistic missile forces. He was also well versed in current electronic-countermeasures equipment and tactics. The North Vietnamese's Soviet patrons would like nothing better than to get their hands on Hambleton.

A great deal has been written about the shoot-down of Bat 21 and the subsequent attempts to recover Hambleton. Nearly all air operations over South Vietnam were suspended as multiple sorties were flown in support of Hambleton's rescue. Over the next week and a half, five aircraft were lost and dozens more sustained battle damage—many never to fly again. Eleven aviators were killed and two captured. Six days into what was to become one of the costliest downed-pilot rescues in Air Force history, General Creighton Abrams, commander of the Military Assistance Command, Vietnam, grounded all helicopters engaged in the effort to recover Bat 21 Bravo. This directive from Abrams came at the recommendations from his senior Air Force commanders. It seems that the North Vietnamese had crossed the DMZ well prepared to deal with American air power. Along with various calibers of ground fire, there were multiple batteries of crew-served antiaircraft weapons. And in addition to the SA-2 SAM missiles that downed the EB-66C from which Hambleton escaped, there was evidence that the North Vietnamese were equipped with the more modern SA-7 Grail man-portable, shoulder-fired antiair missiles. Abrams's directive was issued on 8 April, barely twenty-four hours before Tom Norris began his briefing with Craig Dorman. While Norris and Dorman were unaware of the drama that was unfolding up near the DMZ, a Marine Corps lieutenant colonel was monitoring these events very closely. His name was Andrew E. Anderson.

Andy Anderson was also attached to MACVSOG, and he headed up a small organization called the Recovery Studies Division, and like all SOG entities, it had a cover title—the Joint Personnel Recovery Center or JPRC. On the SOG org chart, Anderson's group was listed as MACVSOG 80. Anderson's mission and that of the JPRC was to gather intelligence on downed flyers and develop plans to rescue them. Like much of MACVSOG and the American military in general, he was under orders to close down his operation and transfer his responsibilities to his Vietnamese counterpart. Yet Anderson saw Bat 21 Bravo and other downed pilots trapped in the middle of the North Vietnamese offensive as one last opportunity to save Americans on the ground. And he had a plan. In a bold move, Lieutenant Colonel Anderson stepped out of his chain of command and called Major General Winton Marshall, vice commander of the 7th Air Force. General Marshall was coordinating efforts to recover the downed airmen. As of the morning of 8 April there were three airmen on the ground, still evading but surrounded by thousands of enemy soldiers.

Anderson met with the general in Saigon that same day and sold him on his plan for a ground rescue of the pilots. That afternoon he was on General Marshall's personal aircraft headed for Da Nang to coordinate the operation. He had a team of Vietnamese Sea Commandos at Camp Fay ready to go, but he would need an American to lead them. The following day, on 9 April, after a day of feverish planning and coordination, he called down to Saigon to speak with Craig Dorman.

"It was really strange," Tom recalled. "I was sitting there in the middle of telling Craig, my new boss, about what we were doing up at Camp Fay, and this call comes in over the STU-3—that's the secure phone line. Craig says, 'I better get this,' and he takes the call. I'm only getting one side of the conversation, but I'm hearing Craig talking about 'downed pilot rescue' and 'behind enemy lines' and things like that. He talks a while longer, then I hear him say, 'Well, it just so happens, he's sitting here in my office—right now and right in front of me.' So about this time I say, 'You need some help with this. If there's an American on the ground in trouble, then I'll do what I can to help get him out.' So my briefing of Craig now turned into the beginning of a rescue mission."

"Anderson had a problem," Dorman recalls of the conversation. "His rescue plan involved moving the pilots to a river that roughly ran between the North and South Vietnamese lines. Two of the three downed airmen were located close to the river, but the enemy controlled both sides of the river. The rescue team needed to move from a secure location, upstream and into enemy-controlled territory, link up with the airmen, and get them back downstream and to a friendly position. Anderson needed a seasoned volunteer who was experienced in working with Vietnamese, and someone who was good in the water—like a Navy SEAL. And I had a problem. I needed Tom's help with all the other stuff that SOG was involved with, but I could see that this was a mission that was going to take priority. And I had only to look across the desk to see that Tom was chomping at the bit."

Tom Norris graduated with Basic Underwater Demolition/SEAL (BUD/S) Class 45 (East Coast), one of the last East Coast winter classes before SEAL training was consolidated on the West Coast on Coronado. Winter classes were tough, with attrition higher than at other times of the year. There were close to seventy-five SEAL hopefuls at the start of training with Class 45—only thirteen Americans and two Turkish officers made it to the end. Tom graduated seventh in the class. He was a good runner and very good on the obstacle course, but he was dead last in swimming. He made the minimum swim times, but the fact that he was usually the last man out of the water on a timed swim was not lost on the instructor staff.

As one of Tom's classmates in Class 45, this narrator saw first-hand how much he suffered. He came down with a stomach flu during Hell Week and for several days could not keep anything down. BUD/S trainees during Hell Week are denied sleep, but afforded all they want to eat—for good reason. A man during Hell Week burns seven to eight thousand calories per day. If he can't keep it down, he's in serious trouble. At the end of our Hell Week, I doubt that Tom weighed more than a hundred pounds. He was barely coherent at the end of that terrible week, but he never quit. Probably more than any of the rest of us, he wanted to be a Navy SEAL.

DA NANG

"After a few minutes on the phone with Anderson," Craig Dorman recalled, "it became clear that Tom was the man for this job on a number of levels. He spoke some Vietnamese and he was one of the few people who had run small units into enemy-held territory. The Sea Commandos knew him and they liked him, and he'd helped to train a great many of them. There were others with those qualifications, but they had either left the country or were days from finishing their tour. Not only was he the right man for the job, he was the only man available for the job."

"The next thing I knew I was on a plane to Da Nang," Norris said of the end of the meeting with Dorman. "It was a nice plane, and I was the only passenger. I think it was a general's plane, T-39 Saberliner, and it was a big step up from the canvas bench seat in the back of a Huey. I felt like a corporate exec. I later learned that it was the same plane that had taken Andy Anderson up to Da Nang the day before. As soon as I got into Da Nang, I was met by the Camp Fay base commander, Commander Graff, and he drove me over to a briefing facility, where a group of us waited for Lieutenant Colonel Anderson to show up."

Camp Fay was a part of the Naval Advisory Detachment, or NAD, that served as a cover organization for the MACVSOG maritime components in the Da Nang/China Beach complex. Activities at NAD Da Nang comprised a small Navy that included swift boats and the Nasty-class motor torpedo boats of the Coastal Security Service, a small-craft repair complex, a training camp for the Chinese Nung tribesmen, and a full range of administrative, logistical, and operational-support services. Camp Fay itself supported the training of the Sea Commandos and served as their main base of operations. One of Craig Dorman's primary duties was the transfer of these boats and these facilities to the South Vietnamese.

"I'd met Anderson once or twice, but I really knew nothing about him," Tom recalled of the SOG Marine. "He was based in Saigon, and I had spent most of my time at Camp Fay or up and down the coast with our Sea Commando teams. He was a short, cocky guy with an easy smile, but he was also very passionate and very professional. And he was all Marine. He walked in about 2000 [8:00 P.M.] that evening, and he gave us an overview of the mission. He had done most of the groundwork and coordination to pave the way for a rescue attempt, and had lined up all the American Air Force and naval support. But there was still a lot we didn't know. The maps we had were crude, and we had very little intelligence on enemy strength in the area where the airmen were on the ground, and what we did know seemed to change hour by hour. We were scheduled to meet with the South Vietnamese military commanders the next day before we headed out to the outpost that Anderson had selected as a jumping-off point. We'd launch the operation or operations from there.

"There was a shooting war going on just south of the DMZ and around the city of Dong Ha. Friendly fire was always a concern, so there were a great many people, on both the American and South Vietnamese sides, to check in with before we could move a team up to the battle line and go out on the mission. We knew by now that this was not just a probe, but a major North Vietnamese offensive. We were coming to understand that they were shooting down a lot of American and South Vietnamese aircraft, so they had brought with them a good air defense capability. This was not good, as American air power was our key strength. Yet we also had to understand that we Americans were in a support role; the battle would be fought and won, or lost, by the South Vietnamese.

"This was Anderson's mission, and he had done a great job of laying out the concept of the operation and how it would be conducted, even to the detailed movement of the recovery squad—my squad—and coordination with the Air Force forward air controllers. It was these FACs who were in contact with the airmen on the ground and would control their movements as a part of the rescue plan. And we were on a very tight time schedule. Anderson had us going after our first airman the following night. Following Anderson's briefing, I now had a clear idea of just what we were going to have to do to get these flyers back. It was doable, but it was not going to be easy. What gave me a lot of confidence was the Sea Commandos I was going to be working with.

"I knew the two senior commandos, Lieutenant Vu Ngoc Tho and Petty Officer Third Class Nguyen Chau, and they were both good men. I'd worked with them before and knew them from our Sea Commando training, so I would be going out with guys I could count on. I knew the other three more junior commandos only by sight, but since Tho and Chau had selected them, I knew they would be good men as well. Two of them were PFCs [privates first class] and fairly new to the Sea Commandos. The third of the three junior men was Petty Officer Third Class Nguyen Van Kiet. Lieutenant Tho had questions about the mechanics of how Anderson wanted us to conduct the operations in the field—how and where we were to move and just how far we were to penetrate into ground held by the enemy. He came to me after Anderson's briefing with his concerns. I told them not to worry, that as soon as we were on our own, we'd do things our way—the way we'd been trained. When he understood that I felt the same way as he did, he was much more relaxed.

"Anderson had a good plan, yet I don't mind saying that I was beginning to wonder just what I'd gotten myself into. All I really knew was that there were Americans on the ground and in harm's way, and we had to do all we could to rescue them. When I was growing up, all I wanted to do was be a jet pilot. That was my dream. It didn't work out and now I was a Navy SEAL on a pilot-rescue mission. Now we were going to see if we could save those airmen on the ground."

Tom Norris was born on 14 January 1944, in Jacksonville, Florida. The family moved to Wisconsin for a short while before relocating to Silver Springs, Maryland, his home of record while he was in the naval service.

"I get asked a lot about my childhood, and what I wanted to be when I grew up. Since I was born a hundred years too late to be a cowboy, I thought about becoming a doctor or a policeman. When it became clear that I would have to go into the military, I wanted to be a jet pilot—a Navy jet pilot—and land on aircraft carriers. Beyond my dream of flying jets, my home life was really very normal and very average. My dad was a teacher, a naval officer in World War II, and worked for the Veterans Administration when he retired. Mom was a teacher, but when Dad went to work for the VA, she stayed home with us boys. And we could be a handful. I remember my parents as loving, encouraging, and supportive. They were strict, but fair. They taught us discipline, respect, and to be responsible, and that you had to work toward goals in life. I have two brothers, and they were, and still are, a big part of my life. Jim is three and a half years older than me, and Kenny is a year and a half younger. Since Kenny and I were closer in age, we were together a lot. And Kenny would do just about anything I would do. I remember one time there was a big storm—the tail end of a hurricane moving up the coast. It hit Maryland with winds of close to fifty miles an hour. I wondered what winds that strong were like, so I climbed a big oak tree near our house, high enough so I was above the roof line and could really feel the wind. And Kenny climbed up right behind me. I was only about ten at the time, so that made Kenny about eight and a half. We caught heck for that—actually *I* caught heck. Kenny was just following me.

"There were two things that were driving forces for us boys: scouting and work. Both my brothers and I were Eagle Scouts. You don't often see three kids in one family make Eagle, but we did it. Our parents encouraged us, and I know they were proud of us. It was something we all did together. All of us had jobs—summer jobs, weekend jobs, before- and after-school jobs. I had paper routes, and I still remember that Sunday-morning edition of the *Washington Post*. It took some doing to cram it all into the front basket and two side baskets of my bike. It was too big to fold and toss. I had to walk each delivery up to the door, so it took some time. And the last week of the month you had to go out after supper and collect subscription fees from people who took the paper, which meant a late night because you had to get your homework done when you got back home. There were no credit cards or direct payments; it was cash or check, and you were responsible to get those funds to the paper. In addition to paper routes and routine chores, I worked at a filling station pumping gas and performing maintenance on cars. I also had a job with a repair shop fixing washing machines and dryers. In college, I landed a job as a railroad brakeman. When I think back on it, my brothers and most of my friends had jobs. It was a thing of pride. At a very early age, we learned to manage our playtime and our sports time around our jobs and school.

"Another thing my dad did was teach us to hunt and fish. I did a lot of that with my brothers and with my friends. It all began with Dad taking us out to the dump and shooting .22s. He taught us gun safety as well as how to hit what you were aiming at. Dad died in 1977 at age seventy. He went to bed and just never woke up. I was home at the time building a deck on the back of the house, so I was there to support my mom with the arrangements and to handle the estate issues. My mom lived in the family home until she passed away."

I visited Mrs. Norris in 1978 when I was back in Washington on a Navy reserve assignment. When I asked her about her boys, she said, "They were all adventuresome and into one thing or another. But

Tommy was both adventuresome and independent. More than the other boys, he could be just plain stubborn."

"I went to Montgomery Blair High School. It was a great high school and gave me a great foundation. I had a lot of really good teachers and made friends that I still have to this day. I was into sports, but being small and skinny, I went out for track and wrestling, finally settling on wrestling. It was what I was good at. I lettered three years and won two Metro League championships. I owe a lot to Montgomery Blair; it set me up for success. It also prepared me for wrestling at the college level.

"My brother Jim ended up at the University of Maryland by way of a year at Ohio Wesleyan University, so I went to Maryland as well. He was in a fraternity, so I joined that same fraternity. It was then that I really got to know my older brother. He went on to law school and became an attorney at the State Department. After two years at a junior college, Kenny followed me to Maryland, so we all graduated from there. I was interested in criminology, so I earned a degree in sociology with a specialty in criminology. During the summer I worked to help pay for my education, and I made the wrestling team as a sophomore. That came with an athletic scholarship, which really helped."

Tom excelled at the sport, capturing two Atlantic Coast Conference championships.

"During the season, I wrestled at 123 pounds. But for the conference tournaments, I went down to 115 pounds. It wasn't easy to make that weight, but I did it. And," he added with that familiar,

Tom Norris shy smile, "I had a few moves that were my own, and they served me very well on the mat."

Tom's size would later prompt a tall, burly SEAL named Mike Thornton to say, on meeting Tom for the first time, "Damn, I didn't know they made 'em that small."

"After Colonel Anderson briefed the group that evening in Da Nang, he and I got together to go over the details of my role in the operation. Since the higher-ups in the American chain of command had given us a green light to go in on the ground, we were given a lot of support, especially, as you might guess, from the Air Force. Because of the many lives and aircraft lost in previous rescue attempts, there were restrictions on the air support. We could count on fixed-wing close air support, weather permitting, but there were caveats on that as well due to the air defenses. And there would be no helos. The mobile air defenses the NVA had brought south with them were just too effective against slow-flying helicopters. No helos meant that we'd have to walk in and walk out. But I have to hand it to Anderson. It was his operation, and he had it very well thought out and very well coordinated. I mean, the airmen on the ground were told of the mission, and they knew what they were supposed to do before I knew what was expected of me and my team. And we all knew that if it was going to happen, it was going to happen very quickly. There were battle lines in place, but no one knew where the enemy would try to break through or in what strength.

"My only issue with Anderson was the same issue I had whenever I worked with the Army or the Marine Corps. They had their own way of doing things, and we in the SEAL teams had our ways of doing things. Neither were right nor wrong, just different, and it had to do with how small units operated. In the teams, when we were tasked with a mission, we felt it was just that, a tasking. Given a mission, we would then plan how we were going to do the job and then we'd go out and do the job. It didn't quite work like that for the Army and the Marines. They often wanted to coordinate what a team in the field was doing from a remote location—make decisions for us on the ground. I didn't see it that way, but it didn't mean we couldn't work together or get the job done. However, once in the field, I felt the tactical decisions were mine to make; once we were out in the field, we'd do it our way. And on this mission, my Vietnamese team leader felt the same way as I did. But one thing we all knew was that there were some very courageous airmen out there on the ground waiting for us."

DONG HA AND ON WEST

"We were up very early Tuesday, 10 April, staging gear, supplies, and radios on the tarmac for the flight north to Dong Ha. The Army had put two Hueys at our disposal to get us up the coast. We might have gotten all of our gear and people into a single chopper, but with all the aircraft being shot down around Dong Ha, helos flying in and out were making the trip in pairs. And thanks to the groundwork by Lieutenant Colonel Anderson, we had the highest priority for on-call support. But Dong Ha was as far as we could go in a helo. Anything farther north or west of there was becoming lethal airspace for helicopters. And at that time, Dong Ha was very much a city under siege."

Dong Ha is a strategic city some eight miles from the southern border of the Demilitarized Zone and about that same distance from the South China Sea. It was the northernmost major outpost along Route

1, the major highway that ran the length of the country. Going south along Route 1 from Dong Ha was Quang Tri City, Hue City, and Da Nang. From Dong Ha north, Route 1 ran across the Dong Ha Bridge up to the DMZ. The primary objective of the NVA's Easter Offensive was to take all of Quang Tri Province and the provincial capital, Quang Tri City, but first, they had to take Dong Ha.

The city was located on the southern bank of the Mieu Giang River, a major waterway that runs west from Dong Ha toward the city of Cam Lo and the Laotian border, and east into the Cua Viet River and on to the South China Sea. The 3rd ARVN (Army of the Republic of Vietnam) Division was tasked with defending the city and the Dong Ha Combat Base located just south of the city. They were doing that, but just barely. The Easter Offensive created a major NVA-ARVN confrontation, and the first real test of ARVN fighting capability and ARVN leadership. The South Vietnamese forces were supported by American advisors and American air power, but it was a South Vietnamese battle.

The NVA, with speed, surprise, and a veteran Army, seemed to have it going their way but for two stumbling blocks. The first was a Marine named John Ripley. On 2 April, the same day Bat 21 Bravo was shot down, Captain Ripley made his way out onto the underside of the Dong Ha Bridge and loaded it with explosives. Hanging from the steel I-beams like a grade-schooler from playground monkey bars, Ripley repeatedly exposed himself to enemy fire to load the bridge and finally drop it into the Mieu Giang River. Ripley was ordered not to blow the bridge by those senior to him in the chain of command. They saw the Dong Ha Bridge as an avenue for a counterattack. But Ripley was on the scene and saw the massing of NVA armor. He knew the South Vietnamese could not stand against it. So he took it upon himself to act. And his actions delayed the ultimate capture of Dong Ha by several weeks. "Ripley at the Bridge" is now Marine Corps legend.

The second stumbling block for the NVA was the spirited defense by some of the ARVN and South Vietnamese marine units. Many of them broke and ran, and some of them were simply overwhelmed by armor and superior numbers of the enemy. Yet there were isolated pockets where South Vietnamese units held on and made the NVA pay dearly. On 9 April, the day before Anderson and Norris arrived at Dong Ha, elements of the 20th Tank Regiment and a well-led battalion of South Vietnamese marines combined to destroy more than forty NVA tanks and kill close to one thousand enemy troops. It was the actions of these South Vietnamese units and their American advisors, along with the courage of John Ripley, that temporarily blunted the NVA offensive and created a window in time for Anderson and Norris to attempt their recovery.

"Once we got to Dong Ha, there was no doubt that both the city and the base were under attack. The Dong Ha Combat Base, the hard-packed dirt airstrip at the base, and the city itself were under a constant North Vietnamese artillery barrage. The only Americans remaining at Dong Ha were advisors who ranged from the divisional to the battalion level. It was through these senior advisors that Anderson had arranged for us to brief the senior Vietnamese commanders on what we were trying to do and to secure the forward outpost from which we would be operating. Our first meeting was with Brigadier General Vu Van Giai, the commander of the 3rd ARVN Division and the senior commander at Dong Ha. Just Anderson, myself, and Lieutenant Tho were at this meeting. General Giai was one busy fellow who had a lot on his plate, and he made it clear at the outset that he had only a few minutes for us. Through an interpreter, Colonel Anderson told him of our mission and reconfirmed that we would be able to conduct our recovery operation from the northwesternmost outpost of his battle line. And through his interpreter, General Giai said that he would support us with transportation and outpost support. He also told us, directly in his broken English, that he thought we were crazy and that our mission had little chance for success.

"Our second briefing was with Colonel Nguyen Trung Luat, the commander of the ARVN 1st Armor Brigade. Again, Anderson conducted the briefing while Tho and I stood at his side. It was a short, ten-minute overview of our plan, hastily delivered to Colonel Luat and a few of his senior staff officers. Luat was tasked with the defense of Dong Ha and, specifically, the western approaches to the city. It was his units, specifically elements of the 20th ARVN Tank Regiment and the Vietnamese 3rd Marine Battalion, that had helped to stall the NVA advance after they had moved into western Quang Tri Province in strength. It was 'his' outpost that we would be working from. Also at the briefing was the senior American advisor to Colonel Luat, Lieutenant Colonel Louis Wagner. It was good to see Wagner there. While the Vietnamese commanders listened politely, I knew they had bigger fish to fry. They really didn't have time for a few Americans on the ground behind enemy lines, nor an American-led ground element that was trying to rescue them. But we could count on the American advisors to be aware of our movements and warn us of any major enemy movements in our area."

Louis Wagner stood with the Vietnamese leadership of the ARVN 1st Armor Brigade during the defense of Dong Ha and later in the defense of Quang Tri City. He was emblematic of those Army and Marine Corps advisors who risked their lives on a daily basis as they worked with their South Vietnamese counterparts in the face of the North Vietnamese offensive. There were, and are, mixed reviews on the courage and effectiveness of the South Vietnamese units during the Easter Offensive. Yet when there was a South Vietnamese army or marine unit that held their ground, or fought a spirited holding action or conducted an orderly retreat, there was usually one of these courageous American advisors on hand to provide support and direction.

During the collapse of the defenses around Dong Ha in late April, Lieutenant Colonel Lou Wagner, though wounded in action, led the ARVN 1st Armor Brigade in a breakout of an NVA encirclement. He was subsequently awarded the Distinguished Service Cross.

"After the two briefings, we saddled up in an M113 armored personnel carrier and headed west on Route 9 toward the city of Cam Lo, some six miles west of Dong Ha. It was late afternoon on 10 April. Cam Lo was now held by the NVA, so both the city and the Cam Lo Bridge were in enemy hands. Our outpost was midway between Cam Lo and Dong Ha, and just east of NVA-controlled territory."

While Anderson was conducting his briefings at the Dong Ha Combat Base and the team was assembling their weapons and radios for the mission, the Air Force was conducting cryptic, clear-transmission briefings of their own for their airmen on the ground. With no hope for a helicopter-borne rescue, the airmen were now being positioned for a ground-force rescue. There were now three of them.

The first was First Lieutenant Mark Clark, call sign Nail 38 Bravo. Clark was in the backseat of an OV-10 close-air-support aircraft that was working against NVA ground targets around the location of Bat 21 Bravo—Lieutenant Colonel Hambleton. On 3 April, a SAM missile struck his OV-10. Both Clark and the other pilot, Captain Bill Henderson (Nail 38 Alpha), managed to eject and safely parachute to the ground. Henderson landed just north of the Mieu Giang River and after a night of evading the enemy on the ground, was captured by the North Vietnamese. They tended his wounds and moved him north in accordance with their guidelines for the handling of captured American airmen. Mark Clark landed on the southern bank of the river and went to ground. He immediately reported his position on his survival radio and that he was safe and well concealed. But he was in enemy-held territory and several klicks (one thousand meters, or a kilometer) west of friendly lines. On 3 April, the city of Cam Lo, located just south of the Cam Lo Bridge, was still in ARVN hands, but units of NVA infantry had crossed the river and had linked up with elements of the Viet Cong. The city fell to the NVA a few days later. Nail 38 Bravo was safe but surrounded by the enemy. Mark Clark was a young, very fit officer, and was the closest of the three to friendly forces.

Just over a thousand meters almost due west of Mark Clark's position and some seven hundred meters north of the Mieu Giang River was Gene Hambleton. On 10 April, Hambleton had been on the ground for close to eight days and was becoming weaker and more discouraged. Perhaps more than anyone, he had seen and heard the ongoing efforts his brother airmen were undertaking to recover him. And the terrible price. Days earlier, he had watched in horror as a CH-53 rescue helo had been struck by a SAM and crashed, killing all six crewmen aboard. His despair must have been unfathomable.

On 7 April, yet another OV-10 flown by First Lieutenant Bruce Walker was hit by a surface-to-air missile. The aircraft, Covey 282, was flying out of Da Nang on an artillery spotting mission. Both Walker and his spotter, marine First Lieutenant Larry Potts, managed to eject from the dying OV-10. Potts never came up on his survival radio, and was never heard from again. Walker landed safely and immediately was in communication as he sought a good hiding place. Yet Bruce Walker, Covey 282 Alpha, was not close to the river, or to Bat 21 Bravo or Nail 38 Bravo. He landed some seven thousand meters north of the outpost from which Anderson and Norris were to launch their recovery operation. He was close to four miles inside enemy-held territory, and well away from the Mieu Giang River.

The three evading airmen had survival radios—URC-64 UHF radios that were their only means of communication. These were unencrypted transceivers, so they were subject to monitoring by the enemy. But they were the downed airmen's lifeline. Air Force airborne forward air controllers (FACs) and close-support aircraft were maintaining near-24/7 communications with them and putting in air strikes around their positions to keep them relatively safe. Since their survival radios transmitted in the clear, the FACs used cryptic transmissions and the careful use of coded phrases to coach the men on the ground through what was to be a waterborne rescue attempt. For Hambleton and Clark, this was relatively straightforward. But Walker had more real estate and a great many more enemy troops between him and safety than did the other two. His recovery seemed at this point to be the most difficult.

"By the time we were in the APC and headed down Route 9, I knew there was a major battle taking shape, and I only hoped we could do our job and get in and out of there as quickly as possible. A little more than twenty-four hours ago, I was sitting in the air-conditioning at SOG headquarters in Saigon, talking with my new boss about what my Sea Commando teams were doing. I was looking forward to a hot shower, a good meal, and a good night's sleep before I headed back up to Camp Fay. Now here I was on a tricky mission, running ahead of a major North Vietnamese offensive to recover airmen trapped behind the lines. I think Colonel Anderson was more aware than I of what was going on, since he'd been following the shoot-downs from the beginning and coordinating things. And I know he was both anxious to rescue these guys, and he was also looking for a success. His organization, the Joint Personnel Recovery Center, was being shut down, even as he was working the problem of this rescue. To date, the JPRC had never had a successful recovery. He wanted to close up shop on a positive note. And I understood that at the time; it was a matter of professional pride for him.

"For me, it was all about executing my part of the mission. It did me no good to worry about all the aircraft that were lost and guys killed or captured, nor the North Vietnamese offensive. My job was to slip through our lines and past their lines, find these airmen, and bring them out. Nothing else really mattered. I was worried that if we got a major armored thrust through our area, we could be in real trouble, but again, you can't get too concerned about what you can't control. Like all SEAL missions, all you can do is hope for the best but plan for the worst. At that point in time, the mission looked difficult but doable. Of course, I knew that could change at any time. Right then, all I wanted was to get to the outpost, get my team ready to go, and then get on with the mission. I'd only managed a few hours' sleep the night before, but when you're getting ready to jump off into the unknown, you're pretty wired up. You don't think much about sleep. I tried to get a little rest in the APC, but it was hot, noisy, and we were getting bounced around a lot. Anderson was studying his maps and the five Vietnamese were dozing fitfully. They'd known nothing but war for their entire life, and this mission, difficult as it might be, was just another day for them."

THE OUTPOST

"It was late afternoon when we turned north off Route 9 and headed for the outpost. It was a good position, about fifty yards off Route 9 and on a hill looking down onto the Mieu Giang River that was some 150 yards below and to the north. The outpost, if you could call it that, was an old circular French bunker—a small concrete roundhouse maybe fifteen feet across. The position was manned by about twenty Vietnamese Army rangers and one very scared Vietnamese second lieutenant. He had three American M-48 tanks that were dug in across a shallow arc just west of the bunker, again in command of the slope down to the river and of the approaches to the position along Route 9 from the west. There were three burned-out T-54 tanks just off the road 150 yards or so from the position. The ARVN rangers pointed to them like they had destroyed them, but we weren't sure whether it was their M-48 tanks that got them or an air strike.

"Weather in this part of Vietnam at this time of year is unpredictable. There are two seasons, wet and dry—or relatively dry. The wet season ends in January and the dry season begins in March. But it's all governed by coastal airflow over the South China Sea and Gulf of Tonkin. This day there was a low cloud cover and an intermittent ground fog. For the North Vietnamese, the weather was everything. When it did clear up, the NVA tanks and armored vehicles were vulnerable to South Vietnamese and American warplanes. Both the South Vietnamese air force and our Air Force flew the A-1

Skyraiders, and they could be deadly for both tanks and troops caught in the open. It was critical for us on the ground as well. When there were low clouds or fog, we could use it to mask our movements. But low clouds and fog meant no air support.

"The Vietnamese crew of the APC was glad to drop us off and head back to Dong Ha, and the young ranger second lieutenant was not all that happy to see us arrive. His orders were to hold the position as long as he could, but he could fall back at any time if he felt threatened by main-force opposition. I think he felt that our arrival there might cause enemy tanks to again probe his position. And their three tanks were very low on ammunition with only a few rounds of main-gun ammo remaining for each tank. And they had almost no food. Colonel Anderson brought along some extra rations so we were able to give them some chow. That bought us some good will. We set up a little TOC [tactical operations center] in the bunker and I guess we sort of pushed them out. Anderson got on the radio immediately with the airborne forward air controllers. The FACs, in some ways, were airborne radio relay links. We could talk to the FACs but not to the airmen on the ground—nor could they talk to us. The FACs were in continuous contact with both of us. They made sure the downed aviators were aware of our plan to come and get them.

"Anderson's plan was simple and straightforward. The airmen were to make their way from their hiding places down to the Mieu Giang River. I was to take my squad of Sea Commandos and work our way upriver into enemy-controlled territory. The airmen, in turn, were to get into the river and float downstream to us, linking up on the southern bank of the river. We knew generally where they would begin their waterborne egress and could be in a position to intercept them. Then we would float with them downstream or to the east, to the outpost and safety. Anderson's plan had us moving in the water, both upstream and downstream. Lieutenant Tho and I weren't too sure about this. We wanted to see the terrain and check out the river. If we found the banks of the river closely guarded by North Vietnamese or the current too swift, we would patrol on foot, not in the river. Anderson and a few of the Vietnamese rangers would be down on the riverbank below the outpost to meet us and escort us back up the hill to the bunker. They'd also be there to intercept the airmen in the river if they somehow got past us.

"So while Anderson talked with the FACs, I got my guys ready to go. It was decided that we would first try for Nail 38 Bravo—First Lieutenant Mark Clark. He was the closest and his recovery seemed like it might be the easiest to manage. Hambleton would be next if we found Clark quickly and had the time to get to him."

On that afternoon of 10 April 1972, the North Vietnamese were still moving troops, tanks, antiaircraft guns, surface-to-air missile batteries, and equipment south. The Paris Peace Talks to end the war were under way, and it was no secret that America was pulling out of this war. The objective of the North Vietnamese was to take as much territory as they could while the talks in Paris went on. Should there ever be a cease-fire, they wanted to occupy and hold as much territory as possible. To do this they had literally committed their entire army, and certainly all of their armor. Their plan was to surprise and overwhelm the South Vietnamese defenders along the DMZ and drive south down Route 1, through Dong Ha to Quang Tri City, and farther south toward Hue and even Da Nang if conditions allowed. At Dong Ha, the South Vietnamese defense stiffened and, thanks to John Ripley, they could not move their armor across the Dong Ha Bridge. And periodic breaks in the weather exposed them to American and

South Vietnamese air power. Yet the North Vietnamese were deter-mined. They were prepared to trade men and material for ground.

With the Dong Ha Bridge down, the NVA swung west with their offensive and began to move armor and infantry units across the Cam Lo Bridge to build up their forces in western Quang Tri Prov-ince. This placed a good portion of the North Vietnamese Army, later learned to be about thirty thousand strong, right on top of the rescue mission. Also farther west, there were crossing points along the Mieu Giang River. So the North Vietnamese were massing forces in western Quang Tri Province where these units could be resupplied from the Ho Chi Minh Trail through Laos. As these forces grew in strength and moved south and east, they threatened to encircle Dong Ha and posed a direct threat to the provincial capital, Quang Tri City.

The three downed airmen—Nail 38 Bravo, Bat 21 Bravo, and Covey 282 Alpha—were all on the ground in a relatively small area west of Dong Ha, east of Cam Lo, and, with the exception of Nail 38 Bravo, Mark Clark, they were north of the Mieu Giang River. All were in hiding among concentrations of North Vietnamese infantry and armor. While the battle for Quang Tri City was shaping up, there was a smaller battle taking place over these three American airmen. It was an odd twist of fate that at this stage of the war, there were two com-peting interests that were on the same side, but at times in opposition to each other. The Americans, including General Creighton Abrams, Commander, Military Assistance Command, Vietnam, and especially his 7th Air Force senior commander, wanted their aviators back. It was a top priority, and in many respects this priority ran up through the entire Department of Defense. On the South Vietnamese side they—and this included their American advisors—were locked in a deadly battle, with tens of thousands of troops committed to fight the North Vietnamese incursion. The South Vietnamese were sympathetic, but for them, the lives of these three Americans were but a minor consideration, certainly not a priority. Yet these considerations affected the larger picture.

The North Vietnamese knew there were American airmen on the ground and that the U.S. Air Force was doing all in its power to recover its own. This tied up air assets that might otherwise be used to attack their units moving south in the offensive. The North Vietnamese knew the general area where the downed airmen were and had bolstered their antiaircraft guns and missile batteries accordingly. These three Americans were serving as bait to bring American and South Vietnamese ground-attack and rescue aircraft within range. Then there was the issue of the Cam Lo Bridge. With the bridge at Dong Ha down, it was being used to ferry NVA troops and armor across the Mieu Giang River. Yet in accordance with standing Air Force pilot recovery doctrine, an area around a downed airman was put off-limits to tactical air strikes. This included the Cam Lo Bridge. Had Bat 21 Bravo and Nail 38 Bravo not been in the area, the bridge would surely have been taken out earlier than it was. Would it have changed the calculus of the NVA push south? Probably not, but it did allow the enemy to more rapidly advance into western Quang Tri Province.

Meanwhile, interest in the plight of the men on the ground and the drama that was unfolding in the search and recovery operations had been growing, especially within those Air Force units still flying combat sorties. While American ground troops had largely left Vietnam, the pilots—Navy, Air Force, and Coast Guard—were still very much in the fight. At air bases in South Vietnam and Thailand and in ready rooms on carriers off the coast, pilots and support personnel alike closely followed the plight of the downed aviators and the radio chatter of the airborne FACs that were their near-constant guardians. The three men now on the ground were becoming well known by their call signs as well as their given names. And while the airspace over the men on the ground was growing more lethal each day, a great many of these pilots were prepared to risk it all to go to their aid. Three of their own were in peril.

It was amid these swirling events that Anderson and Norris set about their efforts to rescue the downed airmen.

NAIL 38 BRAVO

"Colonel Anderson was in constant communications with the FACs, and both Clark and Hambleton were told to prepare to move toward the river," Tom said of their rescue plan. "For Clark, this was no big deal, since he was in hiding on the south bank of the river just a few meters from the water. In fact, Clark was no more than two klicks [two thousand meters] from a South Vietnamese infantry battalion, but they refused to push into NVA-occupied territory to get him. But Hambleton was on the north side of the river, and he had farther to go to get to the river. Hambleton had been down for eight days now, and he was getting weak. Also, he was fifty-three years old. Clark was younger almost by half, yet he had been on the ground almost as long as Hambleton. But since Clark was the closest and most accessible, he would be the first.

"After Anderson assured me that both airmen were in position, or soon would be, we geared up and set out for the river. We were cammied up with faces blackened, a light combat load, and one canteen per man. We expected to be back at the outpost by dawn. Like the Sea Commandos, I carried an AK-47, a few grenades, and some signaling devices. The Sea Commandos were in their tiger-stripe camouflage blouses and blue jeans. We wore blue jeans a lot as they were quieter to walk in when they were wet than our standard-issue cammie trousers. One of the Sea Commando PFCs carried the radio. It was an AN/PRC-77 backpack FM transceiver that we called a 'Prick 77.' The set was waterproof if you didn't hold it underwater for too long and had a VHF line-of-sight capability. It was our link to Anderson and the outpost, and then to the forward air controllers overhead. The Prick 77 had a range of about five miles with the short whip antenna, maybe more if you took the time to set up the longer, collapsible antenna.

"It was about 10:00 P.M. when we left the bunker. There was a solid cloud cover and a moon above the clouds that provided for some illumination. Once at the river, I immediately checked the temperature and the current. Anderson's plan was for us to move upstream, wading or swimming, for no more than a half klick or just five hundred meters. This would put us west of the outpost along the river and inside enemy-controlled territory. But the river was very cold. You don't think of cold water in Vietnam, but this water was draining out of the central highlands, and it was more than a little chilly. We SEALs know how to deal with cold water, but I wasn't sure how the men that we were going to rescue would handle it. With the rainy season just behind us, the current was too swift to swim against. Wading was out of the question; wading upstream in the shallows would have made a lot of noise and made us too good of a target. Lieutenant Tho and I talked it over and came up with a new plan.

"We moved a few meters south away from the river and began to work our way west on foot toward the enemy lines. There was good coverage with stands of nipa palm, bamboo, and elephant grass. There were open areas and an occasional rice field, but we were able to skirt those. The thing about moving at night in enemy territory is that you have to move from cover to cover. When you're in good cover and safe, you need to wait and listen—maybe even as long as five or ten minutes—before moving on to the next stand of cover. It's the way to move in enemy territory and even then, it's only safe to move at night. Also, noise is a big issue. We were very strict about moving quietly and periodically stopped the patrol to listen.

"It didn't take us long to find advance elements of the NVA. They were all around us. We'd gone no more than two klicks when we crossed a shallow rise and saw a column of North Vietnamese vehicles in the distance crossing the Cam Lo Bridge and turning east toward us along Route 9. I thought, 'Uh oh, here they come.' I was about to call in an air strike on them, but they were too close to us and probably too close to Clark. Fortunately, they turned south onto a secondary road, and we continued moving west. We moved slowly in a squad file with Kiet, the junior Sea Commando petty officer, on point. He was very experienced and he moved well. We skirted several North Vietnamese patrols without difficulty. They were sloppy and made a lot of noise. There were a number of enemy troops in the area, so it made for slow going on our part. Another thing that made for slow going was that we had to look for friendly ordnance on the ground. When a pilot goes down in enemy territory, we put in a cordon of protective ordnance in the form of cluster bombs—little bombs that sow a mini-minefield around the downed airman. Some of these are bomblets that are armed with explosive, anti-personnel charges—others disperse chemicals that can incapacitate anyone who trips over them. There were none reported in our area, but still we wanted no part of them. Again, we had to go slow. We also had to stay close to the river because Anderson had preprogramed air strikes and artillery to confuse and disrupt any enemy troop movements that might have learned what we were doing in the area.

"After patrolling for a little more than two hours, I took over on point. We had turned back north, and I was looking for a place along the river where we had good cover but could see upstream to catch Clark as he floated down to meet us. But it was hard to find the right spot and we went upstream farther than Anderson had wanted us to. Actually, a lot farther. He was very emphatic about us going no farther than five hundred meters from his position just downhill from the outpost. We were probably closer to three klicks upstream from Anderson when we found a good place on the bank to wait for Clark. Once we were in position, we settled in to wait for our airman to come to us. I knew we were still downstream from about where Clark would enter the river, and I knew that about this time he would just be getting into the water. If he kept to schedule, we were in position to catch him coming downstream, and that was all that mattered.

"It didn't take Clark long to get to us. Because of our vantage point on the bank of the river, we easily saw him coming. And because the river was cold, we could hear him breathing as well; he was a-huffing and a-puffing. It was now a little after 0100 [1:00 A.M.]. Just as we were getting ready to move down into the water's edge to get him, here comes a North Vietnamese patrol. I glanced down the squad file, and my Sea Commandos had their weapons at the ready. They were looking at me and all I could see were blackened faces and wide eyes. There were six NVA soldiers in the patrol and we could have easily taken them out, but then that would have alerted all the enemy troops in the area. So I decided we would not fire unless they spotted Clark in the water. They didn't. So we watched Clark float by and waited for the NVA to move on. They were making a lot of noise as they moved through the vegetation so they neither heard nor saw Clark.

"Once the patrol had passed, I told Lieutenant Tho and his men to stay hidden while I went after Clark. He was floating and I figured that if I was swimming, I could quickly catch him, so into the river I went. Again, it was cold—really cold. My thinking was that when I got to him, I could stash him in the vegetation along the riverbank, then go back and link up with my commandos. Then we would patrol back to Clark's position, collect him, and work our way back along the southern bank of the Mieu Giang to where Anderson was waiting near the outpost.

"But I simply could not find him! I moved downstream about a klick, looking in branches and overhanging limbs, and he was no-where to be found. I was getting cold and I could only imagine that he would be getting very cold. He had gone into the river at least two klicks farther upstream from where he passed us. So I figured, he's cold and he's tired; I bet he pulled off into the bushes to rest upstream from me, and I simply missed him. So I turned around and began working my way back upstream looking for him. No luck. I reached Lieutenant Tho and the other Sea Commandos, and they were tired, cold, and frustrated. And I'm thinking, 'Now I really have a problem. I went a lot farther upstream than Anderson wanted, and we had patrolled overland rather than staying in the river. Now we'd lost our pilot.' I had no choice but to call Anderson on my radio and tell him that Clark had gotten past us. And that we couldn't find him.

"I had a thing about the radios. Army and Marine commanders like Anderson like to talk to their units in the field and keep up on what's taking place. But if you're a special-operations team sneaking around behind enemy lines at night, the *last* thing you want is a voice breaking squelch on your radio wanting to know your loca-tion or how the mission is going. So I never patrolled with my radio on. Today SEALs have these small radios and sound-cancelling headsets with commo earpieces. We had none of that, and the Prick 77 handset was noisy unless you had it pressed up against your ear. And you can't run a patrol with one ear glued to a radio handset. I was out there to do a job; the radio was for me to ask for help if and when I needed it to do my job. And now I needed help. I told Anderson to have the forward air controller contact Clark on his next radio check and tell him to go to ground on the south bank of the river, and that we would be working our way downstream to him. And as you might expect," Tom said, now chuckling and shaking his head, "Anderson wanted a full report on where we are, how long ago Clark passed our position, and other details. I hadn't the time for this, and talking on the radio is unwise in enemy territory. So I made sure he had the instructions to pass along to Clark, and I turned off the radio. We then began moving carefully downstream.

"I wanted to make sure we didn't miss him as we swept the south bank of the river, so I again called Anderson and requested some illumination well east of our position. I got the illum in short order. It was from one of the Navy ships off the coast, and they put it right where I wanted it—well to the east so we could see downstream. You have to be careful when calling in illumination, as it lights up the bad guys as well as yourself. But they put the single parachute flare right where I wanted it. The flare allowed us to see a ways downstream, but still no Clark.

"Now I had a problem. It was close to 0400 and we had to get back to friendly lines before daylight—with or without Clark. We still had plenty of darkness left, but we had to keep moving. Our searching along the riverbank made us more vulnerable to enemy patrols. But we had no choice. I was in the water along with Kiet, while Tho and the other Sea Commandos began searching along the shore and providing Kiet and me with security as we moved downstream. We were at this for about an hour, and I think we were just past where I had been on my earlier solo trip downriver. And I don't mind saying that I was getting anxious. There was a guy, hopefully in front of us, who had been evading on the ground for several days. He was tired, cold, and scared. I was cold, and as time passed, I was getting worried. I'd run the patrol my way, and looking back, the right way, but still, I'd let him get past me. It was in my mind that I'd not followed Anderson's instructions and I'd been pretty short with him on the radio. So there was a lot riding on our search of that riverbank, *and* there were a whole lotta bad guys in the area. And, of course, there was my team; I wanted to get them safely back to base. Then I saw him.

"I was in the water, just past where I had turned around last time down. Coming around a bend in the river, I spotted this head peeking over the top of an old waterlogged, overturned sampan. I knew it was him, and Kiet saw him about the same time I did. I signaled Kiet to get behind me and I slung my rifle behind. Since it was an AK-47, I didn't want him thinking I was an NVA soldier. I took off my hat and began to talk to him as I approached. He immediately ducked back behind cover, thinking we were the enemy. I had to keep my voice low but I kept talking. 'Mark, I'm an American. My name is Tom Norris. I know you spent some time in Idaho and that you've just floated down the Snake River to get here. I'm here to take you home.' The reference to Idaho and the Snake was part of the cryptic, clear-transmission-text instructions that got Clark into the river and moving downstream. At one time, Mark Clark was stationed at Mountain Home Air Force Base near Boise, and he was familiar with the area and the Snake River."

Nguyen Kiet recalled the meeting with Clark from his position closer to shore. "He was in the water with a camouflage net over his head and I could see that he had an orange life preserver on. He had a .38-caliber pistol pointed at me and for a second, neither of us moved. I turned my rifle barrel away from him so he could see I meant him no harm. Then *Dai Uy* [pronounced 'Dye wee'— Vietnamese for lieutenant] Norris began talking to him and moving closer to him. When *Dai Uy* Tho came down the bank to the water to join us, I went on shore with the others to form a security cordon."

"When he finally understood that I was really an American," Norris continued, "and a part of the rescue effort, you could see the relief on his face. He probably saw the relief on my face as well. I didn't want to face Anderson if I failed to find Clark and get him safely back to the outpost. But Clark was all smiles—he thought he was home free. About that time, Lieutenant Tho came down the bank to the water and scared the life out of him. I said, 'No, no, no, he's with me—he's on our side.' He settled down again, and I had his full attention. Lieutenant Tho and the other guys set out around us in a security fan while I had a talk with our new Sea Commando. I told him where we were, where we had to go to be safe, and how we were going to get there. To his credit, he became a good commando trainee. I said, 'Now listen, stay right behind me. Whatever I do, you do. If I drop, you drop; if I turn, you turn. Whatever I do, you do the same—and do it exactly when I do it. Don't question what I do or my decisions—just follow my lead. We're not home yet, and we got a lot of bad guys to get through before we're safe.' He said okay and he did just that. The guy was really good. He did exactly what he was supposed to do as we worked our way back to the outpost.

"I was able to get a radio call in to Anderson to let him know that we had Clark and were headed back. He again had questions about our situation and location, but once he understood we had him and were returning to the outpost, I again turned the radio off. We had maybe an hour before sunrise and not much more than a klick to go to get back to the outpost—plenty of time unless we ran into trouble. Fortunately, we didn't. I could hear enemy troop concentrations on either side of the river, but they must have felt secure, as they made a lot of noise. We heard them before they could see or hear us, and we managed to skirt these formations and keep moving east toward our outpost.

"You have to be really careful coming back into a friendly position, so I called Anderson and we also exchanged signal lights. Lieutenant Tho and the Sea Commandos also exchanged verbal signals with the outpost soldiers. I knew those South Vietnamese rangers would be on edge, and we didn't want to get shot by our own guys. But we made it in okay. Anderson took charge of Clark straightaway, got him up to the bunker and got him some chow. He was in very good shape, but a little dehydrated—dirty and dehydrated. With Clark safe, I collected my team and made sure that they got a meal and that they were taken care of. A long combat patrol can take it out of you and we still had two more men out there. I had to make sure they cleaned their weapons and attended to their gear and, above all, got some rest. We would all be going back out as soon as it got dark."

In the larger picture, the North Vietnamese Army continued to press their offensive. With Dong Ha holding on, they swung to the west, still moving troops and armor south across the Mieu Giang River on the Cam Lo Bridge and into western Quang Tri Province. They were gaining ground, but at a price. In some sectors the South Vietnamese defense was collapsing, but there were pockets of stiff resistance and an orderly retreat. And there was American air power at work. The North's strategy was to gain as much ground as possible in anticipation of a possible cease-fire that might come from the Paris Peace Talks. But they were trading some of their best infantry and armor units for this ground.

By midmorning on 11 April, Lieutenant Colonel Anderson was able to pass word back through Lieutenant Colonel Lou Wagner at the South Vietnamese 1st Armored Brigade that his team was successful in rescuing one of the airmen. At ready rooms and American air bases across Vietnam and Thailand, from air crews on standby up to General Abrams, they learned that First Lieutenant Mark Clark was safe. From Anderson's perspective, the rescue mission had been a success. For his part, Tom Norris never let on that he had gone much deeper into enemy territory than Lieutenant Colonel Anderson had intended. Neither of them had a great deal of time to savor the success of Clark's recovery. Anderson had to get Clark ready for transport, and Tom, in addition to seeing to his Sea Commandos, was trying for a little rest himself. And both of them had to begin to plan for the next night's mission. Then things began to come apart.

"The South Vietnamese rangers and tank crews were all sitting around resting and playing cards when the first mortar round landed," Tom recalled. "It was maybe a hundred yards west of us. It got my attention, but they didn't seem to care. They'd been fighting for so long that a stray mortar round didn't mean much to them. Then another round fell just to the east, and I knew we'd been bracketed. I yelled for Lieutenant Tho and the others to take cover, and we did just that. But the rangers and the tank crews didn't move; they just didn't see the danger. Then a round dropped right in the middle of us. It was coming from across the river, and in short order we were getting hammered by mortar and rocket fire. Anderson was on the radio trying to get air support or some suppressing artillery or naval gunfire. There was a low cloud cover, so it was hard to get any accurate air support, and for some reason he couldn't get anything else. Clark was safe in the bunker, but Anderson was on top of it on the radio, exposed and trying to get help. It was a mess. The tank crews got in their tanks and buttoned up, and the rangers scrambled for what cover they could find. Some of them went to shallow foxholes they'd dug, while others managed to crawl under the tanks, but they started taking casualties. I was yelling at the tankers to return fire at the North Vietnamese across the river. I was also working with the ranger officer to get his men ready to repel an enemy attack. It was in my mind that the rockets and mortars were a prelude to an infantry ground attack.

"It went on for an hour and a half and it was all pretty confusing. Lieutenant Tho and I were treating casualties and trying to direct the outpost defenses while Colonel Anderson was doing his best to get us some support. Then he got hit with a piece of shrapnel right above his right eye. It knocked him down, but he was still conscious. I examined the wound, but there was no way to tell how far the shrapnel had penetrated into his skull. All I could do was bandage him and try to get him evacuated to a medical facility. We got him into the bunker, where the South Vietnamese officer was on his radio trying to get help. I even got on Anderson's radio, but initially had no luck. The only help in sight were two APCs [armored personnel carriers] that had come from Dong Ha to get Clark. They were sitting on top of a hill about a klick away, but they weren't going to come in as long as we were under attack.

"I moved outside to try to get better radio reception and some air support. There with Lieutenant Tho, we watched mortar rounds splashing around us. We moved to the base of the bunker, just as a round landed where we'd been standing. Unfortunately, a piece of shrapnel tore into the Vietnamese lieutenant's arm, wounding him seriously. I bandaged him up, gave him a shot of morphine, and was finally able to get an Air Force forward air controller, or FAC, on the radio. Suddenly, the shelling stopped.

"The tank crews seemed to be okay, but the platoon of rangers had been hit pretty hard. Three of them had been killed and close to half of the others were casualties. Anderson was still down and Lieutenant Tho was out of action. The APCs finally came in about noon, and we loaded them up with the dead and wounded, and First Lieutenant Mark Clark. Petty Officer Chau also left to help tend to Lieutenant Tho. They moved back east along Route 9 toward Dong Ha. That left me and the three Sea Commandos, Petty Officer Kiet, and the two PFCs to carry on. I was now supported by the three tanks, a very nervous South Vietnamese second lieutenant, and about a dozen very scared Vietnamese rangers. And they had orders to pull out if things got worse. I still had two airmen out there, but I wasn't sure that if I went back out, the battered outpost would be in friendly hands when I got back. As for my three Sea Commandos, they had done well the previous night, but now they were without their leaders. I was now the only American at the outpost. But I had Anderson's radio, also an AN/PRC 77, but with a better antenna. I could still reach Lieutenant Colonel Wagner at the ARVN 1st Armor Brigade, but more importantly, I had a better link with the Air Force FACs. Still, I had to be careful with what I said, as neither my radio nor the one Anderson left were equipped with encryption. The bad guys were listening in."

DRY HOLE

"By late afternoon of 11 April, things had quieted down at the outpost. The Vietnamese officer and his remaining rangers were taking turns on guard duty, and the tank crews were staying pretty close to their tanks. Generally two of them would be sitting on top of the tank while the other two slept under the tank. My three Sea Commandos managed a few hours of sleep, but not much more than that. I got none. With Anderson gone, I was both the TOC [tactical operations center] officer and the recovery patrol leader. I needed the rest, but I also had to stay up with the FACs who were monitoring the location and condition of our guys still out there on the ground."

In anticipation of a possible pickup the previous evening, Lieutenant Colonel Gene Hambleton, Bat 21 Bravo, had moved south from his previous hiding place down to within fifty yards of the Mieu Giang River. On his radio he had followed the FAC-chat and knew that Nail 38 Bravo had been rescued and was now safe. Hambleton had now been on the ground for nine days. He was becoming desperately weak, but the safe recovery of Mark Clark bolstered his spirits. Farther north, First Lieutenant Bruce Walker, Covey 282 Alpha, had been on the ground now for four days. He too was trying to make his way south, but there were sizable troop concentrations in his area. He managed to move east for about a klick, but he could get no closer to the river.

In addition to the movement of NVA troops and armor through the area, the NVA were setting in antiaircraft guns and SAM batteries along the north side of the Mieu Giang River. There were also a number of small villages and fishing hamlets on both sides of the river. Most of the civilians had fled or were preparing to flee the fighting and bombing. Many of these villages were deserted, yet in others there were those who were unable or unwilling to abandon their homes. These civilians often clogged the roads and made it difficult for the North Vietnamese to move vehicles by road and for American pilots to search for military targets among the noncombatants. As time wore on, there were fewer civilians on the roads and more completely abandoned villages.

"Late that evening, the FACs gave me Hambleton's approximate location on the river. They could not give me the location in the clear, but I had a map with predesignated reference points along the river to serve as a guide. They told me that he was now missing some of his scheduled radio transmissions and that his speech was becoming slow and disjointed. Our plan was that we would patrol up to a point on the south side of the river, across from his location, and then have him try to cross the river to us. If he couldn't cross the river, then I'd go across after him. That evening, Kiet carefully briefed the Vietnamese outpost officer on when we might get back to the outpost and reviewed the signals we'd exchange when we did. Working through Kiet, I got my commandos saddled up and we headed off. Like the previous evening, we went down close to the water, then turned west.

"All of them understood a little English, and, of the three, Kiet was the most conversant. And I could speak a little Vietnamese, so we managed. The two Sea Commando privates were relatively new and now looked to Kiet as their leader and to explain things to them. Kiet understood things far quicker than the others, and it was easier for me to make myself understood to him. As we talked through the mission, I would tell Kiet and he would tell the other two. This night I began walking point for the four of us, with Kiet bringing up the rear. The Sea Commando right behind me had the PRC 77 radio, and, of course, once I left the outpost, I turned it off. Initially, we followed pretty much the same route as we did the first night out. After a while we moved in more of a straight line, as we didn't have to follow the bends and twists of the river. Again the going was slow, as there were enemy patrols out. We'd move fifty yards or so, then stop and listen. On the occasions when we spotted an enemy patrol, we just had to wait for them to move on so we could continue moving west.

"To get to a place on the riverbank across from where Hambleton was supposed to be, we had to go a lot farther than the previous night. All told, we had moved some three and a half klicks in a westerly or northwesterly direction—about two miles. It was just before midnight when we got back to the southern bank of the river that was our objective. Hambleton was supposed to be on the north bank of the river, about a klick east or downstream from the Cam Lo Bridge. I couldn't see the bridge from where we were on the south bank, but I could hear the truck traffic moving north to south, so I knew we were in the right place. And I knew we were about a klick from the bridge. I called the FAC who was in contact with Hambleton, and he told Hambleton in their cryptic radio-speak that he was to step out from the shore and into the water where we could see him. Again, I had no direct radio contact with Hambleton. But I think he was too weak to move out to the river or that he just stood up where he was on the bank. But we couldn't see him. So we started moving up and down the southern bank, looking across the river for him, but we just couldn't find him.

"The weather had cleared and we had a partial moon, so we could see across the river. And from where we were on the south riverbank, we had a good field of vision to see anyone in the imme-

diate area on the north bank. I was trying to decide if I should swim
the river and search along the north bank for him, but we really had
a good vantage point from where we were. So I decided that we
would just work our way slowly along the southern bank, first upstream and then back downstream, and search the far bank for him.
After a few hours of moving and looking, I sensed that there was
some kind of a dispute among my Sea Commandos. That's when I
could have really used Lieutenant Tho. Kiet was very steady, but the
other two were getting impatient with being this far upstream and
this far from the safety of the outpost. They wanted to go back. I
couldn't really blame them; there were a lot of enemy troops about.
We would spot company-sized bivouacs and periodically we could
glimpse trucks and tanks moving across the Cam Lo Bridge and
along Route 9. The enemy was all around us. I called the FAC but he
was now having trouble raising Hambleton. A few hours before
dawn, we began to make our way back to the outpost. Neither I nor
the Sea Commandos wanted to be out there in the daylight. I hated
to go back empty-handed, but there was no point in crossing the
river and thrashing around trying to find him. And we were out of
time. We'd just have to try again.

"Once again, we carefully made our way back to the outpost
and Kiet alerted the ranger and tank crews that we were coming
back in. The following day, April 12, was pretty much a repeat of
the previous day. I got Kiet and the others something to eat, and
had them tend to their equipment. I told them to get some rest
because we'd be going back out again after dark. I could tell they
were not all that excited about it, but that was my mission—our
mission. Twice that day we came under mortar and rocket attack,
but the FACs were quick to call in suppressing fire. I think the NVA
across the river knew something was going on at our outpost with

the APCs coming and going. But they also knew that if they fired on us, they'd be inviting air attacks.

"Most of that day I was talking with the FACs and trying to come up with a plan to get to Hambleton. Everyone knew he was getting weaker and that he was having trouble moving. This meant that even if we did find him, he might have a hard time walking out. And he needed to do more than walk—he had to move quietly in a patrol file and take direction from me. It didn't look good, but I had an idea. Maybe we could bring him out by sampan—again if we could find him. During our previous outings, we'd passed through some deserted villages and I knew there were plenty of sampans along the riverbank. But I didn't recall seeing any paddles. Sometimes the Vietnamese don't use paddles, but I knew we'd need them. So that day I radioed back to Dong Ha and asked them to round up some canoe paddles—two of them. I got a lot of 'You want what?' and 'Say that again,' but I finally got through to them. I also asked for some life jackets and medical supplies, and that afternoon they were delivered by APC. The APC also delivered something I really didn't need.

"It was along about midafternoon and I was standing at the side of the bunker talking to one of the FACs about the upcoming mission that night. The weather was improving; that was good for the guys in the air, but not necessarily good for us on the ground. I was wearing only my cammie shirt and boots—nothing else. My blue jeans, which is what I operated in, were hung over a bush drying out. I heard this commotion behind me, and when I turned around, there's this reporter. He had a microphone in his hand and a film crew setting up a camera. I couldn't believe it! I asked him what the devil he was doing here and he said he was with such-and-such news network and that he'd heard there was some kind of rescue going on. They were there to film it. I said, 'The heck you are. I want you back in that APC and I want you out of here now.' Besides the distraction, we could come under attack at any time.

"So he told me, 'We have clearance to be here and permission from some general up the chain of command.' I was just flabbergasted; this was the last thing I needed. So I grabbed my AK-47, which is never very far away, and jacked a round into the chamber. I'm not sure quite what I said, but there was no mistaking my meaning: they were to clear out, and they were to do so now. I must have looked pretty funny there on that bunker with a cammie shirt, no trousers, no underwear—and an automatic weapon in my hand. But he didn't think it was funny. He and his crew packed up in short order and filed into the APC, and they left. That might have been a little harsh on my part, but we were playing for some high stakes here, and people's lives were on the line. I simply didn't need one more issue to deal with. And this was a classified mission. Who the heck gave them permission to be there in the first place?"

BAT 21 BRAVO

"That evening as I was getting ready to go back out, Kiet came to me and told me that the other two Sea Commandos would not go. They said it was too dangerous and that it was not worth risking their lives again to save one American. I was kind of expecting this, and had already decided to not to take any of them back out that night. But I had not told Kiet this. I figured that sooner or later we'd run into an NVA patrol or an outpost, and it would go badly for us. Or the NVA would push through our little outpost on the way to Dong Ha, and we'd have no secure base to come back to. So I told Kiet, 'You stay back here with them and be ready to help me when I'm on the way back in tomorrow morning.'

"He said, 'No, *Dai Uy,* I'm going with you.'

"'Look, Kiet,' I told him, 'this time it could be really danger-ous. I might not get back from this one.' I didn't really think in terms of this as a one-way mission; you don't want to admit that, even to yourself. But it was going to be very difficult. If he too did not want to go, then I wanted to give him a way out—a way to save face. But he would have none of it.

"'If you go, *Dai Uy,* I go,' and that was it.

"'Okay, we go together. You get everyone here ready to help us when we get back to the outpost, and I'll let the FACs know what we're trying to do.'"

A good question at this point in the narrative might be why did *either* of them go? Even though they had returned safely from two previous patrols, they were tempting fate a third time. And this time, they had to recover a man who in all probability could not walk and would be just so much baggage on a combat patrol where stealth and silence were essential. Those of us who know Tom Norris know why he went back; he's simply the caliber of warrior who could not rest if another American was in trouble. No matter what the odds, he would go. He is also someone for whom fear either does not exist or can be so com-partmentalized that personal physical danger does not enter into the calculus. Of course he was going back out.

As for the fate of a downed airmen, or any American in danger of capture, there was some logic in the idea that Norris or Kiet should *not* go back into harm's way. It was known that captured Americans—live Americans—were of value. North Vietnamese Army protocols in place at the time were that captured Americans were to be made safe, medically treated, and sent north—not tortured or killed. The United States was pulling out of South Vietnam and peace talks were under way. Captured Americans were leverage at these talks. While a prize like Hambleton might be the exception in that he might *not* be held by the North Vietnamese but passed along to the Russians for his special knowledge, Americans at risk of capture were not necessarily at risk of death. From my study of downed pilots during the Easter Offensive during the late stages of that war, if an American in enemy territory simply raised his hands and surrendered, there was a good chance he would be taken to Hanoi to wait out the conflict. In fact, two airmen shot down during failed attempts to rescue Bat 21 Bravo did just that, and were repatriated at the end of the war.

Yet Tom Norris was not alone. A great many airmen at sea and at air bases in Thailand and Vietnam were poised and ready to go into harm's way for those evading on the ground. It is simply a part of our culture; we risk all for one of our own—we go back. Regarding Petty Officer Nguyen Kiet, I asked him why he agreed to go back out with this American *dai uy* that third night. His answer was simple and straightforward.

"I volunteered because it was my duty, and it was the right thing to do. If we had left Hambleton there, he would have been captured by the North Vietnamese Army troops."

The situation regarding the NVA offensive on the evening of 12 April had changed little, at least for those working on the rescue of the two remaining downed airmen. The North Vietnamese continued to move armor, trucks, troops, and supplies across the Cam Lo Bridge, but these forces seemed to flow south into western Quang Tri Province rather than east toward Dong Ha. That would come later. While Hambleton was on the ground, the no-bombing, exclusionary zone around him included the Cam Lo Bridge. The North Vietnamese seemed to be making full use of this bridge to move their forces south. They were also fording the Mieu Giang River at crossing points farther west. And these were not the only enemy forces on the move. The NVA had come out of Laos in divisional strength, moving east into Quang Tri Province and driving toward Quang Tri City—the provincial capital.

Hambleton himself was not doing all that well. The night before, while Norris and the three Sea Commandos searched for him, he had apparently been too weak to move down onto the bank of the river where they could see him. It was becoming clear to all that he could not last much longer. The airborne forward air controllers had pinpointed his location and on two occasions had directed that relief packs called Madden kits with food and water be dropped in his area. Two of these kits were scheduled to be deployed, yet only one was released from the drop aircraft. But Hambleton had been too weak to recover it. At one low point, Hambleton struggled onto a sandbar in the river and began to wave a white handkerchief. He was immediately spotted by one of the FACs, who managed to get him on the radio and talk him back into the covering foliage of the riverbank. Throughout the ordeal, Hambleton had been both responsive and defiant. He had even retained his sense of humor. But this was changing. He was missing some of his radio checks, and when he did communicate he was dispirited and sometimes incoherent. Back at the outpost, Norris was able to gather enough from his conversation with the FACs to know that Hambleton was reaching the end of his tether and that he couldn't last much longer.

Both the FACs and Norris were coming to the conclusion that it would have to be this night or never. And Norris knew that he would have to go and physically get him. Hambleton was simply unable to get into the water and float to a rendevous, and when they did find him, it was a near certainty that he would be too weak to walk out.

•   •   •

"Just after dark, Kiet and I saddled up and made our way down from the outpost toward the river. Before we got to the water we again swung west and began to move toward NVA-controlled territory. I now carried our radio, and both Kiet and I were each armed with an AK-47 and a canoe paddle. It took us a half hour to get to an abandoned village that we had skirted the previous night, and, after watching it for a while, we made our way along the water into it. There we found what we were looking for: a small nest of sampans. They were tied up in the river and submerged. They keep them submerged so the wood won't dry out. When they dry out, they crack and leak. We found one that looked seaworthy, emptied it out, and climbed carefully aboard. A sampan is like a flat-bottomed canoe with much less freeboard on either side. In a sampan, you sit cross-legged with your butt in the bottom of the boat. I also made sure we had one of the bail cans that we found along the bank. In a sampan, you paddle for a while, then you bail for a while, as they always leak. We lucked out with this one; it leaked very little. Moving on the water would allow us to avoid area-denial ordnance that may have been dropped in the area to protect the pilots. And it gave us the option of moving Hambleton back downstream by sampan, if and when we found him.

"We had a little more gear this night than we'd had on previous trips up the river. I had an extra canteen and some medical gear, the radio of course, a compass, and extra magazines for my AK. Before we went out, both of us had traded our uniforms for local dress. Kiet had exchanged his tiger-stripe camouflage utilities for a dark khaki shirt like the NVA wear, and I had on a black long-sleeved shirt like most Vietnamese wear when they're on the water fishing. And my blue jeans. We had our gear on the bottom of the sampan and our rifles in our laps. On close inspection, we probably wouldn't fool anyone, but from a short distance in the dark, we looked like a couple of fishermen. On most of the rivers in Vietnam, there was a curfew at night because that's when the Viet Cong moved about. But a lot of Vietnamese villagers along the water snuck out at night to fish. Now, we may not have been fooling anyone, as by this time most of the civilians had left the area, but it seemed like it was worth a try. And if we needed to, we could always leave the sampan and make our way overland. It was a gamble any way you cut it. I'm not a big guy, and Kiet is smaller than me, so there was a good chance we'd be taken for local fishermen.

"Once we settled into the boat and arranged our gear, we began to paddle upstream. The current was swift in places but we kept to the eddies along the bank, taking advantage of the cover along the shoreline. We'd hug either the north bank or the south bank, depending on where the cover was best. Pretty soon, we began to notice activity on both banks. The enemy troops seemed to feel secure and that they had control of the area—which they did—and they didn't try to be quiet. It was an overcast night so it was pretty dark, which was to our advantage, as all we needed to see were the banks on either side of the river. There were some side channels that made for some confusion. At one point, we got lost and had to call on one of the forward air controllers overhead to help us out. Finally, we were able to find our way and move up the main course of the river.

"Being on the water is a lot different from patrolling on land. It was easier going in some ways, but you felt a lot more exposed. We pulled into the bank in the overhanging vegetation several times to check the compass. Kiet would hold us into the bank with his paddle and I'd check the map with a small red-filtered penlight.

The river snaked around a great deal, so by comparing the compass heading with the course of the river, we knew approximately where we were. And from what the forward air controllers had told us before we started, I had a pretty good idea where Hambleton was. At some point earlier that evening, the FACs had managed to get him into the Mieu Gang River, across it, and to the southern bank. I had his new position plotted on my map; we just had to get to him. My plan was that when we got close to where he was, we'd beach the sampan and conduct an area search for him along the bank of the riverbank. Then, about an hour into the paddle upstream, we went into the fog.

"You have to understand that this was our first time on the water, so as we were feeling our way upstream, we were seeing the banks of the river from a perspective that was new. On my map, I had Hambleton's position plotted exactly; I knew right where he was. My biggest challenge was knowing where *I* was on the map. The river snaked around a bit, so with my compass, I could tell generally where I was and generally where I was in relation to Hambleton's location, but not precisely. There was no way I could pull over to a section of the bank of the Mieu Giang and say, 'He should be right here.' It wasn't that easy, and the fog changed everything. It made it easier and harder. It was easier because now we were much safer from being spotted by an NVA patrol or an NVA encampment along the river. But it made our navigation more difficult. There were small streams and tributaries coming into the main channel, and we made a few wrong turns. And with the fog, sound became our primary line of defense. We were making no noise at all, but we could hear a lot of movement along the shoreline.

"The fog allowed us to safely cross Mieu Giang and use the cover on whichever bank looked the best. We were making good time, as we didn't have to stop as often to look for enemy patrols. We were shrouded in fog. Yet I still had to navigate and try to track where we were. Once when we pulled over so I could get a compass heading and check the map, we were suddenly surrounded by tank engines. It was like pulling into a bus station. The fog hugged the water so I could see only a few hundred feet. Just inshore from the riverbank was a refueling station and there were tanker trucks gassing up NVA tanks. They were all camouflaged with tree branches and palm fronds, but they were making a lot of noise. We eased out from the bank and continued upstream, generally working our way west, but with the bends in the river sometimes we were paddling south and sometimes north. And periodically along the bank, we would hear enemy troops talking and hear the movement of troops. By this time I guessed we were in the area where Hambleton should be, so we hugged the southern bank of the Mieu Gang looking for him. The fog kept us safe, but it made searching the bank for him very difficult. Again, I knew where he was supposed to be and had a description of the terrain where he was hiding, but it was hard to see details of the shoreline in the fog—just as it was hard to know exactly where we were. We'd been on the river for about six hours and we'd come a long way. Suddenly the fog broke and we could see. We were just a few meters downstream from the Cam Lo Bridge.

"I thought that by now the bridge would have been bombed to keep the enemy from moving south, but that was not the case. There were no vehicles on the bridge, but there was a procession of enemy troops marching across. I was thinking, 'I hope they continue south and don't turn east down Route 9 and take out our outpost—or cause our little outpost garrison to get spooked and pack up and leave.' But now that I could see the bridge, I knew exactly where I was on the river and I knew where Hambleton was supposed to be from our current location. He was downstream from us about seven hundred meters. The Mieu Giang River flowed almost due east under the bridge for about four hundred meters, then took a bend to the left in a northeasterly direction. Hambleton was on the south shore some three or four hundred meters from this bend in the river. So we drifted downstream from the bridge, and after passing the bend in the river, we began a careful search of the bank where we thought he should be.

"We got to a spot that looked like a good place to beach the sampan and close to where I thought he was. And then we got really lucky. Getting in and out of a sampan is tricky and you have to move slowly and carefully. Once out and onto the bank, I began to slowly make my way along the south bank of the river. I hadn't gone very far and there he was, sitting by a bush some twenty-five meters from the river, waiting for us. He saw me and his face lit up; he started smiling and waving. And I'm thinking, 'Wow, I finally found this guy.' It was sort of like it was with finding Clark. I don't know who was more relieved, him or me. But that feeling came and went very quickly, because now that we had him, we had to get him into the boat and safely back downstream. And having just spent most of the night getting there, we knew there were a whole lot of bad guys between our location and the safety of the outpost—if it was still there.

"My immediate concern was Hambleton's condition and how we were going to handle him. He'd been on the ground for eleven days, and I could tell that while he was very glad to see us, he was weak and disoriented. Daylight was going to be on us very soon. I now had to decide if we were going to lay up here for the day and try to make our way back the next night, or to try for it now. There were risks to both, but I was worried about Hambleton's condition. He had sores on his hands that looked to be infected, and he was scraped, bruised, and dirty. He also had injured his back. I wasn't sure he could last another day, or if the three of us and the sampan could hide out for another fourteen hours or so before trying to get back to base. So I decided we would go for it, knowing that most of the journey would be made in the daylight.

"Hambleton was not in good shape, but he was coherent enough to know who we were and that we had come to take him home. He did pretty much what we told him to do, and it didn't take long to settle him into the bottom of the sampan and cushion him with the life preservers we'd brought with us. Then we covered him up with grass and nipa palm fronds. A sampan is a tricky boat, and, like a canoe, it can be very tippy. Once we were loaded, we had only three or four inches of freeboard, so all movement had to be done carefully or we would take on water. Before we left the bank, I checked in with the FAC on station overhead. I told him in so many cryptic words that we had Hambleton, that even though it would soon be light we were going to try to make a run for it downriver. I also told them that we were going to need some air cover, as there was no way we were going to make it past all those NVA troops and bivouacs without some help. We'd just pushed off the bank when this FAC came back to me and, in a very nice and conversational voice, told me he had no air support for us. I mean, here the whole U.S. Air Force has been trying to get this guy out safely and now that we have a good shot at it he's telling me I have no air cover. I asked about fast-movers [jet fighter-bombers] and I got the same response. Later I learned that the airbase at Da Nang was under rocket attack and no aircraft from there could sortie, but at the time, it was very frustrating. Yet we had no choice but to keep paddling. It was almost dawn and we had to make use of every bit of the fading darkness.

"We had two things going for us. One was the current. Paddling with the current yet staying close to the shore, we were moving quickly in relation to someone standing on the bank. If someone on the near shore saw us, we would hopefully be past them before they had time to react. Second, we looked like two fishermen out for a dawn catch, and we might pass out of sight before a closer inspection revealed who we really were. And that's what happened. We heard movement along the banks and we were probably visible in the dim light, but they didn't react. There were still some patches of fog on the river, and that helped.

"After we were on the river for fifteen or twenty minutes, we were spotted by a patrol that was on the move. The light was good enough that I could see they were NVA regulars. They saw us and yelled at us to stop, but we were past them before they could do much. Kiet and I tried to act like we just didn't hear them, but we were both digging a little harder with our paddles. They didn't shoot, but they started chasing us along the bank. We were moving with the current and they had to crash through a lot of brush. Then we came to a bend of the river, and soon they were both well behind us and out of sight. However, it showed us just how easily we could be spotted on the water. Fishermen or not, they were not going to let us just coast down the river unchallenged.

"Later on we passed some rocket and mortar emplacements, but they were abandoned or the NVA troops manning them were still asleep. I was pretty worried about that area where we encountered the tanks refueling, but when we got there the tanks were gone. The refueling tankers were there, and the soldiers around the trucks were busy camouflaging them. The fog was lifting with the sunrise, and it looked like they were trying to conceal the tankers from attack from the air. At any rate, they were too busy to pay us much attention, which was all right by me. I called in the coordinates to the FAC for future attention by our bombers, and turned off my radio. Right then I was focused on the next bend of the river and searching the shorelines for trouble. It was full daylight now, and very dangerous, but I was starting to think we might make it. Just a few more bends and twists of the river. Hambleton was now starting to moan and babble as he tried to talk. I kept whispering to him to keep quiet—to hang on for just a little while longer.

"All the while, Kiet was doing a great job of paddling up in the bow and keeping a sharp lookout. He would spot something up ahead and signal us into the foliage along the shoreline, and we'd wait until the danger passed. Then we'd move on. Before we got to what I thought to be the last bend in the river, we crossed over to the southern bank so we could be on the same side as the outpost. We'd just cleared the bend when we came under fire from a bunker farther downstream and on the south side of the river. It was a heavy machine gun and it was tearing up branches overhead and putting up water spouts all around us. We had no choice but to put the sampan into the bank and take refuge under a tangle of roots and logs along the shoreline. Somehow Kiet and I managed to keep the sampan in close to shore using a tangle of vegetation for cover. I managed to scramble up the side of the bank to see if there was any infantry in the area. I was worried that they may have been alerted by the shooting and come to investigate. Now that it was light and the fog had lifted, you could see for quite a distance down the river. That NVA gunner had spotted us well upstream of his position. If he'd just waited until we paddled down to his position, he could have easily killed us all, but he engaged us way too quickly. I guess it was a good thing we crossed the river so he could see us coming from a ways off. I don't even want to think what might have happened if we'd stayed to the north bank and come right past him. We'd have been at point-blank range.

"I immediately raised my forward air controller and said we *really* needed some air support. He came back saying that he had some fast-movers [jet fighter-bombers] inbound. I gave him the coordinates of the bunker, which was in a deserted village on the south bank of the river. It stood to reason that if there was one gunner there, there would probably be others. We weren't going anywhere until this gun emplacement got neutralized. The FAC then marked the target with a smoke rocket, and we waited."

Sometimes jets have a hard time spotting targets on the ground, as they're going so fast, so they need the slow-moving forward air controllers to mark the targets. As it turned out, these fast-movers were F-4 Phantoms from the aircraft carrier *Hancock*. The USS *Hancock* (CVA 19) was one of the twenty-four Essex-class carriers built during the Second World War, and *Hancock* was brought out of mothballs for both Korea and Vietnam. The NVA antiair defenses were minimal that morning and in that area. The F-4s were able to saturate the bunker complex with bombs and rockets. But with friendly lines and safety so close, Norris was taking no chances. After the Phantoms had worked over the target, he again contacted the FAC.

"I asked the FAC what else he might have available. I knew that a good bunker can often withstand a bombing and since we had to paddle right by it I wanted to make sure that the gunner was out of action. The FAC said he had a section [two aircraft] of Sandys.

Sandy was the call sign for the Air Force A-1 Skywarriors. They were propeller-driven close-support aircraft that could carry a whole lot of ordnance and had the ability to loiter on station for long periods of time. We loved it when the Sandys were overhead. I told the FAC to paste the target again as well as both riverbanks downstream from the village. By now, I had to figure the NVA forces in the area were on full alert, and we were not that hard to spot on the water in the daylight. I also asked for smoke, and I was in luck. One of the A-1s was carrying some smoke canisters. The wind was out of the east, so I had them put the smoke in on the north bank downstream from us. It was perfect. With the second pasting of the village and the smoke drifting over the water, we were able to continue along the southern bank of the river. When we came out from under the cover of the smoke, we were only about five hundred meters from the outpost. I thought we'd be safer on land and in the foliage than on the water, so we beached the sampan. Kiet helped me get Hambleton out of the sampan over my shoulder, and the three of us began to work our way along the shore and up the hill toward the outpost.

"The smoke the A-1s delivered that day made all the difference. It was not until I attended an A-1 pilots' reunion forty-three years later, in the summer of 2015, that I was able to thank the pilot who dropped that smoke. His name is Ron Smith. After all those years, it was an honor to finally thank him in person for his help during that rescue mission.

"Of course, we again had to be careful coming into a friendly position, but Kiet went on ahead and signaled the ARVN rangers that we were coming in. Several of the rangers and our two Sea Commandos came down to help us up the hill and into the bunker. As we made our way up the hill, we came under small-arms fire

from across the river. But with the help of the rangers and commandos, we made it back to the outpost, and to the bunker and safety.
Once we got Hambleton into the bunker, we helped him to the
floor and covered him with a blanket. He was in and out of consciousness, but I managed to get a little bit of warm liquid down
him. I checked him over for any major wounds, as this was the first
chance I'd had to carefully examine him in the daylight. Anderson
had thought to bring a good medical kit with the team gear so
we were able to dress some of his wounds. I kept telling him that
he was safe now and that things were going to be all right—that
we'd soon have him to a hospital. I think he understood, but he
was totally exhausted. Someone gave him a cigarette and he
seemed to respond to that. I guess if you're a smoker and haven't
had one in a while, a cigarette can really help. It settled him right
down.

"With Hambleton safely in the bunker, I called for an armored
personnel carrier to come and evacuate him, and wouldn't you
know it, we came under mortar and rocket attack again. This was
getting to be a daily ritual, and this time it was very intense. I knew
that the APCs would not come into the area while we were under
attack. And I also knew that sooner or later, these attacks were
going to be followed by an infantry assault. So I called the FAC,
and he was right there. They knew by now that we had Hambleton
at the outpost. The FAC pilot said he had some fast-movers code
named 'Garfish' on call, but he didn't know what or who they were.
I knew exactly what they were and told the FAC to clear them onto
the enemy concentrations across the river from us."

Garfish was the code name for Navy A-4 Skyhawk attack aircraft.
These A-4s were also from the USS *Hancock.* In one of those odd

twists of fate in war, this flight of A-4s was led by one Navy Lieutenant Denny Sapp. Denny Sapp and Tom Norris had become close friends while Norris and Sapp were both in Naval Flight School in Pensacola, Florida. Sapp finished his flight training and qualified as a naval aviator, while Norris left flight training for SEAL training. Neither Sapp nor Norris at the time knew of this coincidence until the incident was recalled years later. Following Vietnam, Denny Sapp went on to become the solo pilot with the Navy's famed Blue Angels Flight Demonstration Team.

"Once the A-4s cleared the target area, the FAC brought in more Air Force A-1 Sandys, and they continued to work over the NVA positions across the river. There now seemed to be no shortage of air cover for the outpost and Hambleton. The mortars and rockets stopped and the APC came into the outpost. The ARVN rangers helped us move Hambleton from the bunker into the APC. I think they felt that as soon as he was gone, the NVA across the river might lose interest in them. With Hambleton in the APC, I now had to start thinking about the third downed airman. He was out there and still evading capture. I called back to the base at Dong Ha, to the American advisor there, and they said he was still deep in enemy-controlled territory. I learned they were going to try to get him to move at night to a safe area, but that it would take some time *and* that he would be moving away from the outpost. It appeared that this outpost would not be a jumping-off point for any future rescue. So Kiet, myself, and the other two Sea Commandos were done there. I held up the APC while we hastily grabbed our gear and hopped aboard.

"As the ramp of that APC came up, I could see the faces of the

South Vietnamese rangers gathered around, waving good-bye. They were none too glad to see us descend upon their outpost, and now they were sad to see us go, which was surprising given that half of them had been killed or wounded during our three-day stay. Or maybe they were just sad to see us leave because we took with us the number-one highest priority for American air support in Vietnam. I often wonder how many of them lived through the NVA Easter Offensive. Or through the war, for that matter. My guess is not many."

The APC with Hambleton, Norris, Kiet, and the other two Sea Commandos rolled into Dong Ha in late afternoon on 13 April. Both the city and the base at Dong Ha were still under siege by the North Vietnamese. Hambleton was immediately airlifted to Da Nang, where a cordon of reporters was waiting for him. When questioned, Lieutenant Colonel Gene Hambleton issued his famous quote that captured the essence of his ordeal: "It was a hellova price to pay for one life. I'm very sorry."

At Dong Ha, Tom Norris, Nguyen Kiet, and the others were busy inventorying their gear, weapons, and radios. Tom was also looking for Lieutenant Colonel Lou Wagner. He knew there was another pilot out there on the ground, and he just assumed that they would be going back out to get him. Wagner, the senior American advisor for the ARVN 1st Armor Brigade, had been their primary contact at the Dong Ha base for the last few days. If a ground recovery operation were to be staged from Dong Ha or the shrinking perimeter around Dong Ha, Wagner would have to be a part of it. As they awaited events at the airstrip of the Dong Ha Combat Base, a reporter found Norris. He was the same reporter Norris had chased from the outpost at gunpoint just two days earlier.

"I'll bet you probably don't want to go back and do that again, huh?" the reporter asked, obviously not knowing Tom Norris.

"I couldn't believe this guy. 'No, *you* have it all wrong,' I told him in no uncertain terms. 'If another American is down and I can help him, then I'm going to do just that.'"

At the time, both Dong Ha and Quang Tri City were threatened by NVA forces coming in from the west. The ARVN outpost at Camp Carroll had fallen on 2 April, which opened the door for a buildup of NVA armor and infantry in western Quang Tri Province. But the situation at Dong Ha was the most critical. They were threatened from both the west and the north. Civilians were streaming south from the city and clogging Route 1 while ARVN forces were leaving the Dong Ha Combat Base along the same route. In some cases, the withdrawal was orderly; in others it was chaos. With the imminent collapse of Dong Ha, the 3rd ARVN Division was positioning itself to make a stand at Quang Tri City. On the evening of 13 April, Norris and his three Sea Commandos were trucked south to Quang Tri City. There they briefed staff officers and an advanced party of the ARVN 3rd Armor Division on the disposition of NVA forces they had witnessed. Then they found a billet and got some sleep. The next day, Norris learned that Lieutenant Colonel Anderson was at Camp Fay in Da Nang, and checked in with him by phone. The tenacious Anderson, who was still seriously wounded, had checked himself out of the hospital and was back on the job. Norris's first question was about First Lieutenant Bruce Walker, Covey 282 Alpha. He was told that Walker was on the ground and still evading, but well north of the Mieu Giang River. There was no immediate chance of a waterborne rescue similar to the recoveries of Mark Clark and Gene Hambleton.

That afternoon, Norris and his team caught a flight from Quang

Tri City to Da Nang and their home base at Camp Fay. Also on that day, 14 April, the Cam Lo Bridge was finally bombed and a section of the bridge was dropped into the Mieu Giang River. And another plane was lost. A Navy F-4 Phantom was brought down by ground fire while attacking NVA targets just north of the Cam Lo Bridge. The aircraft was observed being shot down and crashing, with neither of the crew getting out. No search and rescue effort was mounted.

Back at Camp Fay, Norris readied another team of Sea Commandos for a potential rescue effort, and tracked the movements of Bruce Walker. Walker was able to hide during the day, but moving, even at night, was difficult. There were simply too many enemy troops streaming south for him to work his way south to the Mieu Giang. On Norris's recommendation, Walker was instructed to move east and to move only at night. The plan was for Covey 282 Alpha to get to one of the streams east of Route 1 or even to the coast, where Norris and a rescue team might go in over the beach and get to him. Walker did in fact cross Route 1, but a local villager spotted him and alerted the Viet Cong of the American pilot's movements. In spite of yet another heroic effort by the airborne FACs and close-support aircraft, Bruce Walker was run to ground and killed by Viet Cong irregulars on the morning of 18 April.

AFTERMATH

A great deal of what took place over the course of this rescue ordeal, from the initial shoot-down of the Air Force EB-66C Destroyer aircraft to Gene Hambleton's final journey down the Mieu Giang River with Norris and Kiet, has been written about extensively. This was, after all, one of the costliest and most closely studied downed-pilot search and rescue operations of all time. Yet the details of these writings and re-creations have a decidedly Air Force/aviator-centric flavor to them—understandably so. This rescue mission, which lasted for close to two weeks, had become something of a tar baby, pulling in and grinding up assets, aircraft, and airmen at an alarming rate. So this final attempt by Norris and Kiet to recover Hambleton was followed closely by a great many people—pilots, ground crews, and senior commanders in Southeast Asia and Washington, D.C. The chatter of the FACs and the close-air-support pilots was transmitted and retransmitted to a great many ships, stations, and air bases in the region. Many of those air-to-air and air-to-ground communications were recorded, so there was an audio record of what took place in the air and the saga of the airmen on the ground.

Then there followed the reconstructions by Hambleton, Clark, the forward air controllers, and support air crews after the fact. And one can only imagine the gratitude and emotions of Clark and Hambleton as they were able to put voice to face of the brave FACs and close-support airmen who watched over them during this long ordeal. However costly, the operation provided a rich mosaic of courage, heroism, and lessons learned. But in all that followed, there was surprisingly little coverage about these events from the men responsible for the ground rescue effort—Anderson, Norris, and Kiet. Anderson recovered from his wounds and completed a career in the Marine Corps. Norris and Kiet moved on to other duties and other missions. For the modest Tom Norris and the stoic Nguyen Kiet, this singular rescue mission was simply another combat operation in a tour of duty in a long war.

One thing that has always bothered this narrator in reconstructions of Bat 21's rescue has been the exchange between Hambleton and Norris on that last day—the day Norris and Kiet brought Hambleton out. There are several accounts of just what took place. These accounts or versions differ widely, yet they could only come from interviews of these three individuals and from the FAC airmen and close-support pilots who flew the support missions on the final day of Hambleton's recovery. Tom Norris lived with my wife and me for a time in 1974 when he was detailed to Bethesda Naval Hospital for a series of reconstructive surgeries from wounds received subsequent to the rescue of Bat 21 Bravo. We talked a lot back then about the operation—what took place in the context of two combat leaders who both know and understand the stress and ambiguity of making decisions in small-unit combat. And in working on this book, we've covered this ground many, many times. Of course, my perspective is tainted—Tom is a brother SEAL. I'm always asking, "Why did you do this?" and "What were you thinking when you were confronted with that?" And there are the technical details of the patrol-leader responsibilities. Who carried the radio? How were your comms? Who walked point? How on earth did you keep that many balls in the air after Anderson was wounded and medically evacuated? And, of course, how did you keep going with little or no sleep for days on end? To this last question, Tom says, "Dick, that's why we went through Hell Week. You were there—you know. You can go for days without sleep if you have to." Yeah, I thought, but not working night after night behind enemy lines, and not under rocket and mortar fire when you weren't. At the time he first told me of the rescue, well before there was any talk of the Medal of Honor, I felt that it was simply an incredibly courageous piece of work. Now, more than four decades later, I still feel that way. No, I take that back. Tommy was far more professional and far more courageous than I could have ever have imagined.

PART TWO

NOT WITHOUT MY LIEUTENANT

TRANSITION

Following the rescue of Bat 21 Bravo, the North Vietnamese Easter Offensive continued into the northern and western provinces of South Vietnam, bringing pressure to both the combat base at Dong Ha and all of Quang Tri Province. The North Vietnamese Army continued to trade men and armor for ground below the Demilitarized Zone.

For Tom Norris, there was little rest. On his return to Da Nang and Camp Fay on 15 April, he continued to work with Air Force planners for the rescue of First Lieutenant Bruce Walker—Covey 282 Alpha. Walker had been on the ground for a week when Norris managed to get Lieutenant Colonel Hambleton to the ARVN outpost on the Mieu Giang River and on to Dong Ha. Walker had been dropped a survival pack with food, water, and a replacement radio on 14 April, but heavy concentrations of NVA troops in his area made it impossible for him to work his way south to the Mieu Giang for a Clark/Hambleton-like rescue. After much discussion, the decision was made to move Walker east across Route 1 toward the South China Sea. Norris, Kiet, and the other two Sea Commandos began to prepare for a possible over-the-beach rescue of the third airman. As far as the Air Force was concerned, Tom Norris was the go-to guy if they were to recover their pilot, and he was kept abreast of the developments as the pilot evaded on the ground. When Walker was killed by Viet Cong irregulars on 17 April, planning for his rescue ended. Marine First Lieutenant Larry Potts, the aerial observer and Covey 282 Bravo, was never heard from nor found, and to this day remains missing in action.

Yet the success of the recoveries of Clark and Hambleton generated interest in standing up permanent rescue teams for the recovery of future downed airmen. With the NVA Easter Offensive in full swing, the Air Force and Navy were ramping up their efforts to bring more American air power into play to blunt the NVA offensive. So there was great interest in creating an on-call, pilot-recovery capability that could function in the area around the DMZ and into North Vietnam, Laos, and Cambodia. Tom Norris was at the center of it. There was talk of creating multiple, company-sized recovery elements with Norris heading up the efforts.

"As you might imagine," Norris recalls with a grin, "my stock with the U.S. Air Force was pretty high at that time. They were wanting me to do all kinds of things and promising all kinds of assets and support. But it just didn't make any sense. By late April and into early May, it was pretty much understood that the NVA offensive was massive and that the entire North Vietnamese Army was committed to it. The only way to stop it was to bomb their supply lines, and that meant going back to a campaign of bombing up north and along the supply routes in Cambodia and Laos. So any rescue of a downed pilot would probably be a cross-border operation. I was contacted by the colonel in charge of what remained of MACVSOG, who wanted me to put together a unit for future recoveries. In fact, four enlisted SEALs were to be detailed to MACVSOG to help with this effort. My concern was that pilot rescues would mean going into Laos, Cambodia, or North Vietnam, and that we would never get approval to do these cross-border operations—even to get back one of our own. Additionally, the remaining MACVSOG assets were being turned over to the South Vietnamese, so we were losing American command and control of the Sea Commandos. And we now knew that unless an airman on the ground could be rescued easily and cleanly by a helicopter, his best chance for survival was to surrender and look to be repatriated at the end of the war. So this recovery unit never materialized.

"I still had six months on my tour, so with the SOG/STDAT organization being turned over to the Vietnamese, I was detailed over to the Military Assistance Command, Vietnam, or MACV, to work with the LDNNs or South Vietnamese SEALs."

STALEMATE

During the Tet Offensive of 1968, the North Vietnamese had used a limited number of their regular Army forces and relied on their Viet Cong irregulars to carry the brunt of the fighting. Using unconventional, insurgent-type tactics and avoiding conventional pitched battles had proven successful for the Hanoi government. General Vo Nguyen Giap, the revered North Vietnamese defense minister, had hoped that the Tet Offensive would lead to a general uprising against the Saigon government and their American allies. He was wrong. What took place was a wholesale slaughter of the Viet Cong cadres. While the Tet Offensive was a huge tactical victory for the South Vietnamese and the Americans, it did in fact play out as a North Vietnamese victory in the American press and helped to turn the tide of public support against the war in Vietnam. Just as the NVA traded armor and infantry for ground in the 1972 Easter Offensive, General Giap sacrificed a great many Viet Cong fighters to change American public opinion in his favor during the 1968 Tet Offensive.

By the late spring of 1972, the North Vietnamese Army had dropped all pretense of an unconventional struggle supported by a popular uprising of the people. They were going for a knockout blow. They sent three of their best divisions across the DMZ into Quang Tri Province, and three more divisions soon followed. Their ultimate objective was the capture of the provincial capital of Hue City—an objective they were denied during the Tet Offensive. Three more divisions attacked central South Vietnam from their sanctuaries in Laos, and another three-division force of NVA and Viet Cong came from Cambodia and moved toward Saigon from the northwest. It was an invasion force with 120,000 North Vietnamese soldiers and an unknown number of Viet Cong irregulars. General Giap had rightly guessed that the Americans would not reintroduce ground troops into South Vietnam and that with speed and surprise, the South Vietnamese would be no match for his hardened NVA force backed by armor and Soviet-provided long-range artillery.

The South Vietnamese Army was falling back in April and May 1972—sometimes in good order but often in disarray. All along hastily erected defensive lines, firebase after firebase fell to the North Vietnamese. In the north, following the fall of Dong Ha on 28 April, the South Vietnamese 3rd Division took up positions around Quang Tri City. But it too fell to the NVA, on 2 May. The seemingly unstoppable NVA advance rolled on south toward Hue City, but no farther.

Throughout May, all efforts by the NVA to take Hue failed. And for days on end, North Vietnamese troops were exposed to American B-52 strikes and the growing close-air-support sorties by Air Force tactical fighter-bombers and Navy carrier-based aircraft. By the end of May, the siege of Hue was lifted as the NVA, after sustaining massive losses, moved north back to Quang Tri City.

Farther south, the Easter Offensive experienced similar setbacks. In central South Vietnam, the NVA laid siege to the city of Kontum. Massive B-52 attacks augmented by American and South Vietnamese tactical air, and U.S. Army helicopter tank killers, finally drove the attackers back across the Laotian border. West of Saigon, the third prong of the NVA offensive was halted at An Loc. Under siege and constant artillery bombardment for ninety-five days, the city defenders refused to give way—again thanks to a generous dose of American air power. By the second week in July, the Viet Cong had filtered back into the countryside and the NVA had crossed back into Cambodia.

In Quang Tri Province, South Vietnamese forces had gone on the offensive. South Vietnamese paratroopers managed to fight their way into the citadel in Quang Tri City on 26 July, but were immediately driven back. The battle ebbed and flowed through August until, on 15 September, the ARVN forces finally retook Quang Tri City for good. But there they stopped. Both sides were exhausted. The South Vietnamese had suffered 10,000 dead and more than three times that many wounded. For the North Vietnamese it was far worse. Between 50,000 and 75,000 NVA soldiers perished, and at least that many more were wounded. Close to one in four soldiers of the North Vietnamese Army became a casualty in the Easter Offensive. Over seven hundred NVA tanks and armored vehicles, and a thousand other trucks and support vehicles, were lost. All this for the northern portion of Quang Tri Province; all this for territory that could have easily been taken, as was all of Vietnam, after the Americans and their air power had left for good.

THE VIETNAMESE SEALS

Throughout the Vietnam War, a great many American units created Vietnamese units in their own likeness. There were Vietnamese ranger and marine units. There were Vietnamese SEAL units, as well as explosive-ordnance-disposal (EOD) and small-craft-support units— all fashioned in some way after their American counterparts and trained in their likeness.

The American SEALs were the direct descendants of the underwater demolition teams and so were the Vietnamese SEALs. In 1960, the South Vietnamese Navy created underwater demolition units for harbor and port security duty. The new South Vietnamese frogmen trained in Taiwan, and the first underwater demolition team was formally established in July 1961. Very soon these frogmen, the *Lien Doi Nguoi Nhai,* usually referred to as LDNNs, added special amphibious operations to their mission taskings. The U.S. Navy SEALs were established in January 1962 and soon began advisory deployments to Vietnam. Initially, the SEALs were assigned to train Vietnamese Sea Commandos, or Biet Hai, for cross-border forays into North Vietnam. As the course of the war escalated and the Navy SEALs began rotating combat platoons into South Vietnam for direct-action combat operations, the U.S. SEALs began to take a hand in the training of the LDNNs for duty as SEALs. Beginning in the summer of 1965, formal training started in Nha Trang for the LDNNs under the guidance of Navy SEALs. The Vietnamese trainees, like their American counterparts on Coronado, California, and at Little Creek, Virginia, were vetted with long ocean swims, paddling small craft deep into swampy inlets, punishing runs, and a U.S. SEAL–like "Hell Week." In 1966, small cadres of LDNNs were brought to Subic Bay, the U.S. base in the Philippines, for special, more intensive training.

Throughout the development of the LDNNs, they remained an

asset assigned to the South Vietnamese Navy, and their American advisors were under the direction of the Military Assistance Command, Vietnam (MACV). At the beginning of the Easter Offensive, the MACV commander was General Creighton Abrams. The Vietnamese Navy and their LDNNs had their own cadre of advisors who reported to the Commander, Naval Forces, Vietnam, or COMNAVFORV. The U.S. Navy presence in Vietnam, under COMNAVFORV, also reported to General Abrams. Under this arrangement, U.S. Navy SEALs helped to train and, indeed, operated with LDNN units in the field. Yet their area of operations, with few exceptions, was confined to South Vietnam. The Biet Hai, or Sea Commandos, were different. They were an asset of the secretive MACVSOG organization (which also reported to MACV), but their portfolio extended to cross-border operations. These commandos were trained by U.S. SEALs, like Tom Norris, as well as Army Special Forces and Marine reconnaissance instructors. Speaking with SEALs of that era who trained both LDNNs and Sea Commandos, it was generally considered that the Sea Commandos were a superior force.

In 1971, in keeping with the turnover of assets and command structures to the Vietnamese, the LDNNs, both the frogmen and the SEALs, along with EOD teams and boat support teams, fell under a South Vietnamese command structure. The Americans served as advisors and training cadre to these units. Also during 1971, twenty-one LDNN officer candidates were taken to the United States for training; ten returned as qualified South Vietnamese SEALs to provide junior officer leadership to the LDNN. Operationally, the LDNNs were generally organized in twelve- to fourteen-man detachments with two or three American SEALs as advisors. These detachments were spread across the country, with many of the detachments operating with or near the remaining U.S. SEAL platoons in the lower Mekong Delta.

During the Easter Offensive in the spring of 1972, many of the LDNNs were pulled back to the Da Nang and Hue area. While this was a conventional NVA offensive met by conventional South Vietnamese forces, the LDNNs and their American advisors were being used to good advantage in a reconnaissance role to probe the territory now held by the North Vietnamese. To help bolster the LDNN efforts closest to the North Vietnamese line of advance, Tom Norris was assigned to the northernmost LDNN base of operations—a South Vietnamese small boat harbor at the village of Thuan-An. Thuan-An (pronounced "TWO-wee-non") was a small coastal facility just east of Hue City. Norris arrived there in June 1972. Barely two weeks earlier, another Navy SEAL had been assigned to the American advisory team at Thuan-An. His name was Mike Thornton.

BACK TO VIETNAM

"I arrived back in-country in May 1972," Mike recalled. "Since we were no longer deploying SEAL platoons as stand-alone operational units, there were no longer dedicated aircraft assigned to deploy those platoons. My last two rotations, we had our own assigned transport aircraft and let me tell you, they were something. They were called C-54s, and they were basically piston-engined, unpressurized DC-4 passenger planes. It was about forty air hours from San Diego to Saigon—flying at 9,500 feet. We stopped for fuel in Hawaii, Johnston Island, the Philippines, and Guam. It took forever. But on those trips, we had all our weapons and operational gear with us, along with a whole truckload of box lunches. This time I went to war on a chartered 707 from Travis Air Force Base to Tan Son Nhut, the big air base in Saigon. It was only about a third full on the trip over; most of those transpacific charter flights were bringing guys back. So this trip over was in relative luxury.

"As soon as I got in, one of the SEAL advisors picked me up and took me over to the LDNN training base at Nha Trang—about forty-five minutes from the air base. There were LDNN detachments all up and down the country. Some of them had American SEAL advisors, others did not. But most of the basic training for the LDNNs and some of the sustainment training took place at Nha Trang. I was there for about two weeks and it was a good stop for me. I got to meet some of the South Vietnamese LDNN training cadre working with their new recruits. And it gave me a chance to compare the LDNN program to what I was doing on my last tour, which was *not* to Vietnam.

"Right after my first deployment, I was assigned to the SEAL Team One training cadre on Coronado and worked under some really great SEAL instructors there. I taught—or 'helped to teach' might be a better phrase—advanced demolitions there at Team One in Coronado and small-unit tactics at our mountain training facility in Cuyamaca, some forty miles east of San Diego, just south of the town of Julian. It was a great time for me, and I learned a lot from those veteran instructors. One of them, Al Huey, got pulled from the training cadre and assigned to a platoon headed for Thailand to train the Thai SEALs. He asked if I'd like to go, even though I'd only been back a few months, and I said sure—another rotation, why not? This was in 1970, and while the Team One platoons were still in combat rotation, there was a general feeling that the war wasn't going to last too much longer. If you had a chance to get back overseas, you took it. And I was proud to have been asked to go over and work with the Thais. It wasn't an operational tour like my first one, but it was an important deployment nonetheless.

"The only sticking point was that I'd just gotten married, and she was not too happy about my heading back overseas. But just like

today, if a gal's married to a Navy SEAL, she's going to find that
he's gone a lot. This was not the last time, I'm sorry to say, that I
put my job and being a Navy SEAL ahead of my family. That first
deployment as a married guy was a relationship-tester. At least it
was for me."

During the Vietnam War, the North Vietnamese made liberal use of
Laos and Cambodia as sanctuaries for moving troops and supplies
south to the fighting in South Vietnam. Both Cambodia and Laos
were nations of tribes with weak central governments. The prevailing
Domino Theory at the time had one Southeast Asian nation after another falling to the communists. The next domino was Thailand. The
Thais were our only Asian allies at the time and provided bases for the
staging of U.S. air assets inside Thailand. In turn, we sent training
cadres to Thailand to help them resist incursions from North Vietnam
along the northern and eastern borders. And Thailand, being a Bud-
dhist nation and loyal to the monarchy, proved to be a good ally and a
difficult domino. The communists were never able to gain traction
with the Thai people as they were in other parts of Southeast Asia.

"That trip to Thailand toward the end of the war was a good one for
Team One and a break for some of the enlisted guys who were making combat rotation after combat rotation," said Dick Flanagan.
Lieutenant Flanagan was the platoon officer-in-charge or OIC of
the Thai training platoon. "In addition to our assignment as trainers, we thought we might be able to conduct some joint combat
operations with the Thais up along their northern border. But that
never came about. As it turned out, we were strictly trainers. Mike
worked out very well with the Thai SEALs. He's such an upbeat
guy and big guy, so the Thais really took to him. And for his part,

I think Mike genuinely liked them. Being a good advisor and a trainer means that you have to be a people person and you have to really embrace their culture. Mike did both. It was a good deployment all around, and since it was a nonoperational deployment, I was able to cut Mike loose early so he could get back for the birth of his son."

"This may sound a little strange," Mike recalled, "but I met my wife during basic SEAL training—during Hell Week. We were married right after I got back from my first deployment, and she was pregnant with our son when I went to Thailand. She was having some problems with the pregnancy, and Lieutenant Flanagan was able to let me come back a month early from the deployment so I could be with her when Mikey was born. Lieutenant Flanagan was a great officer, and I really appreciated his letting me come back early. That's why I volunteered to go back as an advisor to the LDNNs. I didn't think I'd put in a full tour with the Thais and hey, it was a chance to get back to where the action was. So I took it. I knew the job was to be an advisor, but I'd talked with some of the guys coming back from working with the LDNNs. They said they were still able to go into the field with them on combat operations. It was a chance to see at least some action. And again, I put being a SEAL ahead of my responsibilities at home.

"So when I got to Vietnam this time, I spent close to a week at Nha Trang working with the LDNNs there and getting the feel for what they were doing in the field. I'd worked with the Vietnamese SEALs on my first tour back in 1969, and I saw a few familiar faces. You have to hand it to those guys; for them, there were no combat rotations. Life *was* combat, twenty-four seven, year in and year out. They fought until they were killed or, as it worked out in the end, we lost the war. While I was in Nha Trang, I also saw the two senior officers who were responsible for those of us who were LDNN advisors. The first of these was Commander Dave Schaible—Uncle Dave. Of course, we never called him that to his face, but he was probably one of the best liked and most respected officers in the teams. He had been my CO [commanding officer] at SEAL Team One when I made my first two deployments. It was good to see him there at Nha Trang."

Captain David Schaible had been an enlisted EOD (explosive ordnance disposal) technician as well as an enlisted Navy SEAL. Then he became a thirty-two-year-old ensign. During his forty-plus years in the Navy, Uncle Dave commanded EOD and SEAL units at every operational level. In the spring of 1972, then Commander Schaible was the commander of CTF (Combined Task Force) 214 and, as a task force commander, he was addressed as "Commodore." CTF 214 was responsible for the American advisory effort for the LDNNs and for the South Vietnamese frogmen, the Vietnamese EOD technicians, and Vietnamese boat support teams. Schaible had just relieved the commander of CTF 214 late that February, but he was a quick study. And while he had to oversee all the units attached to his combined task force, his primary concern was for the eighteen or so American SEAL advisors who supervised the training and operational deployment of the two hundred–some LDNN SEALs. While there was an American exodus from Vietnam in the spring and summer of 1972, it was still dangerous business for those "advising" the Vietnamese. In the early spring of 1971, this narrator was deployed with my SEAL platoon in An Xuyen Province in the lower Mekong Delta. An LDNN detachment was assigned to our firebase to replace a sister platoon from SEAL Team One when they rotated back stateside. The senior advisor, Lieutenant Jim Thames, and three of his senior LDNNs were killed in a Viet Cong ambush shortly after they arrived. A second LDNN advisor was also seriously wounded.

Working with Schaible at CTF 214 was his able assistant, Lieutenant Commander Tommy Nelson, a veteran UDT/SEAL operator who had worked with the PRUs (provincial reconnaissance units). Nelson served as Schaible's executive officer as well as the primary supervisor for all of the LDNN advisors. Both Schaible and Nelson were based out of Vung Tau on the southeastern coast of Vietnam, where the South Vietnamese Navy was located, but they often got up to Nha Trang. In the spring of 1972, both Schaible and Nelson were pushing for their Vietnamese counterparts to move more LDNN and boat support assets north to help counter the North Vietnamese Easter Offensive. This led to a concentration of American advisors and LDNNs at Thuan-An. There were some thirty LDNN SEALs there along with five American advisors—three enlisted SEALs and two SEAL officers. Tom Norris would be the third officer and Mike Thornton would be the fourth enlisted SEAL on the Thuan-An advisory staff.

"The week I spent at Nha Trang gave me a chance to see the training there," Mike said of his return to Vietnam, "and I had a chance to spend some time with Commodore Schaible and Tommy Nelson. Of course," Mike added with a grin, "Commodore Schaible and I had some history. He was the commanding officer at SEAL Team One, and I was—well, you might say that I was not always the model sailor. There'd be the occasional bar fight or a speeding ticket that came to his attention—nothing major, just us SEALs letting off a little steam. So once or twice I found myself in his office explaining, or trying to explain, what had taken place. He was generally pretty understanding, but when he said, 'This time I'll overlook it, but not the next time,' you knew the next time he would hammer you. He was one of the finest commanding officers I've ever served under, and most of the Team One SEALs of my era will tell you the same thing. It was Tommy Nelson who managed the SEAL LDNN advisors, and he was the one that sent me up to Thuan-An. Tommy Nelson is another story for another time, but he was a great operator and respected up and down the chain of command."

Dave Schaible was this narrator's commanding officer at Underwater Demolition Team 22 and again at SEAL Team One. After Vietnam, while I was at the CIA, I had a close working relationship with him when he was then commanding officer of the Explosive Ordnance Disposal School at Indian Head, Maryland. He was one of the finest officers I knew during my time in naval service.

ON TO THUAN-AN

"I caught a hop on a C-130 from Saigon up to Da Nang and a CH-47 Chinook out of Camp Fay on up to Hue. One of the other SEAL advisors met me at Hue and we drove east to the base at Thuan-An. It wasn't much of a base, and both we and the LDNNs lived in corrugated metal Quonset huts—semiround huts that we referred to as hootches. The village of Thuan-An itself straddles the Perfume River that opens onto a long shallow bay that ran north and south with a barrier of dunes between the bay and the South China Sea. Our base was on the western side of the lagoon not far from the town. This allowed our boats access to the South China Sea through a cut in the dunes on the east side of the bay. The only other American presence was an Air Force LORAN station across the bay from us to the southeast."

LORAN (long-range navigation) A and LORAN C were at the time the primary military electronic navigation systems in place. Their precision could range from ten feet to several hundred yards. LORAN was replaced by more modern technologies in the 1980s. But the LORAN navigational sets were for installation aboard ships or aircraft. SEALs had no comparable equipment for precision navigation. They used map and compass, or a local guide, for most land navigation. Moving on the rivers or up and down the coast in a small craft was a piloting exercise. These were the days before GPS and the compact precision afforded today's special operators. Signals from this particular LORAN station were used to guide aircraft on strikes into North Vietnam.

"We Americans, officers and enlisted, all lived in the same hootch," Mike said of his new quarters. "We had a Vietnamese cook who bought all our chow out in the village, which meant we ate a lot of fish and rice. On occasion we'd take one of our LCVP [landing craft, vehicle/personnel] boats across to the Air Force chow hall. The Air Force ate a lot better than we did, but they were always ready to share. I guess with the North Vietnamese Army activity in the area, there was something in it for those Air Force guys to be nice to some Navy SEALs camped across the way. If it came to a fight, they could count on us.

"The conditions at Thuan-An were Spartan but we managed. We had an old pickup truck, and one of the guys got his hands on an Army jeep at the base at Hue. He managed to 'liberate' it before it was to be turned over to the Vietnamese, so we could get around. And someone came up with two window-type air conditioners that worked most of the time and we could sleep cool. With an outdoor shower and privy can that we burned off daily with diesel fuel, we lived as well as most SEALs did in Vietnam. There was a fridge in the hootch for leftovers, chow from care packages from home, and beer. With the heat and the chow the way it was, it was a formula for losing weight. I arrived weighing maybe two twenty and when I left six months later I was down to one ninety.

"The daily routine revolved around getting our Vietnamese LDNN SEALs out for PT [physical training], then getting them to the shooting range or working with them on small-unit tactics. Their abilities were all over the place. Some of them knew how to shoot and move and were tactically sound. Others seemed to have had no training at all. And their officers were a mixed bag. Some of them were damn good, while others got their commission because of family connections. It could be a little frustrating. But we did the best we could with them. As I mentioned earlier, it had been a long war for the Vietnamese with no end in sight.

"The detachment there at Thuan-An was not as busy as I thought it might be. How we and the LDNNs usually worked was that we became friends with the local village chiefs, and maybe even some of the province-level senior people, to develop intelligence. And two, maybe three times a week, we would take the jeep over to the Army base at Hue City to see if we could find some information about enemy movements along the coast. SEAL operations today are much different than in our day, but one thing has not changed: good intelligence leads to good operations. So we did what we could to work with the local leaders for actionable intelligence. The NVA had their own intel network with the Viet Cong, and that's who we were primarily after—the senior Viet Cong leaders in the area. But in June and early July 1972, no one was sure just how far south the North Vietnamese might go. Quang Tri City had fallen to them around the first of May and by mid-May they were probing the defenses of Hue City. If Hue fell, we'd all have to pull out and head south, probably to Da Nang. But Hue held. The South Vietnamese stopped them and the B-52s came in and pounded them from the air. In August we were told that we were winning and the South Vietnamese would soon counterattack to win back Quang Tri City. But no one was sure. I do know that a great many South Vietnamese, including our LDNNs, were afraid that the North Vietnamese Army might just roll over us. The village chiefs were being none too cooperative; they knew we Americans were leaving and no one knew if or when the NVA might come. Even our LDNNs were hesitant about going out on operations. I guess all of us were just waiting to see if the ARVNs had really stopped the NVA and if so, could they push them back north. One of our priorities was to try to capture Viet Cong or perhaps even an NVA soldier to see what might be the status or intention of their forces. Past that, the detachment operationally was not all that busy. We went into the field on an operation maybe once or twice a week. We really had to get creative to find a good reason to operate.

"The LDNN detachment at Thuan-An was organized roughly into two elements or squads. The U.S. advisors would help the LDNNs plan operations and then go into the field with them, so they were really U.S./LDNN joint operations. One of our officers and one or two of our enlisted SEALs would help an LDNN squad work up a mission, then go with them on the operation. And to be honest, it seemed as if it was us Americans who were always pushing for operations. There was an odd mix of Navy SEALs there at Thuan-An. The enlisted guys were all SEAL Team One veterans. The two officers were from SEAL Team Two and while they were both lieutenants, this was their first combat tour. I guess they had us West Coast vets there to keep them out of trouble. But then Tom Norris came to MACV and the LDNN program from MACVSOG.

"When Nasty—that was our name for Tommy—came to Thuan-An, he was put in charge of the SEAL advisory group there. The other two officers and the five enlisted SEALs reported to him, and he in turn reported to Lieutenant Commander Nelson down in Vung Tau. We all worked together pretty well, but having an experienced officer in the mix was definitely a good thing. The two new SEAL officers listened to us veterans; they just about had no choice, as they were totally inexperienced. So after Tommy arrived in Thuan-An, everything went through him before anyone did anything. But Tom Norris was not one to sit back and let others go into the field. He put together his own share of operations and was always looking for ways to get in the action.

"I got to Thuan-An a few weeks ahead of Tommy. Yet we all knew who he was, that's for sure. Everyone knew about the pilot-recovery operation, so he was something of a minor SEAL celebrity. But none of us had ever worked with him. We knew him only by reputation—and in the SEAL teams, reputation is everything. I knew two guys from SEAL Team Two who were in his first platoon—Al Ashton and Chuck Fellers. They said he was a good officer and a steady one, which for us enlisted SEALs meant that he was an officer who would listen to his platoon veterans. That's how it worked between the officers and enlisted men. A good officer was one who would listen and learn, and who could make good decisions in the field. Tom Norris had that reputation. He also had a reputation of being fearless, which is not always a good thing. A little fear going into combat can be a healthy thing. So all us West Coast enlisted SEALs from Team One were glad to see Lieutenant Tom Norris show up at Thuan-An. But man, was he small. He couldn't have been more than a hundred forty pounds soaking wet."

Today's SEALs are bigger than those from the Vietnam era, averaging close to six feet and weighing about one seventy-five or more. But by the standards back then, Mike at six feet two inches and a solid 218 pounds was a big guy. It might be said that Mike was ahead of his time—both because of his size and because he was predisposed for military distinction. He was raised in Spartanburg, South Carolina (population 37,000), which has something of a reputation for heroes. Mike is the fifth Spartanburg resident to receive the Medal of Honor. Yet his name is not on the memorial honoring the town's recipients, as he was not born there. Mike was born in Greenville, South Carolina, on 23 March 1949. Before he was a year old, his parents moved thirty miles west to the town of Spartanburg.

GROWING UP IN CAROLINA

"Spartanburg was my home; it's where I grew up. We lived in town for a short while before Daddy moved us outside of town and into the country. Our closest neighbor was a quarter mile away, so my younger brother and I grew up fishing and playing cowboys and Indians in the woods around the house—chasing cows, building forts, and getting into mischief. My brother was a year younger than me, so we were together most of the time. We fought a lot, but were the best of friends. And I had a younger sister as well, but she was six years younger, so we boys didn't have too much to do with her when we were growing up. She was just our kid sister. My dad was in the construction business and an insulation contractor. He was also the guy who not only took care of our family but our extended family as well. Anytime someone in the family had a problem, it seemed like they would come to my dad, and he would help them. Daddy always said that blood and family came first, something he passed along to the rest of us. He was ten years older than my mom and a World War II vet. He was in the infantry, and served with a coastal artillery unit in the Philippines. I know he worked with boats as well, but he never talked too much about the war.

"Some of my earliest memories were of getting into trouble with my brother, and my dad punishing us. I remember him taking me and my brother out to the well house with a leather belt, but before he whopped us, he would talk to us about what we'd done and why we were being punished. He made sure we knew why he had to whip us. It was his disapproval that hurt more than the whipping. Neither my brother nor I wanted to disappoint him. I forget the swats on the butt, but I can still remember the look of disappointment on Daddy's face. But we did some crazy stuff. One time my brother and I decided to take a ride in Daddy's pickup truck. I was five and he was four. We started the pickup, and I knelt in the seat to steer while he worked the pedals. We got damn near down our long drive to the county road before we rolled off into the ditch. Another time we were playing cowboys and Indians in our barn. We decided to build a campfire in one of the horse stalls and almost burned down the barn. Again, Daddy would first talk to us and then out came the belt. Yet, there was a lot of love in my family. All us kids grew up knowing that our parents really cared for us.

"We did a lot of things as a family—picnics, boating, fishing, things like that. And we went into town to the YMCA, where we all learned to swim. Daddy made sure we knew how to swim at an early age, even though he himself couldn't swim a stroke. Swimming was something that I always seemed to be good at. I was good at other sports, but swimming was my thing. I could swim faster and farther than just about any other kid my age. So I hung out at the pool a lot in the summers and even became a lifeguard. I was always very comfortable in the water.

"My brother and I also watched a lot of TV with the family after dinner. I think it was then that I first got interested in the Navy and becoming a frogman. I remember seeing *The Fighting Sullivans,* about five brothers who were all on the same Navy destroyer in World War II. The ship was hit and four of the brothers refused to leave, searching for the oldest Sullivan. All five were killed when the ship exploded. Now *that's* family. I guess it was not too long after that when I saw Richard Widmark and Dana Andrews in *The Frogmen* and then I was hooked. I always figured that I'd go into the military, so when it came my time to go, I joined the Navy. I still wanted to be a frogman, but that would come later. We liked watching John Wayne and just about any cowboy movie, but I still remember the Sullivans and those Navy frogmen. You ask a lot of guys from my generation in the teams and they'll say the same thing. It all began by watching our heroes on black-and-white, small-screen television.

"I didn't do all that well in school. I couldn't read and I still have problems with it. I'm dyslexic. Back then, they didn't call it that—you were just dumb. For me it meant that I simply couldn't keep up in school. I did okay in math but that was probably the only thing. And I loved history. Otherwise, I did poorly. I had to repeat my sophomore year in high school, and that really hurt my pride. Failing a grade is a blow to a fifteen-year-old boy's ego. I wanted to play high school sports and the coaches wanted me to play. I was tall and lanky then, and they wanted me as a linebacker in football. But my grades just wouldn't allow it. I got As in P.E. and Bs in math, but

Ds and Fs in everything else. I was in summer school every summer. So it's no wonder I got in with the wrong crowd and started getting into trouble. Nothing serious, but we were mischievous—southern country boys drinking beer and making bad decisions. The sheriff was out to the house a few times, and there was a time or two in juvenile court. And I cut a lot of classes. I had seventy-two absences in my senior year in high school. It was hard on my parents, especially Daddy, as he was the one who had to deal with me. He always stood up for me, because that's what families do, but even he could see I was headed for trouble.

"You hear a lot of those stories back then about the judge saying, 'It's go into the service or go to jail.' Well, it wasn't exactly like that for me, but it was damn close. I was running with a bunch of guys who were like me, service classification 1A and waiting for the draft to catch up with them. We all knew we were headed for the military, and we were just having a good time while we waited. Well, Daddy and the judge talked it over. I was headed for reform school, and they both knew it. So my dad took me in to see the judge and he said, 'Son, I'm going to let you make your first major decision in life. You can join one of these fine armed forces or the county has a special school that will provide you with the kind of close supervision that I think you need.' I joined the Navy in Spartanburg and then drove to Columbia, South Carolina, to be sworn in. A few months later, they mailed me my high school diploma—probably because they didn't want me coming back for it."

In talking with Tom and Mike about how they grew up, it's hard to find two young men who were more dissimilar—physically, educationally, temperamentally, and socially. Yet at least for this narrator, three things stand out in these two young lives that were common to both. Both grew up in families that were close and put a premium on what might loosely be termed today as strong family values. They were both loved, and early on they were raised to understand right from wrong—if not always doing the right thing. Second, they both had a brother who was younger but close to them in age. As the older sibling, they were always the leader and they took some measure of responsibility for their younger brother. If there was a scrape or there was trouble, or someone had to answer for the actions of the two, that burden fell to them. Looking out for a younger brother brings a maturity and a personal accountability that both Tom and Mike took seriously. And finally, early on both Tom and Mike stood up for what was right. Like all boys moving into manhood, they got into fights. For both, these fights were often the result of someone picking on their younger brother or stepping in to confront a bully. As young boys, both had an intolerance for anyone who abused or took advantage of someone else. Neither would stand for it. The fact that Mike was a big kid and Tom was not made no difference. Both would step in and take the part of the underdog.

CLASS 49

"I can honestly say I enjoyed Navy boot camp," Mike recalls of his first days in the Navy. "It was four months at the Naval Training Base in San Diego and for me, it was easy. Unlike high school, I could keep up and even excel. There were other guys like me at Navy boot camp who had trouble reading, and the Navy was very good about taking the time to make sure we learned what we had to know. I was a better athlete than most of the other guys, and in the pool I could help others. When I graduated, I went directly to my ship. I was an engineman striker, which meant I was still a seaman, but designated to work with auxiliary gasoline and diesel engines aboard ship. Usually a seaman out of boot camp goes to what they call A-School to learn about his rating—in my case, engines. I didn't test so well, so they sent me straight to my ship, the USS *Brister*. Actually, this was a stroke of luck, as the *Brister* [DER-327] was an old ship and scheduled for decommissioning. I was aboard long enough to put my package in for UDT/SEAL training and within a few months of reporting to the ship, I had orders to Coronado.

"I got there just in time to begin training with Underwater Demolition Recruit Training Class 49. Back then they didn't call it BUD/S, and there were no pretraining programs or indoctrination. You just showed up and jumped right in. I knew I wanted to be a frogman, but I had no idea what I was getting into—how hard it would be. Hell, it was considered shore duty, so I figured that I'd have the weekends off and that during the week after the workday a guy could go into San Diego for a few beers. Boy, was I in for a surprise."

"Mike was a character, start to finish," says his friend, classmate, and teammate Hal Kuykendall. "I remember we arrived for SEAL training with Class 49 in Coronado at the same time. It was around the first of November 1968. We were still over in the old Quonset huts on the Naval Amphibious Base on San Diego Bay. Training began the next day and everyone was turned in early, trying for some sleep, as we all knew the first day of training was a real ballbuster. We got there about midnight, and Mike turns on every light in the barracks. That brought all kinds of complaints from the guys in their racks. Mike just said, 'That's why God gave you eyelids. Why don't you try using them.' He proceeded to take a shower and stow his gear, and then he turned off the lights. I didn't like Mike at first. It took me a while to get to know him and to warm up to him. But start to finish, he was a strong SEAL trainee."

Basic underwater demolition team/SEAL (BUD/S) training at that time was conducted on both coasts. The Underwater Demolition and SEAL teams then came directly under the Navy, and with the exception of Vietnam or other area-specific deployments, the East Coast teams served units of the Atlantic Fleet and the West Coast teams those of the Pacific Fleet. Training on both coasts was conducted at the main Navy amphibious bases that served that fleet—Little Creek, Virginia, and Coronado, California. Without getting into the odd class nomenclature, Mike was in training in Coronado with Class 49 (West Coast) at the same time as Tom Norris and your narrator were training with Class 45 on the East Coast. The training differed organizationally and professionally and in how the phases of training—basic physical training, diving, land warfare, weapons training, and so on—were conducted. But both coasts had a brutal Hell Week. Only about one in five who entered this ordeal made it through to the end. That was the case back in 1968–69 when we went through training, and it's the same today. Class 49 on Coronado began with 129 trainees and graduated eighteen of the original 129 and four who rolled into the class from a previous class. In my Class 45 at Little Creek, we began with seventy-two and graduated thirteen Americans and two Turkish officers. In Class 45, all of us went to the East Coast Underwater Demolition Teams, but for Tom Norris. He had orders to SEAL Team Two. In Class 49, fourteen of the graduates went to the West Coast UDTs, while eight were selectively assigned to SEAL Team One. Mike Thornton was one of the eight.

Perhaps one difference in the East and West Coast training venues was the instructor cadre. Instructors at the two training facilities came from the teams on that coast. Both teams had commitments in Vietnam, but the West Coast combat rotations were far more rigorous than for the East Coast, especially in the UDTs. So there were a great many more combat veterans on Coronado than in Little Creek.

"We had some instructors who were not only good teachers, but they were real characters," Mike recalls. "There was Vince Olivera, who was part American Indian and a plank holder [assigned to the unit when it was first commissioned] at SEAL Team One. He called us palefaces and we all stood in awe and fear of Instructor Olivera. Then there was Dick Allen, a black SEAL who was the Navy boxing champion. He once sparred with Muhammad Ali. When Ali was once asked who hit him the hardest, he said that it was a chief petty officer in the U.S. Navy named Dick Allen. And then there was Instructor Terry Moy, who we called Mother Moy. It seemed as if he was always there watching us, making sure we did everything right and that we put out 110 percent."

"I remember Mike Thornton," said the now-retired Master Chief Petty Officer Terry Moy. "He was one of those strong trainees who was very good in the water. And he was also one of those in-your-face trainees who was just a natural for extra attention by the instructors. Guys like Mike we would single out for more push-ups and more harassment. Basically, we picked on him because we knew he could take it, and it was good for class morale. Like one of us would say, 'Okay, because Thornton here screwed up the evolution, the whole class is going to have to do it over again.' By singling out two or three of the strong trainees for extra attention, it brought the class together as they sought to protect and look out for one of their own. We wanted our trainees to bond as a class, just like they would later be expected to bond as a team or an operational team. Because Mike was outgoing and gregarious, not all of his classmates liked him—especially the more serious ones. But when we picked on him, the rest of the class would rally behind him. Every class has a Mike Thornton or two, and we SEAL instructors used them to good advantage."

"Training was hard, but it was also a lot of fun," Mike says of his Coronado training class. "I didn't have a lot of problems, and I was always very good in the water. But I was not all that good a runner. We had to run four miles for time in boots on the beach, and I was always at the back of the pack, which meant I was out there running with the goon squad after everyone else was secured from the day's training. But during those goon-squad runs, Olivera or Dick Allen or Mother Moy would be out there running with us. So my times came down. By the end of training I was doing 5:40 miles in boots and in the sand.

"Hell Week was hard—maybe an hour of sleep a night if we were lucky, and we were always cold and wet. The instructors worked us in shifts, so they were always fresh. It was a miserable week, but what stands out in my mind as the hardest day in training was the night we tried to get one over on the instructors. We were coming back from the mud flats in south San Diego Bay, back to the amphibious base by way of running on the beach. We were on our own, each boat crew carrying our rubber boats on our heads. The Hell Week class was divided into boat crews, and each crew's constant companion was their IBS [inflatable boat, small]. An IBS is twelve feet long, five and a half feet wide, and weighs 108 pounds. We carried them everywhere. This time it was a race back to the base carrying our boats, and it always paid to be a winner. Well, my crew and another crew figured we'd get a leg up on the instructors and the other Hell Week crews. One of my classmate's girlfriends came over the beach berm with a four-wheel-drive flatbed truck. We loaded two of the boats on the flatbed, piled aboard, and away we went. The plan was to hide out along the beach, then jump back in ahead of the other crews—all rested and coming in first. As we came up the strand highway to the base, this Navy ambulance pulls up alongside us and guess who's in the cab? Vince Olivera and Dick Allen. Well, when we got dropped off, they were waiting for us. They made us pay, and pay dearly. While the other trainees got a meal by the fire and got to doze off for fifteen minutes, we got to do push-ups in the surf, a roll in the soft sand, then more surf push-ups. It's what they call surf torture. The instructors like it when you try to be sneaky, but when you get caught, you pay the price. That night, we paid in full, and I'll never forget it. After that beating, we came together as a crew and started winning boat-carry evolutions without cheating."

For the record, there were *three* crews who took a shortcut that night. The third crew, however, managed to elude the instructors and gain a reprieve from that Hell Week evolution. And as an aside, one of the young women who tried to help Mike and his boat crew in their ill-fated attempt to sneak their boats past the instructors was later to become his wife.

"It was just after we began our last phase of training, the land warfare phase out on San Clemente Island, that we got our team assignments. There were twenty-two guys who graduated in my class—eighteen from the original 129. I remember how lucky and proud I felt when I was given orders to SEAL Team One. Even back then, it was no small thing to be a Navy SEAL. But it's one thing to be a SEAL and yet another to do the work of a SEAL."

THE SUMMER OF '72

"After Tommy arrived at Thuan-An, it seemed like we pressed a little harder for operations. He was a guy who wanted to go out and get things done. And things began to pick up a bit once it was clear that the NVA were not going to be able to take Hue City. Then when the ARVNs finally recaptured Quang Tri City in mid-September, it got even better. Most of our missions were reconnaissance-type missions, and we were always looking to grab a Viet Cong fighter or, better yet, a senior-level Viet Cong cadre. But the LDNN SEALs were still a little reluctant to go into the field. And we all understood that. Many of them had been fighting for a decade or more, and while we SEAL advisors were still there, they knew we'd be gone soon—and by early 1973, we were. Still, while we were there, most of us wanted to go on operations whenever we could, and we were looking for intelligence leads that might get us to a good target.

"A typical LDNN SEAL operation would have us launch from Thuan-An late afternoon in one of the boat-support-detachment junks. These were concrete junks—imagine! They were ferro-cement hulls built in Vietnamese shipyards for the coastal junk force. We had a few of these junks assigned to support LDNN operations. We'd make our way out to the South China Sea and either turn left and go north toward the DMZ or south toward Da Nang. After dark, we'd insert over the beach, patrol to the objective, and then try to get back across the beach and out to the junk before first light. If we went south, we were usually targeting the Viet Cong or looking to capture a VC fighter for intelligence. If we went north, we were probably still looking for a VC target, but maybe grab an NVA soldier. There were still main-force elements of NVA north of Thuan-An and we had to be very careful. Sometimes we'd launch from the junks in an IBS [the same Zodiac-type rubber boats we used in basic SEAL training on Coronado] and paddle in close to the beach. From there it was over the side and a swim through the surf. If the junk could get in close enough, we'd swim ashore from the junk. Most of our operations fell into this pattern.

"In the evenings, we'd sit around with a beer and recall the old days when we deployed as SEAL platoons to conduct direct-action missions. Yet we knew those days were over. Back then, we usually operated in SEAL squads of six to seven SEALs with a Kit Carson Scout or two [Vietnamese Army scouts who used to be Viet Cong but came over to the Vietnamese Army under an amnesty program], a couple of LDNNs, or a local guide. My first platoon was Charlie Platoon and we were in-country from December 1969 through July 1970. We worked out of a place called Dong Island, and it was a great deployment. We had solid platoon officers and our platoon leading petty officer was Barry Enoch, one of the finest SEAL operators at Team One. When I made my first deployment, he was my sea daddy. It was the same for all of us on our first combat tour, and it was an active tour. Seems like we'd be out every other night, and most of the time we made contact. I remember we took down a few province-level Viet Cong cadre types, and one time we had good intelligence and were able to take down an entire VC grenade factory. Jumped right in the middle of it; it was great."

"I was one of the eight from Class 49 to go to SEAL Team One along with Mike," recalls Hal Kuykendall, "and I was with him in Charlie Platoon. And it truly was a great platoon. Us new guys, and even the veterans, worshipped Barry Enoch; he was a great leader and a great teacher. Mike fit right in. He carried the squad M-60 medium machine gun and about eight hundred rounds of ammunition—often more. Sometimes a whole operation would depend on getting the 60-gunner into position where he could command the target. And Mike loved it. I was the radioman in my squad. I walked right behind the squad leader and Mike walked behind me. When he put that 60 into action, it was like poetry. He'd settle into a nice three-to-four-burst rhythm—sort of a cadence.

"I can remember more than one firefight, where we were shooting and ducking—sometimes more ducking than shooting. But Mike would be right there, working that 60 with a big grin on his face. There were plenty of times when I was really scared, but I'm not sure Mike ever was. He was reliable and brave, but I'm not sure he ever knew or understood fear like the rest of us. He was a great teammate and my God, he was strong. None of us could believe how much ammo he carried. Sometimes he'd go out with a thousand rounds, or more. That's close to eighty pounds of just ammo. And he'd swim canals with that load! He'd just shrug and say, 'You don't want your 60-gunner running out of ammo, do you?' We got through a pretty active tour with no one getting killed. Then a couple of the guys stayed behind to break in the new platoon while the rest of us packed up and left. They were two of our best, and one of them was killed in a helo crash with three other SEALs. We all took it hard when Rich Solano was killed, but I think Mike took it the hardest. Mike was a guy who really cared for his teammates."

"Mike was a solid platoon SEAL from start to finish," recalled Tom Boyhan. Then Lieutenant Tom Boyhan was Charlie Platoon's officer in charge. "He could get a little wild when he wasn't in the field, but so could a lot of us. But [Barry] Enoch only had to say a word to him, and he'd settle right down. But Mike was a sled dog; I've never seen anyone carry that much ammo. It was unbelievable. And he was reliable in a fight. I only saw him falter one time. It was during a daylight operation, and we didn't do too many of those.

We were in these motorized skimmers that were something like a Boston whaler only with shorter gunwales. It was a Viet Cong small-craft boatyard of some sort, and we decided we'd just drive in and take it down—surprise them in the daylight. It was an audacious play, but it worked. The VC just watched while we came down the canal, and we were in the middle of them before they knew it. Then the shooting started. Before they could get organized to resist, we had the upper hand.

"We formed a loose skirmish line and began to work our way through the objective. I heard Mike's M-60 get off a few rounds, then it went silent. The bark of an M-60 is very distinctive; it's psychological as well as a fire-superiority weapon. When it was quiet, something was wrong. I looked around and Mike was on one knee. He had the weapon's receiver in one hand and the barrel in the other. M-60s are designed for a quick barrel change, and so the barrels twist off with a quarter turn. It seems his first few rounds had unseated the barrel. 'No problem, Lieutenant,' he yelled with that wild Mike Thornton grin, 'I'll have it fixed in no time.' And he did. Soon he was back on line and had his 60 rhythmically barking out short bursts. After we finished the mission, he apologized for letting his gun go down for a few minutes."

"Those of us at the LDNN base in Thuan-An all came to know both Tom and Mike well," recalled Ryan McCombie. Then Lieutenant Ryan McCombie was one of the SEAL officers from SEAL Team Two who was cutting his teeth as an LDNN advisor on his first combat deployment. "Both were great SEAL operators, and they were both very different guys. Tom was quiet and serious, yet he had this great, wry sense of humor. He rarely drank and never used foul language, which was probably one reason the guys in his first platoon took to calling him 'Nasty.' We of course picked right up on that nickname. But he was all about getting the job done. After Tom arrived, we began going out a little more frequently. Mike was easygoing and gregarious—always ready for a laugh or to kid around. I'm proud to have served with them both and proud to call them friends today. As for Mike, he could be a rowdy sailor as well as a crack Navy SEAL. I remember well the first and only time I went out for a few drinks with Mike Thornton in Vietnam.

"Today, SEALs generally deploy in an alcohol-free environment. This began with General Order Number One initiated by General Norman Schwarzkopf in the Gulf War—no alcohol in the battlespace. Probably a good idea, but in Vietnam that was not the case. Alcohol was readily available. For us back then it was usually a cold beer or two after we came in from an operation or at the end of the training day. But one day, it got a little past that. Not long after Tom arrived in Thuan-An, I received word that my first child had just been born, and that mother and son, Ryan, were doing just fine. So we decided to celebrate. We took the LCVP over to the Air Force base where there was a bar just outside their gate that catered to American servicemen. And we started drinking. It was probably one of the only times that we really got drunk. At any rate, a few Army Special Forces soldiers came in for a beer and a bowl of rice, and being SEALs, we started giving them a hard time. Well, one thing led to another, and pretty soon the Army guys began to get a little fed up with us. And rightly so. Then the team leader, a Special Forces major, takes out his .45 and says it's time for us to drink up and leave. He probably had no intention of using it; it was just for show. But he did take the gun out of his holster. So Mike slaps it out of his hand, picks the guy up, and throws him out the window. The bar was built out over a tidal inlet, so the Army major lands in a few feet of water and a whole lot of mud. Mike hands the pistol to one of the other Army guys and says they might want to go out and re-trieve their officer before the tide comes in and washes him away. All the while, he's got this wild grin on his face. That's just how he was."

Ryan McCombie went on to serve for twenty-six years in the Navy and the Navy SEAL teams, retiring with the rank of captain. He now serves on the board of trustees for his alma mater, Penn State Univer-sity. When both Tom Norris and Mike Thornton speak of good naval officers they've served with during their SEAL careers, Ryan Mc-Combie is at the top of that list.

The main force fighting around Quang Tri City continued through mid-September, when the NVA finally quit the outskirts of the city and consolidated their positions along the southern bank of the Cua Viet River. The Easter Offensive had taken the starch out of both the North and South Vietnamese forces, and by the first week of October they had settled into static lines of defense. While this left the north-ern portions of Quang Tri Province under North Vietnamese control, the provincial capital had been retaken. Hue City, and by extension the LDNN base at Thuan-An, was safe—for the time being. With Quang Tri City now under ARVN control, the question arose as to what might be the next move in driving the North Vietnamese back across the DMZ. It seemed logical that the ARVN would continue north along Route 1 to recapture Dong Ha. Or through the north-central part of the Quang Tri Province toward the city of Cam Lo. Yet efforts to push the enemy out of western Quang Tri Province were frustrated by the NVA's use of Laos as a sanctuary and for resupply. And now that the NVA were in a defensive posture, their superb long-range Soviet artillery made the prospect of any further push north a costly offensive.

"There was a great deal of talk about landing the Vietnamese marines north of the NVA line of defense at the mouth of the Cua Viet River in an Inchon-like maneuver," recalled Ryan McCombie. "Or even a seaborne assault to retake the Cua Viet Naval Base as a step to recapturing Dong Ha. Some thought any amphibious landing behind the NVA lines would be a feint and an attempt to fool the NVA into thinking it would be a major amphibious effort while the Vietnamese rangers attacked Cam Lo or Dong Ha from the west. But no one really knew what was going to happen—if anything. A couple of times a week, two or three of us would take the jeep into Hue City to talk with the Army advisors there. They didn't know much more than we did, but we were getting more requests for intelligence on enemy movements along the coast north of Thuan-An. It was that need for intel that took Tom Norris down to Vung Tau late that October."

MISSION TASKING

"The summer of 1972 and into the fall was a very tense time for all of us in the Hue City area," Tom Norris recalled. "We knew the Paris Peace Talks were under way, but that really meant little for us at the operational level. We were focused on the next mission. Gradually that summer, and certainly when we got into September, we knew the North Vietnamese were not going to overrun Hue. We continued to operate in the fall much as we had that summer, conducting a lot of coastal reconnaissance operations. When we did go up north of Thuan-An, we went at night, and when we went ashore, we were careful to avoid any large concentrations of NVA. But exactly where the enemy was, and in what strength and configuration, was unknown to those at MACV or to the South Vietnamese.

"For me personally, I went out on very few of the operations. I left that for Ryan and Doug Huth, the two assigned SEAL Team Two officers. They needed the experience in the field and, given just how few operations we were running, there was no need for me to go out. Then on 25 October, I got a message from Commodore Schaible that he wanted to see me and that I was to get to Vung Tau as soon as I could. The next day, a couple of the guys drove me down to Da Nang, where I caught a helo from there directly to Vung Tau. Vung Tau was a coastal city some fifty miles southeast of Saigon. It was an old city with a lot of intact French architecture. There was a nice, crescent-shaped harbor, and it was very picturesque. It was also home to the Coastal Surveillance Command, what was more commonly referred to as the Brown Water Navy, and Commodore Schaible's CTF 214, which included the LDNN advisors.

"Uncle Dave had me take a seat in his office, and I could tell he had something on his mind. 'Tom,' he said, 'my counterpart [the Vietnamese commander of the LDNNs] wants to run a SEAL reconnaissance mission to the mouth of the Cua Viet River. Specifically he, or he and his superiors in the South Vietnamese Navy, want to know about the defenses and enemy disposition around the Cua Viet Naval Base. He wants a Vietnamese LDNN officer to head up the reconnaissance team. I want you to run the operation to ensure the mission gets done properly, but this needs to be seen as a Vietnamese operation.'

"I knew what this meant. It meant that we would run the operation, and when we got back, the Vietnamese officer would report what he saw and learned to his superiors. His American officer counterpart—in this case, me—would also report what took place, but from all outward appearances it was to be a Vietnamese show. That was okay with me, as we had some terrific LDNNs, and as long as I could choose the team, American and LDNN, I knew things would work out once we were in the field. But I was a little iffy on just why we needed to go up there, as we already had much of the information needed for any kind of an assault on the Cua Viet base.

" 'Sir,' I told him, 'I think we already know what's going on up there, as we had teams in that area shortly before I got to Thuan-An. I'm not sure we need to mount an operation to go and get what we pretty much already know.'

"So Uncle Dave gives me that knowing, patient smile of his and says, 'Tom, that's not what I asked you. I asked if you could lead an American-LDNN reconnaissance patrol up to the Cua Viet Naval Base and report back on base defenses and enemy disposition.'

" 'Yes, sir,' I replied. 'I'm sure we can do that.' Thinking quickly, I added, 'So long as we can pick the team, we can make it happen. And for this kind of reconnaissance, I'd like to keep it to a small team—say, about five guys. Two American SEALs and no more than three LDNNs. I'll probably take Mike Thornton along as the other American.'

"I got another patient smile and Commodore Schaible replied, 'Good choice.' "

MISSION PLANNING

"When Tommy got back from Vung Tau," Mike remembered, "we all wanted to know what was going on, but he was pretty close-lipped about it. Yet we knew it must have been some kind of priority for him to go all the way down there to get briefed for a single mission. The other two officers assumed that one of them would be tasked with the operation, but it didn't work out that way. Tom came to me the next morning and said that we would be doing a recon of the Cua Viet Naval Base. He said that he'd be the American officer on the operation and that I would be the only other American SEAL. He also said that while it was to be a Vietnamese operation with the LDNNs nominally in charge, we would go along as advisors and to coordinate the fire support and help out. As we both knew, we'd basically be running the operation. In the eyes of the South Vietnamese it was an urgent mission, but we would have a few days to prepare for it. Up the Vietnamese chain of command, they wanted to know the strength and disposition of the NVA at the Cua Viet Naval Base and what kind of force might be needed to retake the base.

"The senior LDNN officer at Thuan-An, Lieutenant Quan, was a great officer with a lot of experience. He was the obvious choice to head up the Vietnamese side of things. Tommy asked me to choose the other two LDNNs, and there were two at Thuan-An who I had worked with during my first tour with Charlie Platoon. They were seasoned fighters and very reliable in a firefight. I knew we could count on them. I was a little surprised that Tommy was going on the operation, as I knew he liked to give good operations to the other two officers. But I also knew he was getting close to the end of his tour, and I just assumed he wanted to get in one more good operation before he rotated back home. As I recall, it was Ryan McCombie's turn in the rotation, and he was a little pissed that Tommy had decided to take the mission himself. But Tommy was in charge and that was his prerogative—or, as I later learned, his direction from Uncle Dave. Now that we had the team set, we had to get ready for the operation. My job was to get the LDNNs and our equipment ready to go and make sure the boats were ready to put to sea; Tommy had to plan the operation."

The U.S. Naval Support Activity Cua Viet River, more commonly called the Cua Viet Naval Base, was established in March 1967 to provide support to the combat base at Dong Ha and the firebase installations in northern Quang Tri Province. The Cua Viet River was a major river complex just south of the Demilitarized Zone. In addition to the Cua Viet, there were a series of estuaries just south of the Cua Viet between Dong Ha and the South China Sea. The waterway becomes the Cua Viet River just west of Dong Ha with the confluence of the Cam Lo River and Quang Tri River. In order to supply Dong Ha and even Quang Tri with fuel and other supplies, the Cua Viet base was set up as a maritime transshipment installation. Oceangoing, shallow-draft ships and seagoing landing craft, like LSTs (landing ships, tank) could land there and off-load stores and fuel bladders. From there these needed supplies could be loaded onto smaller, riverine-type landing craft for transit west, upriver.

The base itself was a crudely constructed facility with sandbagged plywood huts and a small pier complex for supporting swiftboat operations. Situated on the southern bank of the Cua Viet River, the base was sited among sand dunes and sparse coastal vegetation. Ships making the almost one-hundred-mile journey from Da Nang to the Cua Viet facility had to contend with shifting sandbars and artillery fire from North Vietnamese batteries that had taken up positions inside the DMZ on the northern bank of the Cua Viet River. The base was the northernmost naval base in South Vietnam, and protected from direct assault by the Marine 1st Amphibious Tractor Battalion. Their PM5 amtracks were gunned with 105mm gyro-stabilized howitzers. Additionally, there was only a small naval security detail that manned sandbagged machine gun emplacements. Yet the base really depended on U.S. air power and naval gunfire for its defense. It was

more of a beach landing facility than any kind of harbor, and the sailors and marines there lived in near-field conditions. In late 1971
the U.S. Navy turned the facility over to the South Vietnamese. They
continued to operate the facility in support of Dong Ha until Dong
Ha and the Cua Viet base were overrun in the Easter Offensive. Now
with Quang Tri City back in South Vietnamese hands, the ARVNs
were looking to retake both Dong Ha and the Cua Viet Naval Base.
And since any retaking would be an ARVN or South Vietnamese marine operation, they wanted a thorough reconnaissance by their own
troops—in this case, the Vietnamese LDNN SEALs.

"What they wanted," said Tom Norris, "and what Schaible was asking for was some idea of just how well fortified the NVA had made
the Cua Viet base. Was it lightly garrisoned or had they really dug
in? Was the base manned by second-tier garrison troops or were
they a seasoned NVA infantry unit? We knew they had held the
base for close to five months, but in what kind of strength? Had
they erected any new defenses? We could do this, but we'd have to
be very careful. And I wanted it to be a single-night reconnaissance
operation. So we needed to get onto the beach as soon after dark as
possible, patrol into the area and do our recon, and then get back
out before first light. I figured that if we left Thuan-An early afternoon and got up there at best speed to be off the coast at dusk, we
could get in and out of there quickly and accomplish our mission,
again in a single night. As for Mike, I wanted him along on the
operation, as I knew we would be going in heavy, with a radio, cam-
eras, a night-vision scope, and enough ammo to fight our way out if
we got caught. I could have taken Brooks or Chambers or Woodruff—
they were all good men. But I wanted Mike, as I knew that he was

good in the water, that he could carry a lot of gear, and that he was reliable in a firefight. But all of what I knew was by reputation. I'd never been on a mission with him; this was to be our first.

"It was not a particularly difficult mission," Norris continued, "and it was certainly something we'd done before, so we knew the drill. In general, it was about a fifty-mile transit from Thuan-An up to the Cua Viet River in our boats; with a max speed of about eight knots, that was a little more than six hours. The plan was to get well out to sea, so no one on the beach would know if we were going north or south. Once we turned, in this case north, we'd make our way up the coast and then turn west to come back into shore. Then we hoped to be on station off the southern bank of the Cua Viet as soon as possible after dark. We'd then leave the junks and paddle in close to shore in rubber boats, and swim ashore from the rubber boats. We'd insert, do our job, and get out before first light. We didn't have to be back at Thuan-An before first light, but we sure as heck wanted to be back across that beach and away from the coast before sunup. I was told I'd have offshore Navy support in the way of two destroyers, so if we were a little late in getting out of there, I'd have some friendly, on-call fire support. I was getting into the planning when Mike came to me. 'Hey, sir,' he said, 'we got a problem.'"

"The LDNNs came in all varieties of experience and capability and courage," Mike recalled of the Vietnamese assigned for the mission. "On this operation, we had three very good ones. Lieutenant Quan was a first-rate LDNN officer, and Deng and Quan [an enlisted LDNN, no relation] were two guys I'd worked with on my first tour and was with them again in Thuan-An. Deng and Quan were good to go, but the problem was with Quan, the officer. The night before, he was in a tuk-tuk accident and banged himself up pretty good—enough that he'd not be able to go on an operation for another few weeks. This left us without our best LDNN officer."

"Losing Lieutenant Quan was a blow," Tom confirmed, "because he really was good. But this operation had to have a Vietnamese officer—someone who could be seen to be in charge, and who could report what we found to his LDNN boss down in Vung Tau, or anyone else in the South Vietnamese military who needed the information. This was a 'now' operation, and we had to find someone else to go. So we turned to Lieutenant Thuan. He was the next in line, both in seniority and in experience. Thuan was one of the LDNN officers who had been sent to the United States for SEAL training and returned to be an LDNN team leader, so his English was very good. I'd been out with him a few times on other reconnaissance operations, and he hadn't done too badly. But none of us had ever been with him in combat. As it turned out, he'd had very little actual combat experience. But he was eager to go on the operation. His family had connections in the South Vietnamese government, which was not surprising. Many South Vietnamese officers owed their position to family influence. From the South Vietnamese perspective, this was an essential operation, and I think he saw this as a chance to be involved in something important."

"My job was to make sure the three Vietnamese were ready to go," Mike said, "while Tommy planned the operation from the top down. We didn't generally tell our LDNNs where we were going, just when to be ready to go, although Lieutenant Thuan probably had some idea. They didn't really understand operational security like we do. You could never be sure that they wouldn't tell a friend or relative where we were going and have that information get passed along to the Viet Cong and on to the NVA. The bad guys had a very well-developed intelligence network. And they had a lot of locals in their employ. So we often told our LDNNs that this was a secret mission tasking and that they would get the full briefing on the operation just before we went out."

"This was to be a straightforward reconnaissance mission," Tom said of the planning process, "and similar to those we'd done many times before. Since it was a reconnaissance and intelligence-gathering operation, we'd be on the lookout for the opportunity to capture an enemy soldier and bring him back with us for interrogation, but a clean body snatch is hard to do. Yet if the opportunity presented itself, we'd make the grab. And it was critical for us to remain undetected. If we made contact, then the operation was blown.

"I looked to the Navy for two things. The first was navigation. The Navy ships offshore, usually destroyers, had good radars and very accomplished radar operators. I counted on them to direct us from an offshore location to our insertion point, in this case a point on the beach on the South China Sea just south of the mouth of the Cua Viet River. They couldn't always see the rubber boats—in this case the IBSs—in the water, but the Vietnamese junks assigned to the LDNNs painted pretty well on radar. We relied on the destroyers to get our junks a few thousand yards off the beach from where we wanted to go ashore. Once on station, the Navy radar operators would give us a magnetic heading to follow to get to our planned insertion point. We'd then paddle in close to shore, usually outside the surf line, and from there, swim in to the beach. The junks would wait for us offshore. If for some reason the junks got out of position, the destroyers could vector them back to our beach entry point for a pickup. The second thing the Navy did for us was on-call fire support. I would give them the map coordinates of several locations in and around the target area. Then if I needed fire support, I could have them shoot a predesignated set of coordinates and then adjust the fire from there to where I needed it. For the most part we worked well with the destroyers, and they had five-inch guns. It was like having a mobile, floating battery of 105mm howitzers. A five-inch/.38-caliber naval gun could send a fifty-five-pound projectile about nine miles or so and, depending on the ship, they could be very accurate. If it was a newer ship with five-inch/.54-caliber guns, it was a seventy-pound projectile, and they could accurately shoot up to eleven miles.

"So ahead of this mission, I set up a navigation plan that had the destroyers picking us up at the mouth of the Thuan-An barrier inlet and tracking us north to the mouth of the Cua Viet. That would get us to a position due east of our insertion point and provide magnetic compass heading for us once we headed toward the shore in the IBSs. Once we were ashore, they were to stand by to seaward while we conducted the recon mission. At least that was how it was supposed to work.

"Early on the afternoon of 30 October, I briefed Mike and a SEAL named Bill Woodruff with what we call a patrol order. A patrol order goes over the operation start to finish, from leaving the base—in this case the LDNN small boat harbor at Thuan-An—to the return to base. The patrol order is a formatted mission briefing that details the timeline, radio frequencies, support assets, the insertion and extraction plans, actions in the target area, emergency procedures, and all the like. Once aboard the junks, we would brief Lieutenant Thuan, and he would brief the other two LDNNs. Then Thuan and I would brief the junk captains. When we operated from junks, we always had a SEAL advisor aboard one of them. On this operation Bill Woodruff, or Woody as we called him, would be with the junks start to finish. Like all the LDNN enlisted advisors, Woody was a solid SEAL operator.

"I recall asking him at the patrol order, 'Are the boats ready to go?'

"'Yes, sir. They're fueled and standing by pier side. The crews know we'll be out for the night and that they'll probably not get back until late morning—maybe tomorrow afternoon.'"

The primary boat-support element for the LDNNs at Thuan-An was the Yabuta junk detachment. In addition to the more modern small-craft combatants in the South Vietnamese Navy there was the junk force. The junks, all told some 450 of them, came in various sizes and configurations, but the most numerous were the thirty-six-foot Yabuta-class junk. Some seventy of the Yabutas, including those at Thuan-An, were constructed of ferro-concrete—cement reinforced with steel mesh. These seven-ton concrete craft mounted a .30-caliber medium machine gun, a .50-caliber heavy machine gun, and a 60mm mortar. They were powered by a three-cylinder Grey Marine diesel engine, and while the concrete Yabutas were slow, about eight knots all out, they were remarkably seaworthy. The Yabutas and the junk force formed the backbone of the "Market Time" operations that sought to stop the movement of military supplies by boat from north to south during the Vietnam War. Those detailed for maritime special operations supported both American and LDNN operations. My SEAL platoon in the lower Mekong Delta used the Yabutas on occasion for insertion and extraction. Junk force detachments usually had an American advisor aboard for most of the war, and operated in two- or three-craft detachments. At Thuan-An in 1972, there was no assigned American advisor for the Yabuta detachment.

OVER THE BEACH

"Most of our operations used the junks for insertion and extraction," explained Bill Woodruff. "Sometimes they could get in close enough to the beach or into a river inlet so that the team to be inserted could jump over the side and wade ashore. They had a draft of only two feet. But they didn't handle well in the surf. If there was a surf up, the guys would have to swim in to the beach, or if there was a need to be silent and have a lower profile going in, we'd use an IBS to paddle in and the team would beach the IBS or go over the side of the IBS and swim ashore. In the latter case there would be others in the rubber boat to paddle the IBS back out to the supporting junks.

"The junks operated in twos or threes for mutual fire support, and if one broke down there was another to tow it back home. That happened more than once. Whenever we used the junks on an operation, one of us would remain with the junks to make sure they stayed on station and to act as a radio relay for the team ashore. Most of us would rather be ashore on the op, but we each took our turn staying back with the junks. The night of 30 October, when Tom and Mike went up north, I was with our two junks."

"We got under way sometime midafternoon and probably cleared the breakwater at Thuan-An a half hour later," Mike recalled of the start of the operation. "We went well out to sea before turning north, probably four miles or so. The junk captains knew these waters pretty well. Even when we had Navy ships vectoring us to a point offshore where we would launch the IBSs, we still relied on the local knowledge of the junk skippers. Now that they knew where we wanted to go, they headed north, paralleling the shore toward the Cua Viet. The junks were always moving up and down the coast, so we passed pretty much unnoticed. It was close to a seven-hour transit this time, but it seemed longer. Again, the plan was for the junks to remain well offshore and we would close the beach in the IBSs. The IBSs would take us in just outside the surf line and we'd swim in the rest of the way.

"Things began to go wrong just before we got ready to insert. One of the Navy ships that was supposed to be guiding the junks to a point off the Cua Viet got called away for a gunfire support mission farther south near Quang Tri City. So that left only one ship to guide us in, which is not as good as having two ships that could provide cross-vectors. But they got us to what they thought was the drop-off area, off the coast just south of the mouth of the Cua Viet River. At first, the junk skippers weren't sure about this positioning. They knew the coast, but it was dark and we were several miles offshore. The shoreline was pretty much featureless. After some consultation, they agreed that we were off the Cua Viet. Unfortunately, that was not the case. We were off the coast and just south of a river mouth all right, but it was the Ben Hai River—a river just below the boundary between North and South Vietnam and the midpoint of the DMZ."

Tom, Mike, and Bill Woodruff all have similar recollections of thinking they were south of the mouth of the Cua Viet when they were actually at a seemingly identical location near the Ben Hai, some ten miles to the north. To this day it is unclear to them whether it was the U.S. Navy or the junk captains that caused the team to insert below the wrong river mouth. Given the navigation tools available in 1972, this was understandable. For the Navy, the radar paint for both locations was similar; for the junk captains, it was a very dark night.

This narrator was able to inspect the deck logs of the ships tasked with supporting various phases of the operation, including those of the USS *Morton* (DD-948), the primary supporting vessel. These records indicate that they had indeed spotted the junks offshore and just south of the mouth of the Cua Viet River. But the reality was that this was not where they were.

In retrospect, it seems inconceivable that they could have been that far off. In today's special-operations and maritime-navigation world, with GPS trackers and satellite-phone technology, precision navigation is taken for granted. Yet the team was spotted offshore on the wrong beach. More than once I led SEAL operations where we inserted on the wrong place on a river or even the wrong river. It happened often back then, and it happened to Tom Norris and Mike Thornton on the evening of 30 October 1972. This error set in motion the events that would change the lives of these two Navy SEALs.

In the reconstruction of this operation, the team had gone ashore just north of the southern boundary of the Demilitarized Zone between North and South Vietnam, and three miles south of the mouth of the Ben Hai River. This DMZ was established by the Geneva Conference of 1954 that officially ended the first Indo-China War and French influence in the region. This conference established the Democratic Republic of Vietnam in the north and the Republic of Vietnam in the south—North and South Vietnam. The agreed boundary between the two was the 17th parallel, but in practice, this boundary followed the course of the Ben Hai River. The zone itself was five kilometers (about three miles) to either side of the Ben Hai River that ran from the South China Sea near the 17th parallel, west to the Laotian border. Throughout much of American involvement in Vietnam, the North Vietnamese militarily occupied the northern portion of the DMZ and often portions south of the 17th parallel.

RECONNAISSANCE

"Tactically, our insertion went pretty well," says Mike of their approach to the shoreline. "The junks took us in to about four thousand yards off the beach, where we boarded the IBSs. There were five of us on the insertion team and four LDNNs who would paddle the IBSs back out to the junks. It took us close to an hour to work our way inshore. There was a three- to four-foot surf running. Just outside the surf line, we slipped into the water and swam ashore. Once on the beach, Tommy sent me up the beach gradient to the top of the berm to check things out. I waited a few minutes to make sure the coast was clear, then signaled the others to cross the beach. We all then moved about fifty yards into the beach scrub for better concealment. As I recall, it was about 2230—10:30 P.M. on the 30th. The tide was low, so there was about fifty yards of flat beach to cross.

"I was carrying the starlight scope, a bulky first-generation night-vision device [designation AN/PVC-1] that allowed you to see relatively well at night. It was the size of a loaf of bread and weighed eight pounds. Tommy told me to scout the beach area to see if I could find any of the features we were looking for or expecting to find—like the mouth of a river. I went north about two hundred yards from our position, and the same distance to the south. And with the starlight scope, I could see a good ways up and down the beach. No river mouth and nothing looked familiar. Tommy moved inland just a short distance to look the area over with his binoculars. Neither of us saw anything that told us where we might be."

"We didn't know where we were," Tom said of their position on the beach, "but it just didn't look like we were anywhere near the Cua Viet River or the Cua Viet Naval Base. At night on unfamiliar ground, it's easy to be fooled. The river and the base facility could be just a few hundred yards farther into the bush. So now I had a decision to make. Do we call the junks and have them send the IBSs back in to extract us, and go looking for the right place to insert? Or do we patrol farther inland and look for some landmark to tell us where we were and perhaps the location of the Cua Viet Naval Base? I decided that we'd stay on the beach and conduct a reconnaissance patrol. We'd do what we could to avoid the enemy, and if we were lucky, we'd find the Cua Viet and that would lead us to the occupied naval base. And there was always the chance that we might come upon an enemy soldier we could capture and take back for interrogation. In retrospect, probably not my best decision in the field, but it was the one I made that night. It seemed the right thing to do at the time.

"I know Mike didn't agree with me," Tom recalled of that fateful decision, "but it was my call and I made it. And Mike stood by me. When I said we'd continue on, he said, 'Okay, let's get 'er done.' We were out to gather intelligence, and since it was late, I knew we would never be able to extract, determine our location, and reinsert at the right location in time to do the recon. We'd have to spend the day on the junks and try again the next night, or go home empty-handed. So I reasoned that we could check out this area and get back to the beach for pickup before first light."

"We set up in our standard patrol formation and moved inland," Mike said. "We moved due west for about a mile. Tommy was on point, followed by Deng. Deng had the radio, so he would always be close to Tommy. Then came Lieutenant Thuan, Quan, and myself. When we were out with the LDNNs, we always tried to keep them between us—an advisor up front or with the guide if we had one, and one of us serving as rear security. The LDNNs were in their standard tiger-striped camouflage utilities and flop hats. They all carried M-16 rifles and maybe two hundred rounds of ammo and a few grenades. Up front, Tommy was in a cammie top, blue jeans, and a floppy hat that Kiet had given him. It had a bullet hole in it, and I think he wore it for luck. Tommy favored an AK-47 and carried his spare banana magazines on his chest in an NVA-type vest. He also had two LAAWs [light antiarmor weapons—rockets carried within disposable launching tubes] and his standard load of grenades and signaling devices. I was the mule. On a recon patrol, I carried a CAR-15 carbine and just over eight hundred rounds of 5.56 ammo, along with an assortment of a dozen fragmentation, CS [a type of tear gas], and smoke grenades. I also had three LAAWs and the starlight scope. All of us carried a medical kit and an inflatable UDT over-the-head life vest.

"I also had our silenced weapon, a .22-caliber automatic pistol with a suppresser attached to the barrel. We called it a hush puppy. The hush puppy used downloaded, subsonic ammunition so there was no sonic crack when you fired it. It also had a slide lock to freeze the action of the weapon so no sound would escape from the ejection port. It was a very-close-range weapon. Even if you were close enough to hear it, it was hard to tell which direction the sound was coming from. But you had to get close to use it."

"About a mile into the patrol we began to see a series of bonfires up ahead," Tom recalled, "fires that usually accompanied bivouacked troops. As we got closer, we began to see a series of fixed bunkers. Now moving slowly, I could spot four small bunkers and one really big one. We still didn't know where we were, but I was now certain that we were not close to the Cua Viet or the Cua Viet Naval Base. These were large, permanent North Vietnamese Army installations—not hastily constructed defenses of an invading Army."

Mike continued: "When we saw the bunkers, Tommy called us in for a field briefing and said we were going to work our way past the line of bunkers and any troops that were in the area and try to get some idea of their disposition and strength. This meant we had to tighten up the patrol and move slowly. Tommy knew how to move around and through enemy formations—he'd demonstrated that on his pilot-rescue operations. It took nerve and confidence on his part, but it was something he was good at. Yet it was still a dicey game. Lieutenant Thuan, Deng, and Quan, and for that matter, Tommy, were small, so all of them could pass for a North Vietnamese patrol in an encounter at night. I spoiled any chance of that, and I was carrying all the damn gear in the world. But Tommy knew what he was doing. Deng and Quan were solid, and they knew the drill. But the Vietnamese lieutenant was clearly nervous. His eyes were as big as saucers."

"We turned north to skirt the bunkers," said Tom, "and we moved very slowly. We didn't see any troops and assumed they were huddled inside the bunkers. We were well inside North Vietnamese–controlled territory, so there was no reason for them to suspect anything. As long as we were careful and didn't bump into one of their patrols, we were pretty safe—or as safe as you can be in a situation like that. It was well after midnight, and after we had moved about a mile and a half north, I saw this lump on a sand dune up ahead of us. So I halted the patrol and called Mike up. 'Is that what I think it is?' he said, and I said, 'If you mean that tank up there, yep.'"

"We were about a hundred yards from it," Mike said of the tank, "maybe a little more. I got out the starlight scope and checked it out. There were bonfires not too far from the tank, so I could see it clearly. It was a T-54 and I could see the lettering on the side and the red star on the turret. So Tommy says, 'I think it's about time we got the heck out of here,' and I said, 'Roger that, sir.' It was about 0300 and we only had about three hours or so of darkness left. It was time to leave."

"We turned east and began working our way back toward the beach," Tom said. "I put Mike on point and I took up a position in the rear of the patrol. The patrol order was Mike, Quan, Lieutenant Thuan, Deng, and myself. Mike had the starlight scope, and I knew that the closer we got to the water, the thinner the covering vegetation would be. He would be able to pause and survey the ground ahead and make sure it was clear of any NVA as we moved. I also had to be on the radio. I was able to raise Woody and let him know that we were on our way out and that we might be needing some fire support at any time. We were moving slowly and carefully, yet we wanted to make our extraction before first light."

"As we moved east," said Mike, now leading the patrol, "we picked up a stream that was heading in our direction. There were trees on the banks to either side and it gave us good cover. So we waded into the stream. The water was three to four feet deep, and I was worried that if it got any deeper, it would be an issue for Quan and Deng. But as we got closer to the coast, the creek widened and became shallower. I knew we were not far from the ocean, as I could hear surf in the distance. Then I heard something else—voices, and they were close by. I halted the patrol and Tommy came up to my position. We listened awhile, and then he sent me up the southern bank of the stream for a look-see. There was good cover in trees along the bank. Not far from our position was an encampment with NVA soldiers moving about. There was a scattering of huts and bunkers, and soldiers moving in and around the structures. They also had a commanding view of the beach where our stream emptied into the sea. There was no way we could cross the beach without them seeing us.

"I made my way back down into the streambed and told Tommy what I'd seen. He sent me to scout the area north of the streambed to see if we could safely move in that direction to avoid the NVA troops now to our southeast and behind us to the west. I scrambled out of the stream and made my way onto a series of sand dunes north of the streambed. It was getting to be just past 0400. I immediately saw a large lagoon and that our streambed had skirted the southern bank of the lagoon. After surveying the area with the scope, I made my way up to a tall dune that had a large abandoned bunker on it. It was not a bunker in the concrete or earthen-log type of construction, but a volcano-like, big foxhole made of sand. It was some twenty feet high with some inside shoring at the base. The 'rim' of the bunker afforded a 360-degree vantage point, and it was a good defensive position. Inside, at the base, the walls were thick, solid sand, and there was a tunnel at the bottom for additional protection—probably from offshore naval bombardment. I scrambled back down and worked my way south to where Tommy and the others waited in the streambed. I told him what I'd found."

"By the time Mike got back to me, it was coming up on 0430. And now I no longer had comms with Woody and the junks. The PRC-77 was a line-of-site radio and good for only about five miles—maybe seven if you had a good elevated position. And it sounded like Mike had found just such a place. It was looking like we might not get off the beach before daylight and would have to lay up for the day. His bunker also sounded like that might be a good place for that as well. I told him to take us there and he did."

Mike: "I led the patrol north from the stream across a field of shallow dunes to the one tall dune with the bunker. It was close to a quarter mile from the stream, and it put that much more distance between us and the encampment to the south. The dune and bunker were pretty isolated and looked like a good place to hide. It was about 0500 when we got there. Tommy immediately got on the radio trying to raise Woody or one of the offshore Navy ships. Deng stayed there with him and I set security with the other two LDNNs. I put Quan just north of the bunker with the starlight scope. He had good command of the beach to the north of our position. With the scope he could see a long way, and I could count on Quan to keep a good lookout. Lieutenant Thuan and I set ourselves south of the bunker, between Deng and Tommy and the streambed. Thuan was on a small dune forty yards behind me and on the seaward side of my position. We were well positioned if someone approached from the south. Our western flank was protected by the large lagoon that was maybe a mile long north and south, and a half mile across. We were in a good defensive position. And so far, the bad guys didn't know we were there.

"The terrain was a lot like that on the Silver Strand where SEAL Team One and the BUD/S training unit are now located on Coronado. Lots of sand, scrub grass, and several smaller dunes between us and the trees along the river. The bunker itself was maybe two hundred and fifty yards from the ocean and close to that same distance from the lagoon. Farther north, the land between the ocean and the lagoon narrowed. Lieutenant Thuan and I had taken up positions behind small dunes maybe a hundred yards south of the big dune with the bunker."

"At this point," Tom recalled, "I still didn't know where we were. Up on the dune near the bunker, I had good contact with Woody. We had a good position and I didn't want to try to cross the beach unless I knew where we were so the junks could pick us up.

I knew once we went into the water, we couldn't use the radio and there'd be little chance of them finding us. Once out of the line of dunes, there was a flat stretch of beach we'd have to cross—about a hundred yards of it. Unless I knew where we were so I could get the junks in to pick us up or so I could call in gunfire support, our options were limited. We'd have to hide out for the day and try to extract the next night. All this was going through my mind when Quan came running back to the bunker.

"'*Dai-Uy* Norris,' he reported, 'with the starlight scope, I see two men coming down the beach. They are quite a way off, but they are headed our way.'

"I took the scope and spotted them as well. Then I sent Deng to get Mike and Lieutenant Thuan. We'd now have to decide what we were going to do with these guys. Waiting for Mike and Thuan, I watched them approach. They were not together. One was in the lead and walking down along the water's edge while the other was walking along the high-tide line near the first line of shallow dunes and maybe trailing the guy near the water by a hundred yards. They were kind of moseying along and not in too big of a hurry. When Mike and Lieutenant Thuan got there, we talked it over and decided that one of these guys could be our captured NVA soldier, maybe both. But if we were going to take one of them, we would have to take them both, or take one and kill one. So we came up with a quick plan. It was a little after 0530, so dawn was approaching. Official sunrise that day was 0545, and I could see the sky to the east beginning to get light. We needed to grab these guys before full dawn—while it was full dark. We would be coming from the west against the dark backdrop of the dunes, and they would be silhouetted to the east. I needed to stay with the radio. It was looking like we were not going to extract anytime soon, but I did need to try to contact the ships. If things got ugly, we'd need their support. Deng would stay with me and Mike, and the other two LDNNs would go after the two NVA."

"We kind of drew it up in the dirt," Mike said of the plan, "or in this case, the sand. Quan and I would first take out the trail NVA soldier. We'd hide in the dunes just above the high-water line and take him as he passed us. He was our primary candidate for capture. Then Lieutenant Thuan would handle the second NVA, the guy along the water. I gave him the hush puppy, and his job was to walk up behind him and either capture him or kill him. It was still dark and we had the noise of the breakers to cover the sound of our movements. Well, the first part of the plan worked fine. Quan and I moved down to near the high-water line and squatted in the grass. The guy was paying very little attention, just walking with his head down—same as his buddy down by the water's edge. It was easy. He walked past us, and I stood up and started walking, ducking in behind him. When I got close, I took him down with a butt stroke of my rifle. CAR-15s have a collapsible, hard plastic stock, so I had to make sure I didn't break my gun. I kept my hand close to the butt and just whacked the shit out of him. He went down like a sack of cement.

"Quan took charge of him and I started moving down the beach, running along the dune line, waiting for Lieutenant Thuan to make his move. But he did nothing. The lead NVA soldier was walking along the water past where Thuan was positioned along the dune line, and I was waiting for him to do something. I don't know if he could see me, but I was waving my arms trying to get him to move. The NVA soldier was paying no attention at all, just strolling down the beach, head down and probably tired after a long and boring patrol. With the noise of the surf, Thuan could easily have just walked up behind him and shot him. Instead he comes out onto the open beach and yells at him.

"*'Ngung lai! Den day!'* Stop! Come here!"

"Well, the guy takes off running, and I start chasing him. I have the angle and I'm running down the beach gradient after him, but he's got a pretty good lead. Yet I'm closing in on him. I glance back at Lieutenant Thuan, and he's headed back for the bunker. The NVA soldier is running south along the beach into the growing dawn. I can see he's picked up a trail and making for the trees that mark the bank of the streambed. And I can't let him get there. He stops and fires a couple rounds at me with his AK-47 and keeps running. I keep chasing him and am only about twenty-five yards from him when he gets to the tree line. I stop, take a knee, and put two rounds into his back. He goes down. I race up to drag him off to the side and hide his body. The shots may or may not have alerted other NVA in the area. Quite often, they fire rounds into the air as a means of signaling. At least that's what I hoped. But no such luck. Just as I got to him, a whole squad of NVA came charging from the river bed right at me. So I turn around and start hauling ass the other way. Now they're chasing me! The sun was just starting to come up.

"But my lieutenant had my back. Tommy watched the whole thing unfold from his post up on the big dune. He grabbed one of his LAAW rockets and ran down to one of the lower dunes and took up a firing position. He sent a rocket into the trees above the pursuing NVAs' heads, and that caused them to stop and take cover. I don't think he hit any of them, but that was not his intent. He just wanted to get them off my tail, and he did. Now we had a whole other issue on our hands. As near as we could tell in the growing light, there were fifty or so bad guys in that encampment and they were all swarming out of the encampment, across the creek bed, and after us. For the moment, that rocket caused them to duck for cover. And with Tommy and Deng covering me, it gave me a chance to get back up into the shallow dunes just to the south of the bunker.

"I got to a good position where I could engage them as they came from the cover of the trees by the stream and tried to move north on our position. Quan had taken our prisoner back to the bunker and left him with Deng. Then he took up a position just seaward of me, and together Quan and I watched as the bad guys began to work their way up to where we were. I sent Lieutenant Thuan to a security position to the north bunker, guarding against anyone moving on our location along the beach from the north. By this time, I knew I couldn't count on our LDNN lieutenant in the coming fight. And a fight it would be, as we had all those NVA from the encampment to contend with."

Tom: "With Mike and Quan in position to engage the enemy, I got back to the bunker and got on the radio. It was now light enough to clearly see our surroundings—the beach, the other side of the lagoon, and the tank. I knew we might be able to deal with the NVA infantry, but not with a tank or artillery or whatever else they might have. Now we really needed that fire support. I raised Woody on the radio and told him to get some spotting rounds on some of those predesignated coordinates. Woody said the ship had radioed him and said they were shooting at first one and then another of the preassigned spots. But I could see no impact from the rounds. From his position offshore, neither could Woody. I knew we were not where we were supposed to be, but could we be that far off?"

THE STAND IN THE DUNES

The confusion that accompanied the insertion of the team carried over to the early daylight hours of 31 October. The Navy ships offshore supporting the operation were a heavy cruiser and a destroyer: the USS *Newport News* (CA-148) and the USS *Morton* (DD-948). On the evening of the 30th, the *Newport News* received orders to steam south and support the ARVNs at Quan Tri City, who were fighting to hold the provincial capital. That left the USS *Morton* alone to provide navigation and on-call fire support for the SEALs ashore. The *Newport News* did not return until just after dawn on the 31st. The ships that performed naval gunfire support, or NGFS, were assigned to sectors along the coast of Vietnam. Collectively, these sectors were called the gun line. They responded to calls for fire from units ashore and conducted harassment and interdiction fire missions—putting rounds on suspected enemy troop concentrations. On the morning of 31 October, the USS *Morton* was relieved of all her normal NGFS duties and was standing by to support the SEAL team ashore.

When Tom asked for fire support in the form of rounds on one of his predesignated coordinates, Woody relayed that request to the *Morton*. The *Morton* complied, sending white phosphorous spotting rounds to the designated coordinates—a set of coordinates near the Cua Viet Naval Base and along the coast just south of the Cua Viet River. But that was several miles south of where the beleaguered team was engaged by a superior NVA force. Neither Tom nor Bill Woodruff spotted the fall of shot. At this time Tom was out of radio range of the *Morton,* and Woodruff, standing just off the coast in his junks, was just barely within radio range of the destroyer. So early on, all requests for fire support went through Bill Woodruff.

At the time, neither the team ashore nor Bill Woodruff on the junks knew they were that far north of their intended insertion point.

Tom kept asking for spotting rounds, and Woody kept relaying those requests to the *Morton*. But neither saw the rounds fall. Meanwhile, the team ashore was giving a good account of themselves, but their situation was precarious.

"Aside from being outnumbered ten to one," Mike recalled, "we had a few things going for us. First of all, they didn't know how many of us there were. Both Quan and I would take a shot or two, then roll over a few times and take another shot from another location. Then we'd move again, and maybe toss a grenade at them. Second, we had position. We were in a scattering of shallow dunes that provided us, and them, with cover, but we had a slight elevation advantage. Quan and I gave ground, but we made them pay for it. They were close to us, and you could see one of them peek over a dune, then duck back down before you could get a shot at them. But we would aim at the exact spot where they had peeked, and wait. They'd invariably pop their head up in the same place, and we'd squeeze off a round. More than once I saw the top of the guy's head come off. We sent a lot of NVA pith helmets flying that morning."

"Mike and Quan were doing a great job of giving ground and killing bad guys," Tom said of the engagement. "When I wasn't on the radio, I too was looking for that head to pop up a second time and fire. We killed a lot of those guys with head shots. I think we were lucky that morning with this opposition. You always wonder just how good the guys are you're fighting, and these guys weren't all that great. And that stands to reason. Most of the crack infantry units were engaged in what was left of the Easter Offensive and the fighting around Quang Tri City. I think these were some guys from a rear-services battalion or some support element. They were brave and they kept coming, but they made a lot of mistakes.

And they paid for it. But time and the numbers were not on our side.

"Meanwhile, when Deng wasn't shooting, he was interrogating our captive inside the bunker. He'd finally regained consciousness, and we had him tied up securely. I gave Deng our map and told him, 'Have this guy point out where we are.' The guy didn't really want to talk, but Deng can be persuasive when he needs to be. Finally the guy points to where we were—on the coast just south of the mouth of the Ben Hai River. At first I didn't believe him and told Deng to ask him again. Same thing: near the mouth of the Ben Hai. We didn't have exact coordinates, but I now knew where we were. And then it all made sense—the permanent bunkers, my inability to talk to the ships at sea, and why we couldn't see the spotting rounds. We were just too far north! I immediately raised Woody on the radio and told him where we thought we were. Then Deng got on the radio and told the junk skippers where we were. Now it was a race. Could those ships get support fire up to our location before the NVA got to us? Thank God we had Bill Woodruff on the junks relaying our new location out to the gunfire support ships."

Bill Woodruff recalls the events of around dawn on 31 October: "When those ships began putting in spotting rounds on predetermined locations south of the Cua Viet, where the team was supposed to be, and Tom didn't see them, I knew we had a problem. Then when Tom called and said he thought they were just south of the Ben Hai, it all fell into place. That was the big 'aha moment' for me. I radioed the ships, specifically the *Morton,* that the team ashore were south of the Ben Hai River and not south of the Cua Viet. Not being sure just where they were, I asked the *Morton* to begin walking spotting rounds up the coast. I knew Tom and Mike were in serious trouble. Tom is a very cool customer, yet I could tell over the radio that he was both frustrated and anxious. But again, he was very cool about it. I told the junk skippers to close the coast a little to see if we could see anything. They didn't like getting close to shore in the daylight, but we moved in a little closer."

"We continued to shoot, move, and give ground," Mike said of the fight ashore, "and they kept coming. But we killed a lot of them. We'd been engaged for close to two hours, and now Quan and I were back to within about twenty-five yards of the bunker. I was well down through half my ammo and was starting to wonder how much longer we could keep this up. Then this grenade comes sailing over the dune I was using for cover—it was one of those Chicom [Chinese communist] grenades that are chemically timed and can take as long as ten seconds or so to go off. Well, I grab it and toss it back at them. I was thinking that I had the better of the exchange when the same grenade comes sailing back at me. It landed less than a dozen feet from me, and I knew there was no time to throw it back. I rolled into a ball with my back to it and it went off. The sand absorbed most of the blast, but I took some shrapnel. Later on, they dug six pieces out of me. I yelled like I was hurt, which I guess I was, and then waited. Less than a minute later, four of them came charging over the dune. But I was still in the fight and I had a fresh magazine in place. As they ran at me, I shot all four of them."

"I heard the grenade go off and I heard Mike yell," Norris said of the exchange. "Then I heard the pop-pop-pop of Mike's CAR. I yelled, 'Mike, are you all right?' and he yelled back, 'I just got four more. That makes thirty-one. How many you got?' That was Mike Thornton. Keeping score in the middle of a firefight. But he had killed a lot of them—all of us had. And these last ones that Mike shot seemed to have taken the fight out of the rest. Those still alive pulled back and we had a break in the fighting.

"I now had intermittent radio contact with the ships. It seemed that I was talking with one ship, and after a lengthy exchange, telling them where I was—telling them our general location—that guy would go off the net. Then someone else would come up on the net and I'd have to go through the whole setup again. Finally I got one guy (which turned out to be the USS *Morton*) who stayed with me. But even he would fade in and out. As it turned out, the ships were coming up the coast and we were talking at the extreme range of the PRC-77. At that moment in time, I was starting to relax a little. We had a good defensive position, and the NVA who attacked us from the encampment across the stream seemed to have had enough of the fight. We had a captured enemy soldier and help was on the way. I'd been worried about that tank, but it didn't move—maybe it couldn't move. Mike was hurt, but I knew Mike. He'd fight right through it. As soon as I could get some naval gunfire in the area to cover us, we could try for a daylight extraction. But it was too good to last. Mike, who was keeping an eye on things with my binoculars while I was on the radio, said, 'Hey, Nasty, I think we might have a problem.'"

"Several trucks pulled up right across the shallow lagoon from us," Mike said. "They were maybe a half mile away from us, but in the early-morning light we could see NVA soldiers spilling out of the truck beds. I stopped counting them when I got to seventy-five. They quickly fell into ranks and began to deploy. Some of them went north to work their way around the north end of the lagoon and others went south, moving past the tank and heading for the creek bed and the south end of the lagoon. It looked like they were going to be coming at us from two directions. Our dune and bunker had served us well in our earlier skirmish, but there were a lot of smaller dunes to the south that would afford cover for a force attacking from that direction—the same dunes that Quan and I had used as we fought our way back to the bunker. Unless we got some help or moved, we were sure to be overrun by this new larger force.

"In the daylight we could see a single large dune about four or five hundred yards to the north. It was by itself with no smaller dunes around it to provide cover for an attacking force. It looked to be a better fighting position than where we were at the moment— one that might be easier to hold. The bad guys would have to come across close to a quarter mile of open sand to get to us. Tommy decided we'd try for it, and I agreed."

"Normally when we conduct fire and maneuver, we leapfrog with two elements, one moving and one covering," Tom said of the plan to relocate to the more defensible dune. "And we normally move short distances depending on the available cover. But there was nothing between the two dunes but open ground. So I told Mike to take Quan and Lieutenant Thuan to make for the dune to our north. Deng and I would cover them while they moved. And I was still on the radio trying to get some spotting rounds into the area so I could adjust fire onto the bad guys. Mike, Quan, and Lieutenant Thuan took off, but it looked like the NVA would get to Deng and me before Mike and the other two got to the next big dune. There were just a lot of bad guys swarming up through the dunes trying to get to us. Deng was shooting and I was talking when a white phosphorous round dropped right in the middle of the enemy soldiers working their way toward us. After all the frustration of trying to get naval gunfire to us, this round dropped right where I needed it."

THE DESPERATE HOURS

In helping Tom and Mike tell this story, I found that the events that took place just after the team made contact with the enemy and their

dramatic escape out to sea proved to be the most difficult to recon-
struct. Stephen Ambrose, one of our most prolific chroniclers of war,
once said that two men fighting side by side in the same engagement
will invariably provide two totally different versions of what took
place. Their accounts might lead one to believe they had been on two
different battlefields, in two different wars. So it was with a patch-
work of interviews of those in the fight ashore and those supporting
that fight offshore that this story unfolds.

Prior to their killing of the second NVA soldier, Tom and Mike
had been working together in close proximity. Once the shooting
started, they still worked together, but, for much of the time, in two
separate maneuvering elements. They had different responsibilities:
Mike was focused on security and fighting off the NVA attacks. Tom
was on the radio, which was their lifeline for support and escape. So
their perspectives on what took place differ. For much of the time,
they were fighting two different engagements. And close combat can
both accelerate and distort time frames; it tends to alter the focus of
those involved. They no longer have the luxury or the time to step
back and see the big picture. When the bullets are flying, there tends
to be a tunnel-vision view of events and a constant shifting of priorities. And these events took place more than four decades ago.

The supporting elements, while in little or no danger, felt the
pressure of trying to sort through the unknowns and ambiguities so
they could help the beleaguered team ashore. Bill Woodruff, on the
junks, could only wait offshore from the insertion point, monitor and
relay radio traffic, and be prepared to move inshore to retrieve the
team if they could fight their way off the beach. And after Tom's radio
went silent, it fell to Woody to try to anticipate the movements of the
team ashore and to guess what their fire-support requirements might
be. And how he could position his two junks to pick them up if by

some miracle they did manage to get into the water? The Navy ships offshore knew there was a team ashore, and after dawn on 31 October, they knew they were in trouble. Yet they could do little unless they had the exact location of the team and/or the NVA elements in close proximity. Initially, they had neither. Damage from friendly fire was on everyone's mind—certainly for the plotting and fire-control teams aboard the ships offshore. It seemed that the fog of war that accompanied the insertion of the team in the wrong location had now descended on them as they tried to break contact with an aggressive and persistent enemy. No one, including Tom and Mike, knew their precise location. Yet as the day wore on, it became increasingly clear that if they did not get some help in the way of fire support, they were not going to make it. With this in mind, it might be helpful to take a closer look at the ships that were the key vessels supporting the team ashore and that participated in the recovery. Then let's take a few minutes for a brief primer on naval gunfire support—NGFS.

There were just the two ships: the USS *Newport News* and USS *Morton*. They were part of a flotilla of U.S. Navy ships patrolling the South China Sea and supporting mainly South Vietnamese Army operations ashore. The admiral in charge of this flotilla, called the gunline commander, was embarked in *Newport News*. It is believed that the USS *Newport News* responded to a call-fire mission near Quang Tri City the previous evening and did not get back on station and up to the DMZ until the daylight hours of 31 October. The *Newport News* had recently suffered a serious gunnery incident. On 1 October they sustained an in-barrel explosion on the middle barrel of turret number two. The explosion of the 260-pound projectile set off seven hundred pounds of powder, causing a devastating flash fire. Twenty sailors were killed and sixty-two wounded. As a precaution, the captain flooded her magazines. The ship immediately made for the U.S. Naval

Base Subic Bay in the Philippines for repairs. She was back on the gun line scarcely three weeks later, but with only the six 8-inch guns in turrets one and three still functioning. The *Newport News* also had a secondary battery of twelve 5-inch/.38-caliber guns in six twin mounts. Even in this crippled condition, she was still the most potent force on the gun line. Yet the *Newport News* fired no rounds in support of the SEALs ashore. The deck logs of the big cruiser confirm that she took no part in the gunfire support that day.

The USS *Morton* was a modified Forrest Sherman–class destroyer with two 5-inch/.54-caliber gun mounts, and was the primary NGFS ship supporting the SEALs. Most nights, the NGFS ships were assigned targets and fire missions in support of the fighting ashore. On the night of 30 October, the *Morton* was relieved of all such duties. She was standing by for on-call fire missions for the team ashore.

Both ships were manned by veteran crews, and a great many of the officers and enlisted sailors serving in these ships were on their second and third gun-line rotations. This experience was especially evident in all the stations that supported the NGFS mission. On the *Newport News,* their expertise extended to the fourteen-man medical department, which had been severely tested during the explosion in turret number two just a few weeks earlier.

Naval gunfire from a seasoned ship like the *Morton* can be very accurate. Most naval gunfire missions fall into two categories. The first entails shooting to a set of targeted grid coordinates ashore, as with a harassment and interdiction mission. The second category involves getting a spotting round into an area near the target so a spotter, on the ground or airborne, can adjust the rounds onto the target. For both, precise and continuous navigation is required. Adjusting the fall of shot is a matter of trigonometrics. The spotter looks for the "splash" of the spotting round, usually white phosphorous or "Willy Pete" projectile. From his position, a spotter on the ground calls in the adjustments, left or right—add or drop (long or short)—so many hundreds of yards. If the call-fire mission is in mountainous terrain, the adjustments can be up or down. Aboard ship, the gunfire support team has to know only the location of the spotter and the gun orders of the last shot fired. Then with a simple device called a grid spot converter that looks like a circular slide rule, a conversion is made from the spotter's reference to the target, and to the ship's range and bearing to the splash of the last round. Then adjustments are made to the fire-control solution, and new gun orders are issued. This process also has to be adjusted for the course and speed of the ship. In this case, the *Morton* was steaming north at ten knots. It wasn't that she couldn't move faster, but a higher speed would hamper precise radar navigation and degrade accuracy.

Today, support platforms are afforded the luxury of GPS accuracy in both navigation and on-demand, precision-guided weapons. Back in 1972, the delivery of ordnance in close proximity to friendly troops required teams of well-trained and highly skilled professionals.

"Early on, I didn't know just where the guys on the beach were," said Bill Woodruff of the kinetic events that began just after dawn on the 31st, "and neither did they. But I knew they were in trouble. Tom was looking for naval gunfire, and I was relaying his request to the ships. They were coming up from the south, moving from the area off the Cua Viet toward the mouth of the Ben Hai. The ships were using alphanumeric call signs that changed often, so I really didn't know what ship I was talking to. As they worked their way north, I kept calling for spotting rounds along the beach. The ships complied, but no one saw anything. As dawn became daylight, I could tell from Tom's voice on the radio that their situation was going from bad to worse."

"Some of this new group of NVA soldiers moved off to the north, moving along the west side of the lagoon," Tom recalled, "and a good many came south around the southern tip of the lagoon to where Deng and I were pinned down in the bunker. They were my immediate concern. There was just no way the two of us were going to be able to hold them. My plan was for us to keep them at bay while Mike and the others got to the second dune. Then Deng and I would make a run for it while Mike covered us. I don't know how many of them there were, but there were a lot. As they moved on our position, they had to be tripping over the bodies of their buddies we'd killed in the previous firefight. I'm sure that made them mad, but I also hoped it would make them a little more cautious. And about then, I *really* needed some gunfire support."

Aboard the USS *Morton,* Lieutenant (junior grade) Ed Moore had just come on watch to relieve the gunnery liaison officer, or GLO. "I walked into CIC around 0700 and immediately noticed that the CIC [combat information center] NGFS team was much more relaxed than normal, sitting around and chatting among themselves. Since I was the CIC division officer, I was used to seeing them busy, shooting a current mission or preparing for the next NGFS mission. Something was up. I began the relieving process with a briefing by Lieutenant (JG) Jack Johnson. Jack was the *Morton*'s communications officer and a Naval Academy classmate. Jack said we were assigned a special mission to support a Navy SEAL operation in case they needed gunfire support for their assigned mission and for their extraction. We had been exempted from all other gunfire support duties during this operation. He showed me where the planned extraction point was plotted on our NGFS chart laid out in CIC. He also mentioned that it was believed the SEALs were inserted north of that point, and it was uncertain at that time exactly where they were located. It seemed strange at the time that we would not know where a team of SEALs had been inserted, but I didn't question it. That was the situation when I relieved the watch. We had been assigned an NGFS frequency to monitor in case they needed *Morton* to provide gunfire support.

"The navigation and NGFS plotting teams had all done their job," Moore recalled, "so the ship had a good fix on its location and we were ready to shoot once we had a target. The captain has the final say on when to fire; our batteries were released only on his authority. With all our navigation and fire control systems set, we could obtain his release of the guns very quickly. This was a very seasoned and proficient group of sailors aboard *Morton,* and they knew their jobs. We were just waiting to hear from the team of SEALs ashore.

"Shortly after I relieved as the GLO, 0720 or so, we got a call on the assigned VHF radio frequency asking for gunfire support. We were used to receiving fire missions in a very specific format that followed a preset dialogue as followed by both spotters ashore and NGFS personnel aboard ship. It was obvious that this call was not going to follow that procedure, and that the SEALs ashore needed immediate gunfire support. I asked my sailor on the radio for their grid location, and he asked them. The response was that they did not have a grid location but were on the beach somewhere south of the Ben Hai River. Our only option was to fire spotting rounds in their vicinity, and hope they would spot one and then direct our fire from that point." In anticipation of this fire mission, the *Morton* then began to reshuffle its ammunition—Willy Pete or spotting rounds in their after mount and high explosives in their forward mount.

During much of the *Morton*'s journey up the coast, south to north, while its crew were putting in spotting rounds, they were in direct communication with only Bill Woodruff on the junks. He relayed radio traffic from Norris to the *Morton*—the information that neither he nor Norris could see the fall of shot from the spotting rounds. Once Norris made his way to the high ground near the bunker and the *Morton* had moved farther north, the ship came within range of Norris's radio. As the North Vietnamese closed in, Tom was able to speak directly with Ed Moore on the *Morton*.

"We began by firing spotting rounds farther north than what we had previously thought would be their extraction point—where we had assumed they would be coming out," Moore said of the NGFS mission, "and then worked our way north along the coast. We fired the first round, alerted the SEALs just before the impact or 'splash,' and got a negative reply. So we moved up the coast several hundred yards and fired a second Willy Pete round. Again the response was negative visual. We continued to do this for about four or five more rounds. On the last round, we moved the round much farther up the coast. This time the SEAL on the radio said, 'I see it! I see it!' We waited a couple of seconds, then radioed back, 'Interrogative spot, over?' We assumed that he would give us instructions to move the fall of shot onto the target. The response we got back was, 'Shoot! Just shoot!' This was around 0745 on the morning of 31 October."

Ed Moore then made a crucial decision. Without going to the *Morton*'s skipper to release the batteries, he decided to shoot.

"I called down to gunnery plot and told them, 'Fire for effect, ten rounds HE [high explosive], fuse quick.' Plot asked me if I wanted to walk them around a bit for better coverage and I said yes. When I got their 'Plot set,' I immediately told them, 'Plot shoot, ten rounds.' The first round was fired immediately, followed by a round about every three seconds. All ten rounds were in the air within a minute. The entire operation, from the first call for fire until we fired for effect, lasted less than half an hour.

"We heard nothing more from the SEALs ashore. We called and asked for their status and to ask them for any spots, but they were silent. For the next hour, we called them every five minutes, and after that continued to monitor the frequency, but heard nothing. Later we were contacted by an offshore spotter and asked to put more rounds into the area, but we never heard from the SEALs ashore. We didn't talk much about that NGFS operation; we all assumed that they had either been overrun or we might have inadvertently killed them with one of our rounds. I never received any feedback on the mission while I was assigned to the *Morton*. It was only recently that I learned of the events ashore that day and about Tom Norris and Mike Thornton."

Ashore, Tom Norris was busy. "I was getting ready to fire my last LAAW rocket at a pocket of advancing NVA troops. My thought was that I would fire the rocket, and then Deng and I would make a run for it. I didn't like our chances making that run over open ground to the north, but we had no other option. Then I couldn't believe it! This round dropped out of the sky right in the middle of the NVA advancing on our position."

Tom recalls a variation of the radio exchange with the *Morton*. "When the spotting round landed just in front of me and right in the enemy's line of advance, I told them to shoot—to fire for effect.

I can understand the ship's reluctance to fire, as that spotting round was very close to us. I was asking for naval gunfire right onto our position—those rounds could have hit Deng and me just as well as the bad guys. But we had no choice. The guy on the radio came back and said, 'Understand fire for effect?' And I said, 'Absolutely. Put it on us.' And he said, 'Are you sure?' And I said, 'Just get it in here!' I went back to getting the LAAW ready to fire. I could hear the ship shooting, but that's the last thing I remember."

At that point in the fight, Tom Norris took an AK-47 round into the left side of his forehead. The bullet entered his skull at the orbital socket of his left eye, tore out a section of his skull exposing his brain, and cut a shallow furrow along the brain itself. Deng saw his officer go down and the extent of his head wound. His lieutenant had been shot dead. Knowing there was nothing he could do, he made for the others, who had just taken a position on the next tall dune to the north. As he ran he took a round through the radio he still carried on his back, knocking him down. The round destroyed the radio and saved his life, but fragments carried through and into his back. Deng picked himself up and kept running. It took him close to ten minutes to reach Mike.

"Where's Tommy?" Mike asked Deng when he reached them. "Where's the *dai uy*?"

"*Dai uy* dead," Deng replied.

GRIT TIME

The firefight had begun about 0545 that morning, and the first high-explosive rounds from the *Morton* arrived on target just after 0745—seconds before Tom Norris received his head wound. So the team had been fighting for two hours at that time, and the fight was far from over. All of them had been up for twenty-four hours and were running on adrenaline. On learning that his lieutenant was dead, Mike Thornton had a decision to make: Do I consolidate my position on the defensible dune? With the enemy at least partially occupied with the naval bombardment, do we now make for the water? Or do I go back for the body of my lieutenant and my friend? Logic dictated one of the first two of these options. Yet the Navy SEALs, then as now, have a covenant that they leave no one behind, and Mike was not about to violate that covenant. He immediately went back.

"I told Quan and the others to wait here, that I was going back for Tommy. They tried to stop me, saying that it was no use—he was dead. I believed them; I too thought he was dead. But I wasn't going to leave him behind; we never leave anybody behind. So no way was I going to be the first to do that. Had I been wounded or dead, he'd have come back for me. That's who we are. Deng said he was dead and I had no reason not to believe him. It didn't matter. And what if, by chance, he was still alive? I could not have lived with myself if I had left him behind not knowing, or what the NVA might do to him if he were still alive. That whole area south of the bunker was littered with bodies, and they would be looking for revenge.

"I had close to a quarter of a mile to cover, and the last part of it was uphill, but I ran all the way. The initial salvo from the *Morton,* although I didn't know at the time that it was the *Morton* shooting, had made the bad guys think twice about advancing on that dune with the bunker. When I got close, I saw them moving carefully toward the bunker. From where I was I could see they were flanking the bunker and moving in from the east or the beach side as well as from the south. I saw Tommy lying on the west side of the bunker. Two guys were climbing over the top as they moved in from the east. They moved cautiously, and got to within a few feet of him. I shot them both, and moved to where Tommy was. He had an unbelievable head wound. The whole side of his forehead was gone, his brain was visible—you could actually see it. The front lobe of his brain was kind of pushing out through his skull. I could now see why Deng said he was dead. I sure thought he was. I picked him up, put him over my shoulder, and started running. I also grabbed his AK-47, as I knew I was getting low on ammo. I hadn't taken more than ten steps from the bunker when there was this explosion behind me from a naval gunfire round. The concussion picked us both up in the air, lifting Tommy off my shoulder, and tossed us forward ten or fifteen feet. I literally saw him leave my shoulder and fly through the air. When I landed, I sat there for a moment stunned, trying to orient myself and catch my breath. Once I sorted myself out, I crawled over to where Tommy was lying in the sand."

"I never saw or heard those initial rounds from the *Morton* land," recalled Tom. "After I told them to fire for effect, I went back to trying to get the LAAW rocket launcher extended so I could use it. Then I was hit. The round just picked me up off of the side of the bunker and dumped me on my back. I knew I was hit, but I didn't know how bad. I began scrounging around to find my rifle to shoot back. I was starting to have tunnel vision, and I was fighting to stay conscious. I kept saying to myself, 'No, no, no, no!' because I needed to shoot; I needed to cover my guys. I fought it for a few seconds, then boom, I just went out. And the next thing I remember, Mike's over top of me and I'm looking up at him."

"After Tom called for the fire for effect," Bill Woodruff said of the NGFS salvo, "we heard nothing more from them. The *Morton* called them; I called them—nothing. Their radio went dark. I think the NGFS team on the *Morton* felt they may have killed them with friendly fire, and I didn't know what to think. We had drifted south of where we had inserted them, so my two junks were chugging north along the coast. We now knew roughly where they were—just south of the Ben Hai River, *not* the Cua Viet. Now I wanted to get up to a location off the coast so if they were alive and could make it to the water, we would be there for them.

"I tried to put myself in their position—no radio, hopefully still alive and fighting. And I figured they'd probably need more gunfire support. So I called the *Morton* and asked them to put more rounds in to where Tom had last called for them. If Tom, Mike, and the others were still alive, some more 5-inch rounds in the area would give the enemy something to think about.

"The round that had knocked us down landed on the southeastern side of the bunker," said Mike. "Thank God there was a portion of that dune between us and that round or we'd have both been killed. It must have raised havoc with the NVA still working their way toward the bunker. Once I got to Tommy again and started to pick him up, he spoke to me for the first time. He said, 'Mike, buddy,' and it was then that I knew he was alive. I said, 'Can you run?' and he says, 'I can run but I can't see.' But he really couldn't run, and he blanked out again. I put him in a fireman's carry and took off for the dune to the north where I had left the others. I heard him talking now and then, and guessed he was fading in and out. But I knew he was alive. And I put all my energy and focus to covering the ground between where we were and the other dune."

The *Morton* continued to put rounds into the area at the request of Bill Woodruff and then by the direction of an Air Force airborne

observer in an OV-10 Bronco spotter aircraft. Yet with the few
SEALs among the many NVA moving in the area, there was the ever-
present danger of friendly fire. And with no radio communication,
that danger increased. It is uncertain after these many years just how
many rounds of high explosive the *Morton* fired that day. The *Newport
News* arrived on station sometime that morning, but there is no record of the big cruiser ever taking part in any NGFS activity. The *Morton* did move in close enough to the beach to take counterbattery
fire in the form of rocket-propelled grenades. In all probability, these
were Russian-made RPG-7s with a maximum range of one thousand
yards. It is doubtful the *Morton* was ever that close to the beach, but
the ship moved out to seaward just to be safe. There were some reports
of soldiers running along the beach, but with no clear identification,
the *Morton* declined to take them under fire.

"I knew we weren't safe, not by a long shot," Mike remembered, "as
I could now see North Vietnamese deployed on the beach to the
north, coming at us. When I got back to the dune, Deng and Quan
were waiting for me, providing covering fire. Lieutenant Thuan was
nowhere in sight; he had already made for the water to escape. But
God bless Deng and Quan. They waited for me and were still in the
fight, even though Deng was wounded.

"They said, 'Mike, what do we do now?' and I said, 'We swim.'
But first we had to get to the water, and the bad guys were now coming at us from the north and the south. Rounds were starting to
kick up sand around us, and we had 250 yards of sand and open
beach to cross before we got to the water. And we'd be under fire
the whole way. I had just one full magazine left for my CAR, and I
knew Deng and Quan were low on ammunition. So off we went.
Now we were leapfrogging with bounds of thirty to forty yards,

first me carrying Tommy and then the two of them—running, then dropping to one knee to shoot. I remember taking measured, single shots, hoping that I could make my ammo last until we got to the water. All the while, rounds were kicking up sand all around us. I had Tommy in a fireman's carry, and I still had his AK-47 clutched in one hand, my CAR in the other. I could feel there was a magazine or two left in Tommy's AK ammo vest, and that was my fallback when my rifle ran dry. Just as I got into the water, I took a round in my left calf. The round tripped me, and pitched me forward, tossing poor Tommy into the shallows. I got to my feet, picked him up, grabbing him around the waist with one arm, and we staggered into the water. I fired the last rounds from my CAR and tossed it aside, along with my combat vest. I now had no rifle, no grenades, no nothing—just Tommy and Tommy's AK. But there was no time to get Tommy's AK-47 into the fight; I was totally focused on getting through the four- to five-foot surf that was then running."

From Tom: "As you might imagine, what took place after I got shot was pretty much of a blur for me. I was going in and out of consciousness. I remember there was a lot of shooting going on— from Mike and from the others nearby. I also remember the impact of rounds from the naval gunfire. But it was hard for me then, and now, to put the sequence together. I remember getting to the water, trying to run through the water, and that Mike had me around the waist, moving me forward. I remember the rounds coming in and splashing all around us. I could see them and hear them. I could even hear the action of the enemy AK-47s, 'Cha-cha-ching! Cha-cha-ching!' I'm thrashing around, reaching for whatever I could find to shoot back with, but there was nothing I could do. It was frustrating and, of course, I was having trouble seeing. I really didn't know at the time that I had only one good eye. The blood from my head wound kept washing in my eyes and I remember dunking my head in the water to wash it off, but then I'd get all bloody again. I was aware there was another guy in the water nearby, but I was having a hard time seeing him. I kept ducking my head in the water to wash the blood off so I could see. I'd be awake, then things would close in and I'd fade out. It was like a dream sequence."

From Mike: "I kind of used Tommy like a surfboard. I pushed him underneath the water through the oncoming waves to get him through the surf zone. My worst fear was that I'd somehow lose my grip on him and have the waves carry him back to shore. Once we cleared the breakers, I tried to find his life vest and get it over his head, which was no small task given he had this big head wound and I could see his brain. Here the bullets were still splashing around us and I was looking for his damned life vest. I never did find it, as he for some reason had tied it to his leg. So I took my vest (these were UDT-type, horse-collar rubber inflatable vests) and managed to get it over his head. I partially inflated it, as I wanted to keep his head up, but not too high, as they were still shooting at us. All the while, I was kicking and pushing him out to sea. Pretty soon we were in the offshore swells and that gave us some cover from the guys firing at us from the beach. I'll never know why those guys didn't come into the water after us. They just stood on the beach, plinking away at us. I guess they were hoping for a lucky hit. Then maybe we'd turn around and give up. But we kept swimming."

"When I came to in the water, I knew that Mike had me and that we were clear of the surf zone. The water was warm and sort of lulled you along. Then suddenly, Mike was not there—he'd swum off."

"There were still bullets singing through the water, so we were still in range," said Mike. "I could see Deng out in front of me and Lieutenant Thuan was nowhere in sight. I was thinking that if we got out of this, I was going to have a serious talk with our Vietnamese officer, but that would have to wait. Then I noticed Quan off to my right—to the south. He was lagging back and splashing about so I knew he was in trouble. I left Tommy and swam over to him. Quan had been shot through the buttocks and the round had lodged in his thigh. Later we learned that it had gone into his femur. So he was in a lot of pain and couldn't swim. I grabbed him and got back to Tommy, and now I had two of them to push through the water. I got Quan's life vest inflated so now I knew he, like Tommy, wouldn't sink. I tied a line around Tommy so he was tied to my back and I pushed Quan ahead of me. And there was nothing to do now but swim seaward. It was like SEAL training and Hell Week—kick, stroke, and glide, although there was not much gliding. With every stroke, I waited for a round to catch me in the back of the head, but with every stroke, we were that much farther from the beach."

"I somehow knew we were in deep water and aware that there was no more gunfire," Tom said of one of his bouts with consciousness. "With the exception of Mike panting and an occasional grunt from Quan, it was quiet. I again ducked under to wash off the blood and looked around. I could see and hear Mike and Quan, and then I found Deng nearby. But what about Thuan? Where was Lieutenant Thuan? A SEAL officer always has to keep track of his men—always. This goes back to our basic SEAL training where our SEAL instructors did unspeakable things to officers in training if they could not account for their men, no matter what the conditions. So it's hammered into your DNA: always account for your men. And I was missing one."

"Every time Tommy woke up it was, 'Mike, you got everyone? I count only four of us; where's the other guy?' I'd say, 'I got them, I got everyone,' and he'd drift off again. Then when he awoke again, it was, 'Mike, you got everyone? Do you have all of them?' And I'd say, 'Dammit, Tommy, I got 'em all, okay? They're all accounted for.' That seemed to calm him down and he'd drift back off to sleep. I really didn't know where Lieutenant Thuan was, and about that time I really didn't care. But I had this growing urge to wring his neck if I ever did see him again."

"I remember that Mike was getting a little irked at me as I kept asking him if he had everyone," Tom recalled. "I don't blame him. He was hurt, and he had to swim for me, Quan, and himself. Finally, after he'd once again assured me he had everyone, I guess I relaxed a little and drifted off. I don't remember much of the day after that."

"After we got out of small-arms range of the beach, all we could do was swim. After a while, Tommy quit pestering me about whether we had everyone. Deng and Quan kept asking, 'Mike, what do we do, what do we do?' and each time I said, 'We swim—we just keep swimming. We'll swim south, all the way to Thuan-An if we have to.' They were starting to give up and said, 'But, Mike, what happens when we get tired?' and I told them that when it got dark, we'd swim ashore and rest. But for now we keep swimming—that we were going to be all right. I was now towing both Quan and Tommy behind me, swimming a breaststroke so I could use my arms. I kept checking on Tommy, and it looked to me like he was going into shock. But all I could do was keep swimming. We were now well into the swells. The ships were well out to sea, and I could occasionally catch a glimpse of them when we rode over the crest of a swell.

An early photo of Mike Thornton, here at the age of four. Always a talkative fellow, Mike began at an early age.

(Courtesy of Mike Thornton)

Senior Class photo of Tommy Norris at Montgomery Blair High School, Maryland, 1962.

(Courtesy of Montgomery Blair High School)

Tommy Norris as a varsity wrestler at the University of Maryland, 1966. For tournament competition, Tommy wrestled at 115 pounds.

(Courtesy of University of Maryland)

Basic Underwater Demolition/SEAL Class 49, West Coast, 1969. Mike Thornton, standing seventh from left, graduated from BUD/S training about the same time as did Tommy Norris who trained on the East Coast. *(Courtesy of U.S. Navy)*

Basic Underwater Demolition/SEAL Class 45, East Coast, 1969. Front row, far left is Dick Couch; front row, far right is Tommy Norris. *(Courtesy of U.S. Navy)*

Charlie Platoon embarked on a Light SEAL Support Craft. The LSSC was fast and had .30 caliber armor, but was gasoline powered and an explosive fire hazard as a SEAL combat craft.

(Courtesy of Tom Boyhan)

Fifth Platoon, SEAL Team Two, in Vietnam, 1970. Kneeling on the far right is Tommy Norris.

(Courtesy of Mike Jukoski)

A single squad of SEALs from Charlie Platoon, SEAL Team One in 1970, with captured Viet Cong flag. Standing right to left, Barry Enoch, Mike Thornton, Lieutenant Tom Boyhan.

(Courtesy of Tom Boyhan)

Then Lieutenant Mike Jukoski (center) and Tommy Norris (right) in Vietnam in 1970. Jukoski and Norris served as Platoon Officer and Assistant Platoon Officer of 5th Platoon, SEAL Team Two.

(Courtesy of Mike Jukoski)

Mike Thornton with Charlie Platoon, SEAL Team One, in 1970. He's holding the Vietnam-era SEALs' weapon of choice—the Stoner Rifle.

(Courtesy of Mike Thornton)

Always the fierce warrior, Mike Thornton was also a willing friend of the Vietnamese people. Following the Vietnam War, he helped to resettle numerous loyal Vietnamese in the United States.

(Courtesy of Tom Boyhan)

Nguyen Kiet atop a burned out NVA tank. Photo was taken by Nick Ut at the Vietnamese Ranger outpost between rescue missions, April 1972.

(Courtesy of Nick Ut)

A very tired Tommy Norris, standing center, watches as Colonel Hambleton (Bat 21 Bravo) is unloaded from an armored personnel carrier after the journey from the Vietnamese Ranger outpost back to Dong Ha, April 1972. *(Courtesy of Nick Ut)*

Tommy Norris and Nguyen Kiet at Dong Ha, just after they brought Colonel Iceal Hambleton out from behind the North Vietnamese Army line of advance, April 1972.
(Courtesy of General Louis C. Wagner, Jr., US Army Retired)

LDNN (Vietnamese SEAL) advisors having a beer at Cat Lai, Vietnam. Back row: Ryan McCombie, Mike Thornton, unknown, John Brooks, Tommy Nelson. Front row: Commodore Robert Stanton, Doug Huth, Tommy Norris. *(Courtesy of Mike Thornton)*

Then Petty Officer First Class Mike Thornton and then Commander (Uncle) Dave Schaible pay an office call on the Chief of Naval Operations, Admiral Elmo Zumwalt, shortly before Mike was awarded the Medal. *(Courtesy of U.S. Navy)*

Petty Officer First Class Mike Thornton is presented the Medal of Honor at a White House ceremony. Flanking Mike is President Nixon and his wife, Gladys.

(Official White House Photo)

Lieutenant Tommy Norris is presented the Medal of Honor by President Ford at a White House ceremony. Attending the ceremony are Tommy's parents, two brothers, sister-in-law, and niece and nephew.

(Official White House photo)

Mike's official Medal of Honor photo, taken soon after he was commissioned as an ensign in the United States Navy.

(Courtesy of U.S. Navy)

Tommy's official Medal of Honor photo, taken shortly before he was medically retired from the United States Navy.

(Courtesy of U.S. Navy)

Tommy Norris, with Ross Perot standing by, receives the Boy Scouts of America Distinguished Eagle Scout Award, 2011. Eleven men who were Eagle Scouts have been recipients of the Medal of Honor. *(Courtesy of Rob Kyker)*

Mike Thornton, Bob Kerrey, and Tommy Norris —the three Navy SEAL Medal of Honor recipients from Vietnam. Photo taken in Dallas, 2014, at a Medal of Honor banquet.

(Courtesy of Rob Kyker)

I wondered if anyone knew we were still alive. I wasn't sure about the Navy, as they might give up or get called away for another fire mission, but I knew Woody would not stop looking for us. I just had to keep everyone together and keep us moving."

RECOVERY

It is unclear just how long Mike, Tom, Deng, and Quan were actually in the water. A reconstruction of events has them entering the water sometime around 0830, and by 0900 they were out of small-arms gunfire range. The four were picked up by the junks around 1130. So they had been fighting on the beach for approximately three hours and in the water for about three hours. Yet nothing had been heard from them since a North Vietnamese bullet had silenced their radio at about 0750 that morning.

"Before Tom's radio went dark," recalls Bill Woodruff, "he'd radioed his approximate location. My junk skipper had spoken with Deng on the radio, so he had a rough idea of where they were as well, and he was not happy about it. He knew it was a bad area with lots of NVA. So we moved up the coast and came in closer to shore. I had no option but to move inshore and look for them. My junk skippers certainly did not like being in that close. As we searched along the coast, I was getting a lot of calls from the *Morton,* as they were still putting in rounds ashore. I was between them and the beach and moving back and forth between them and where they were shooting. Naval gunfire protocols require that there be no friendlies on their gun target line in case there is a short round. But that's where I had to be if these guys managed to get off the beach and into the water. The ship kept telling me to move away, and

I kept telling them to shoot over me. We got into a little shouting match over the radio, but I had to stay where I was—just in case we could rescue them.

"Then about 1030 or so we're maybe a thousand yards or so off the beach, a lot closer than any of us liked to be in the daylight. We get a few RPGs shot at us, but we're just out of range. Then we see this guy in the water. We maneuver over to pick him up and it's the Vietnamese officer, Lieutenant Thuan. We get him aboard and he tells me that Lieutenant Norris was killed fighting the NVA, and that Mike Thornton went back to get him and never came back. He said he thought that the others, Quan and Deng, had followed him into the water, but he didn't know where they were. Of course I'm wondering what the hell he's doing here without his men, and how was it that he was the only one who escaped. He was clearly scared and babbling on, but I had no choice but to pass this information along to the *Morton*. I asked them to keep shooting; if there were any chance for them at all, those 5-inch rounds might provide the diversion they'd need to break contact. But it didn't look good. I was in radio contact with my other junk and ordered them to keep moving ahead of us and to keep searching along the coast. No matter what the Vietnamese lieutenant said, we were not going to give up."

Word passed from the *Morton* to the *Newport News* that there was one American killed in action (KIA) and one American and two Vietnamese missing in action (MIA). Aboard the big cruiser, the admiral who was in charge of all NGFS activity off the coast of North and South Vietnam, the gun-line commander, ordered the *Newport News* south. With the uncertainty of the team ashore and the need for the heavy cruiser's big 8-inch guns in support of the heavy fighting around Quang Tri City, it was a logical decision. The *Newport News* began to steam south, leaving the *Morton* to sort out the missing SEALs thought to still be ashore. Word of the death of Tom Norris and the MIA status of Mike Thornton was passed to Commodore Dave Schaible in Vung Tau and back to SEAL Teams One and Two stateside. It seemed as if one and likely two more SEALs had been killed in the decade-long Vietnam War.

"I was between a rock and a hard place," said Bill Woodruff of learning the fates of Tom and Mike. "We don't leave our people behind or unaccounted for. My junk skippers wanted no part of getting any closer to shore and risking damage to their crafts. My duty was to try to get to the guys ashore, but how? And the four LDNNs that were aboard the other junk in my two-junk force were none too keen about going ashore. Had I ordered them to do so, they probably would have refused. Yet we never leave a teammate behind. So we continued to skirt the coast just out of small-arms range and look for swimmers. And God knows what I would do if we failed to locate them. It didn't look good, and I was scared—really scared."

"It seemed like we were in the water forever, and I was exhausted," Mike recalled of the ordeal. "When we were on the crest of a swell, I could see ships farther offshore, but I could only catch a glimpse of them now and then. Deng again asked me, 'Mike, what are we going to do?' and I said we'd just keep swimming—that the junks were sure to spot us. He says, 'What if they don't find us? What if they went back to Thuan-an?' Both he and Quan were about at the end of their tether. The Navy ships were well out to sea, so our only friend on that big ocean was Bill Woodruff. I knew Woody would be looking for us. I knew he'd never leave us—not Woody."

"It was about 1130 and I saw the *Newport News* begin to move off to the south," Bill Woodruff remembered. "Then my junk skipper got a call from the other junk that was off to the north and slightly inshore from us. We were about a half mile apart so as to better search the area. They said they had swimmers in the water and were going to get them. You can't know what that meant. Now it remained how many and in what condition."

"I saw the one junk and Deng and I began yelling and waving," said Mike, "but they had spotted us and were already headed our way. But we still kept yelling and waving. Tommy was out cold and Quan just held on, fighting the pain. It seemed like it took them forever, then they were alongside and I was looking up into the faces of the junk crew and the other LDNNs. They hauled up Deng and Quan, and then I helped them to pass Tommy up and over the side. You could see by their faces that they thought he was dead. At that point, I wasn't sure myself. But he was still breathing. As I got on the radio to call Woody, I saw that the cruiser was headed south. I didn't know much about ships, but I knew that cruisers carried a doctor aboard and the destroyers didn't. And Tommy needed a doctor. I told Woody to call that cruiser and get them turned around, that Tommy was alive but he wouldn't be much longer without medical help. Woody got the *Newport News* turned around and headed back our way. We headed out to sea to meet them. Tommy was in a bad way, but he was still hanging in there. By now the other junk was chugging alongside us, and I could see Woody, radio handset in hand, smiling and waving. What a sight he was! Quan was bleeding and in a lot of pain and Deng was hurt, but he was a tough kid. I just hoped we could get Tommy aboard the cruiser in time."

"That cruiser was a big ship," Bill Woodruff recalled. "You know it's big when you see just how much bigger it is than the destroyers. But when you come alongside her in a thirty-six-foot Yabuta junk, I mean it's *really* big. We came alongside the port quarter, back by the number-three turret. She was still headed north, making bare steerageway, perhaps a knot and a half. Once alongside you don't see the ship anymore, just a big gray metal wall that's about fifteen feet high. Both junks were alongside together and they put a Jacobs ladder over to each one. Deng and Lieutenant Thuan scrambled up first, Deng from the other junk and Thuan from the junk I was on. But it took some doing to get Quan and Tommy up to the deck. A line with a loop was lowered for Quan and he was pulled aboard. For Tommy it was a Stokes litter that was hoisted up to the main deck, sailors lifting from above while Mike and the other junk crew tended the trailing lines to steady the litter. I just got a glimpse of Tommy, and I could see even from a distance that he was in a bad way. Once the team and myself were aboard the *Newport News,* the junks cast off. The junk skippers were anxious to get back to Thuan-An, and their mission here was done.

"There was great relief up the chain of command that all of the team had been recovered, even if the life of Tom Norris still hung in the balance. And no one was more relieved than I was. If they'd not made it out, I'd like to think that I would have had the courage to go back for them. Maybe I could go up the coast a ways, then insert after darkness and try to recover them. It would have been more than dangerous, maybe even a suicidal mission. But that's what we SEALs do, we go back. And I was right there, right offshore, but thanks to Mike Thornton, I never had to make that call. I give thanks to Mike every day that he did what he did, and I never had to face that decision. When you look at it, with the information Mike had, *he* made an illogical decision. It was a brave decision, but given the facts at hand, maybe a foolish one. But he did what heroes do, and I didn't have to face the what-might-have-been. Thanks, Mike."

Bill Woodruff completed his tour of duty as an LDNN advisor and rotated back to SEAL Team One, one of the last SEALs to leave Vietnam. After his enlistment was up, he completed his college degree and returned to the SEAL teams as an officer; he served there for another twenty years. After leaving active service, he completed his law degree and is now an assistant U.S. attorney in the District of Columbia.

TRIAGE

"I was a first class corpsman on the USS *Newport News* when we got the call in sick bay that there were wounded coming aboard," recalled Chuck Zendner. "We had a crack medical department on the ship, with a great deal of experience. Don't forget, it was exactly a month earlier we suffered that turret explosion. We put twenty shipmates in body bags and treated sixty-two wounded sailors. Prior to that we'd been on the gun line on and off for seven months. There were fourteen of us including our physician, Lieutenant Greg Fulchiero. He always ensured that we knew exactly what to do in any emergency and under any conditions. And he was a great doctor. If we needed a head doctor, he was a head doctor—or a bone doctor or a surgeon or whatever. So the five SEALs who came aboard needing medical attention was a walk in the park for us."

Dr. Gregory Fulchiero graduated from the University of Pittsburgh in 1966 and from Hahnemann Medical College and Hospital in 1970. After completing an internship at Allentown General Hospital, he

came on active duty in the Navy in 1971. Like so many general medical officers, or GMOs, he was plucked out of residency and served as a general practitioner aboard ship or at a shore facility. Following his service on *Newport News,* he completed his orthopedic residency in 1977. After a thirty-year career in orthopedics in Altoona, Pennsylvania, Dr. Fulchiero passed away in July 2012.

"When they came aboard, they were a pretty scruffy lot," Zendner continued. "My job in handling casualties was triage. I saw them first, evaluated them, and sent them on to a senior medical person, corpsman or doctor, for treatment. I remember seeing this one American, and I couldn't believe his head wound. His forehead was simply blown away. I had two thoughts: one, it was a good thing he was in saltwater or he'd have bled to death. My second thought was, this man will not be alive in the morning. He went straight to Dr. Fulchiero, who was waiting for him in surgery. There was this big guy who was with him, and he carried him from the fantail to sick bay. We had to force him to let go so we could treat him. He wanted to go in to surgery to be with him."

"When we finally got up on the deck of the *Newport News,*" Mike recalled, "I was pretty amped up and wanted them to take care of Tommy right away. I think they figured that he was a goner and that with that head wound, he would never make it. They wanted to check me over and check the others over and I told them flat out: Tommy comes first; the rest of us can wait. I carried him straight into sick bay and the doctor went to work on him."

"Then we started checking the other four," said Corpsman Zendner. "One of the Vietnamese was sitting in a pool of blood and we got right on him. He had a nasty bullet wound in his buttocks. Another was uninjured, and the third Vietnamese had only some shrapnel lodged in his back, which was an easy fix. We treated them, cleaned them up, and got them into bed. While we were treating the Vietnamese SEALs, I kept my eye on the big American. I finally got him to sit down so we could look him over. I saw blood on his pant leg and when I cut into his trouser leg, I saw a bullet hole in his leg. My eyes got big and I called another corpsman over to look at it. I said that we'd better treat that and the SEAL said something like, 'Yeah, whatever.' He just didn't seem to care. But he did care about the others and kept asking about them, especially his lieutenant. We knew he was a lieutenant because the other big American SEAL said he was. He had no rank insignia on him."

"After they initially treated my leg," said Mike, "I got word that Captain Zartman, the skipper of the *Newport News,* wanted to see me in the captain's quarters to brief him and the admiral, the guy who was the gun-line commander. I went up, and I don't know what they expected, but I was a mess—wet, dirty, still running on adrenaline, and dripping all over the captain's nice rug. They looked at me like I was from another planet, which in a way I was. I told them what had happened as best I could, and they called a corpsman to take me back to sick bay. Tommy was in surgery for close to two hours. They got him stabilized and some IV fluids in him, and heloed him off to the medical facility at Da Nang. I stayed behind with the LDNNs to see that they were taken care of. Lieutenant Thuan had almost gotten us all killed, and I don't think he ever fired a round the whole time. Deng and Quan fought well start to finish. None of us would have made it without their courage and loyalty. They were just great fighters."

"With the junks on their way back to Thuan-An, I was left on the cruiser," recalled Bill Woodruff. "I waited for Tommy to get through what little they could do for him aboard the big ship and

boarded the helo with him for the trip to Da Nang. He had a bandage around his forehead and eye, but nothing across the rent in his
skull. You could see his brain. He was fading in and out on the hour
flight to Da Nang, and we had to shout over the sound of the tur-
bines. When he was conscious, he was coherent. I think he was
more tired than in pain, at least that's what he said. After all, he'd
been up for about thirty-six hours. And I tell you, it was really
strange talking to someone who'd just been through what he'd been
through, and the fact that you could clearly see his brain."

"We spent the night on the cruiser in their sick bay ward,"
Mike said of his stay on the ship. "I sat up with Quan for a while.
He said, 'Mike, whenever I go out with you, we get into trouble.' I
told him, 'I guess that's true, but I always get you back home, don't
I?' The next day we were standing off Thuan-An on the *Newport
News*. They sent a junk out for us and by late afternoon of Novem-
ber 1, we were all back at the LDNN base—all but Tommy."

"We left the gun line late that November and headed home,"
said Chuck Zendner. "The turret explosion and the loss of our shipmates was still foremost in our minds. But I still never forgot those
SEALs—the lieutenant with that terrible head wound and the big
SEAL who was hovering over him."

AFTERMATH

Word that Tom, Mike, and the LDNNs had been overrun and were
KIA or MIA reached the SEALs at Vung Tau, Thuan-An, and the
stateside SEAL teams. This narrator recalls those incoming overseas
messages when I was at SEAL Team One, priority messages saying
that a platoon or a team in the field had been hit. They were dreaded
communiqués. I even sent a few of those messages while on deployment. Sad business. At Thuan-An, Ryan McCombie was mustering

the other SEAL advisors and LDNNs for a recovery effort. It's with a great sadness and sense of purpose that a team has to kit up and get ready to go out to try and recover a team that's been hit. I've done that as well. It's dangerous, gut-wrenching duty. Imagine the relief that McCombie and the other SEALs at Thuan-An felt when they learned that all five were safe and on board the *Newport News*.

As for Tom Norris, his medial odyssey was just beginning. There was little that could be done for him on the *Newport News*—or even in Da Nang, for that matter. He needed the attention of a neurosurgeon and there were none at Da Nang or anywhere else in Vietnam. The closest physician with this specialty was at Clark Air Force Base in the Philippines. Tom was ferried by helo from the *Newport News* to the medical facility at Da Nang late in the afternoon of the 31st. A casualty-evacuation aircraft, a C-141, was laid on to fly him to Clark Air Force Base the next day, if he made it through the night.

"I managed to get down to Da Nang just a few hours after Tommy got there," said Ryan McCombie. "There was not a lot they could do for him other than keep him quiet and keep him pumped with fluids and pain meds. They periodically chased me out of the ward where they were treating him so they could irrigate his head wound and what was left of his left eye. But he was not allowed to go to sleep. The doctors said that with a head wound like that, if he went to sleep, he would likely slip into a coma and not wake up. So I sat up with him all night, talking to him. It was kind of distracting, talking with someone whose brain you could see. He would fade in and out, and he said he was not in any pain. Yet with Tommy, you never knew. He could be very stoic and not admit that he was hurting. But he was tired—and no wonder. By the next morning, the morning of 1 November, he'd been awake or mostly awake for forty-eight hours. And he was for the most part coherent. I tried to kid him, saying that when they operated on him, this was his chance to improve his looks. I even offered to go along so they could use me as a model—then maybe half of him would be good-looking.

"I rode with him in the ambulance over to the big C-141, where they took him aboard for the trip to Clark AFB. He was still awake, but just barely. I said the standard line when someone left Vietnam, 'See you back in the world,' and he answered, 'See you back in the world.' Then I went back up to Thuan-An to finish my tour. By early spring of 1973, all of us were back home, back in the world. Some of our LDNNs managed to get out before the NVA came south for good; others were left behind and made to suffer under the new communist regime."

Through the efforts of the Navy SEAL community, a great many of the LDNNs, along with some Kit Carson Scouts and interpreters who served in combat with us, managed to leave Vietnam and come to this country. Some made it onto helicopters during the last chaotic days of the final North Vietnamese push south. Others crowded onto junks or were repatriated through Thailand. Lieutenant Thuan and Quan made it out and today are U.S. citizens. The North Vietnamese caught Deng and executed him.

"I received a call that morning from our ER [emergency room] that there was an inbound head wound," recalled then Major Walter Grand. Grand was the only neurosurgeon in the region and stationed at the hospital at Clark Air Force Base in the Philippines. All massive head wounds came to him. "When he arrived, we took him directly into the OR [operating room]. At the time, general military/battlefield protocol held that the patient needed to be or should be conscious going into surgery. And I was surprised that someone with that serious of a head wound would be conscious and conversant. Fortunately he was. He was still dressed in his operational gear, which were blue jeans and a black T-shirt of some kind. As I was conducting my initial examination, I remember that he was conscious, but just barely. I could tell he'd been through a lot. Then, he seemed to become more alert and asked, 'Sir, can you tell me about my men. I know we got all of them off the beach, but can you tell me if they're okay.' He called me 'sir' because he could see I had on my major's oak leaves. I'd been told that he was a SEAL lieutenant. I didn't know about his men, but I said I'm sure they're going to be fine. And I told him, 'Son, you've got a pretty bad head wound, but we're going to get you fixed up.' I don't know why I called him 'son' at the time except that he looked so young. After all, I was thirty-two at the time and he was twenty-seven.

"I worked on him for about six hours, perhaps seven. The bullet had torn away a section of his skull from the left orbit—the eye socket, back to close to his ear. There was irreversible damage to his left eye. The brain itself had a long laceration to the frontal left lobe. Nothing could be done with his left eye but to remove the remnants of the eye and debride the left orbit. There was little else I could do but find and remove the remaining bone fragments, clean up and debride, and sanitize the surrounding tissue, and use the remaining skin and scalp tissue to cover and close the wound. It was critical to create a sterile sac and skin closure over the exposed brain to ward off infection. With this kind of wound, there was the ever-present danger of infection. Past that, his survival and recovery were chancy. It all depended on how much trauma the brain had suffered and the will of the patient. From what I'd seen, this SEAL had plenty of willpower.

"When I made my rounds the following morning, I was surprised to see him up and moving about with assistance. I asked him how he was feeling, and he sort of shrugged. His head was still bandaged up with only his right eye visible. On removing the bandage and inspecting the wound, we talked and I sensed that he didn't know that he no longer had a left eye. I was reluctant to tell him, as he'd endured a great deal. But he was a pretty tough fellow, so I told him that we were unable to save his left eye. He thought about it a few seconds, then said, 'Do you think they'll kick me out of the Navy because of that?' I said that I couldn't really answer that, but I took it as a good sign that he still wanted to be a SEAL."

Following his service in the Air Force, Dr. Wally Grand went on to become the director of the Brain Endoscopy Center and clinical professor of neurosurgery, pathology, and anatomical sciences at the State University of New York at the University at Buffalo School of Medicine and Biomedical Sciences. He has lectured widely on endoscopic neurosurgery and minimally invasive brain surgery for residents and neurosurgeons in Buffalo and throughout the United States, Europe, and Asia. He is now seventy-six and still practicing.

"Mike and I invited him to a Medal of Honor dinner in New York in 2009," Tom recalled, "and it was great to see him again after all those years. What a nice man. We got to talking about the operation, and he said, 'You know, when you came in, we just went through the procedures. To us, you were pretty much a dead man, but you just wouldn't die. We did what we could as best we could, but none of us thought you were going to survive.'"

Because of Tom's condition, his parents were flown to Clark Air Force Base to see him. His condition was still critical—too critical for a

transpacific flight. Yet he remained cognizant and positive, and was able to reassure his parents that he would come through this. When he did begin his journey back to the United States, it was a leapfrog odyssey from one hospital to the next. Along the way, a great many doctors wondered why he was still alive. But again, he simply refused to die.

Tom was admitted to Bethesda Naval Hospital just outside of Washington, D.C., in early 1973. From 1973 through most of 1975, he underwent a number of major surgeries, and from 1976 to 1978, a number of minor surgeries. Bethesda was close to his home in Silver Spring, Maryland, so family visited often and he could return home between operations. For a portion of that time, between 1973 and 1978, Tom lived with your narrator. He also lived for a period with Ryan McCombie. Both of us remember Tommy as the perfect house guest, always looking for projects to stay busy and to help out around the house.

Lieutenant Tom Norris was medically retired from the U.S. Navy in April 1975.

PART THREE

THE AWARD AND LIFE
AFTER THE AWARD

ABOVE AND BEYOND

There is a saying among Medal of Honor recipients that it's more difficult to wear the Medal than to earn the Medal. While the criteria for earning this highest of all military awards for heroism is steep and singular, much is expected from those who wear the Medal. Yet it all begins with heroism in combat. The action for which a recipient receives the Medal is often a life-changing event—literally. Since the beginning of World War II, 60 percent of all awards have been posthumous. That ratio between living and posthumous awards since Vietnam even more dramatically favors the posthumous. For those who do survive and are privileged to live with this distinction, theirs becomes a life before the award and a life after. Most find that it is both a heavy burden and a humbling one. In all cases, there is change. America has evolved to bestow nobility on those who achieve success in the media, political, and corporate worlds, but it confers a very special status for those who receive the Medal of Honor.

Like America and its military, the Medal has evolved in its form and the criteria for which it is awarded. Yet since 1942, it has been reserved only for those in combat action, and the requirements have been somewhat standardized. Public Law 88-77 of 25 July 1963 codified those requirements. A recipient has to "distinguish himself conspicuously by gallantry and intrepidity at the risk of his life above and beyond the call of duty." Such conduct must occur under one of the following circumstances:

1. While engaged in action against an enemy of the United States.
2. While engaged in military operations involving conflict with an opposing foreign force.
3. While serving with friendly foreign forces engaged in an armed conflict against an opposing armed force in which the United States is not a belligerent party.

Awards are usually initiated by the commander in the field, documented by at least two eyewitnesses, and passed up the chain of command in a highly regulated and formatted process as detailed by Title 10 of the U.S. Code. Recommendations for the Medal are made in compliance with specific procedures established by the service secretaries, and these recommendations are passed along, with supporting documentation, to the chairman of the Joint Chiefs of Staff. Once endorsed by the chairman, the recommendation for conferring the award is passed on to the secretary of defense.

Given the rigorous criteria for the award and the public honor afforded a recipient, there has been controversy over who does and does not qualify for the Medal. There are statutory time frames for submission and the awarding of the Medal, yet exceptions have been made to those existing parameters. Without getting into the controversy and, yes, the politics of the Medal, the criteria for the award, since the conferring of the first medal in 1863, have become increasingly more stringent. Yet who receives or does not receive the Medal is subjective. In the words of General David Petraeus, "There's a band (gray area) there, and the difference between the Medal of Honor and the Distinguished Service Cross (or the Navy Cross or Air Force Cross—the Army, Navy, and Air Force's second highest award for valor) is sort of in the eye of the beholder on a given day. And that's tough. But decisions do have to be made." Which actions do or do not qualify for the Medal today are ongoing and contentious. For his actions at the bridge at Dong Ha in 1972, then Captain John Ripley received the Navy Cross. A great many Marines of the Vietnam generation feel his courage merited the Medal of Honor. This unique award, the Medal of Honor, does represent our nation's highest notion of valor and service above self, and is the very essence of patriotic service.

As one Army recipient told me, "I wear this decoration for all those who served with me, and served with great honor and distinction. It's not my Medal; it's our Medal."

The Medal itself is awarded in three service-centric designs, one for the Army, one for the Air Force, and one for the Navy, Marine Corps, and coast guard. All three are cast in a burnished brass alloy. Each medallion costs the taxpayers about thirty dollars. According to the U.S. Institute of Heraldry, the naval service medal is "a five-pointed bronze star, tipped with trefoils containing a crown of laurel and oak. In the center is Minerva, personifying the United

States, standing with a left hand resting on fasces (a bundle of wooden rods that symbolize power and jurisdiction) and the right hand holding a shield blazoned with the shield from the coat of arms of the United States. She (Minerva) repulses Discord, represented by snakes. The Medal is suspended from the flukes of an anchor." Surrounding the depiction of Minerva is a circle of thirty-eight stars representing the thirty-eight states at the time of the Civil War. The Navy medal, as with the Army and Air Force versions, is suspended by a sky-blue ribbon with thirteen stars for the thirteen colonies. For all still in uniform, the military ribbon worn with other military ribbons on the uniform of the day is a sky-blue entry with five stars. The civilian decoration is a lapel button in a modest six-sided light blue rosette with thirteen white stars.

The Medal confers a number of benefits on the recipient. One is a monthly pension that, with the recent cost-of-living increase, amounts to just under $1,300. There is a 10 percent increase in the recipient's military retirement pay. Sons and daughters of recipients, if fully qualified, may attend a service academy without regard to quotas of the normal nomination process. Most states (forty) allow for free vehicle license registration and a special license plate that identifies them as Medal of Honor recipients. In addition to other travel, ceremonial, and burial benefits, there are those that are granted by custom, not by statute. A recipient is rendered a salute by those in uniform, even by those senior to the recipient. And then there is the reverence afforded by the public at large to our greatest heroes.

The Medal is presented by the president in the name of Congress, which is one reason the award is sometimes referred to as the Congressional Medal of Honor. The president, in a formal ceremony, presents it to the recipient or, in the case of a posthumous award, to his or her family. By convention and practice, the ceremony is accompanied by a visit to the capital with pomp and ceremony associated with the formal White House presentation. And the recipient and/or his or her family is treated to a trip to Washington and a night on the town at government expense. Yet even with the standardization of the criteria for the Medal and the statutory benefits, each award is different and each recipient is different.

MIKE THORNTON AND THE MEDAL OF HONOR

Since Mike received his Medal first, let's look at Mike's award. The action for which he received the Medal of Honor took place on 31 October 1972. His Medal was presented by President Richard Nixon in a White House ceremony on 15 October 1973. The citation reads:

> For conspicuous gallantry and intrepidity at the risk of his life above and beyond the call of duty while participating in a daring operation against enemy forces. PO (Petty Officer) Thornton, as Assistant U.S. Navy Advisor, along with a U.S. Navy lieutenant serving as Senior Advisor, accompanied a 3-man Vietnamese Navy SEAL patrol on an intelligence gathering and prisoner capture operation against an enemy-occupied naval river base. Launched from a Vietnamese Navy junk in a rubber boat, the patrol reached land and was continuing on foot toward its objective when it suddenly came under heavy fire from a numerically superior force. The patrol called in naval gunfire support and then engaged the enemy in a fierce firefight, accounting for many enemy casualties before moving back to the

waterline to prevent encirclement. Upon learning that the
Senior Advisor had been hit by enemy fire and was believed to be dead, PO Thornton returned through a hail of
fire to the lieutenant's last position; quickly disposed of
two enemy soldiers about to overrun the position, and
succeeded in removing the seriously wounded and uncon-
scious Senior Naval Advisor to the water's edge. He then
inflated the lieutenant's life jacket and towed him seaward
for approximately two hours until picked up by support
craft. By his extraordinary courage and perseverance, PO
Thornton was directly responsible for saving the life of his
superior officer and for the safe extraction of all patrol
members, thereby upholding the highest traditions of the
United States Naval Service.

Tom described Mike's actions in his own words. "Mike did good
work that day—courageous work. He was heroic and he saved my
life. It's a given that we don't leave a team member behind, but it's
more than that. Mike had every reason to think that I'd been killed.
He also had responsibilities for the other members of the team. Yet he
risked his life to come back for me. But you know, Mike's one heck
of a fighter; he really is. If you get into a dangerous situation, which
we certainly were that day, you want a guy like Mike Thornton with
you. I'm only glad that I got hit instead of him, as he would have
been a big man to carry off that beach. The Medal of Honor? Absolutely. Not just because I wouldn't be here if he hadn't done what he
did. His actions were in keeping with the precepts and requirements
for those who receive the Medal."

On reflecting on his actions that day—the actions for which he
was awarded the Medal—Mike put it this way: "The teams are a

brotherhood and our teammates are our brothers. Tommy and I both have brothers, but I think our blood brothers feel a little short-changed because of the bond we SEALs have for each other. So when Deng got to me on the beach that day and said that Tommy was dead, I didn't really think about it. I just told the others to wait there while I went and got him. We're trained from day one to look after our swim buddy and our teammates. This was simply a reaction to how we were trained. I did nothing more than to look out for my teammate that day. And in the back of my mind I was thinking, 'What if he *isn't* dead? Then what?' We'd killed a lot of NVA soldiers that day. What would they do to Tommy if he *was* alive and they captured him? Proud to be a recipient? Of course. Do I think I deserved it? No—I was just doing my job. Had I not done all I could for Tommy that day, how could I have lived with myself? Maybe in my heart I didn't really believe he was dead or refused to admit it. Or maybe I had to know for sure. Either way, I couldn't leave him behind."

Mike's Medal of Honor ceremony and the events surrounding it were like Mike himself: unique. In addition to his family and a few other SEALs and their families, Mike wanted Tom to be there at the White House when he received his award.

"Mike really wanted me to attend his ceremony. Even though it was close to a year since I'd been shot, I was still undergoing treatment. At that time, I was in the Bethesda Naval Hospital. I'd been in and out of the hospital so many times and had so many procedures, I'm not sure if I was recovering from one operation or getting ready for the next one. At any rate, Mike came to see me at Bethesda. We asked the doctors if I could go and they said no. Given my condition, and even the prospects of my recovery, which was no sure thing even at that point, they said it was not a good idea for me to leave the hospital. Well, it's bad business to tell a SEAL that he can't do something. 'Can't' is not a word in our vocabulary. So we made a plan, kind of a domestic SEAL operation."

"Late the next night I sort of kidnapped Tommy out of the hospital," Mike continued. "It was just another nighttime SEAL mission. My folks were up from South Carolina and staying at the Madison Hotel with my wife and kids. I checked Tommy in under a false name so there was no way they were going to find him. Once they knew he was missing, the search was on. They called his parents and then SEAL Team Two in Norfolk, and no one knew where he was. There were no cell phones back then, so we were on our own."

"The night before the ceremony," Tom recalled, "we had a night on the town—Mike and his wife; myself; his parents, brother, and sister; and a few friends. We headed for Georgetown and made a night of it. There was this poor Navy junior grade lieutenant assigned as Mike's escort officer. He was supposed to drive us around to wherever we wanted to go and pay for whatever we wanted to eat and drink. And Mike was buying drinks for us and everyone around us. The lieutenant kept saying, 'Sir, I'm not sure we're supposed to be doing this,' and Mike would reply, 'Hey, it's my night, right?' Our escort officer, who even though he was an officer and Mike was an enlisted man had to address him as sir, said, 'But sir, that's a big round of drinks,' and Mike would just laugh and order another round. Mike even ordered him to have a drink. When the lieutenant said he couldn't, that he was on duty, Mike put a drink in front of him and said, 'Mister, I'm in charge here, and I order you to have a drink with me.' The only guy who didn't have a drink that night with Mike was me. That part of the doctor's orders I did follow. We finished the night in some upscale restaurant in Georgetown with Mike ordering expensive bottles of champagne for our table and every table around us. We spent a lot of money that night. I sure hope that young officer didn't get into trouble for the cost of that evening. But when Mike's on the town, he knows how to do it up big."

"The next day we showed up at the White House for the ceremony," Mike recalled. "And we were made to wait like a group of tourists. I was getting a little upset with the process, but Daddy told me to settle down and wait things out. Then we were all taken into the Oval Office and I was presented with the Medal. I'll never forget President Nixon saying, 'Mike, what can I do for you?' And I said, 'Well, Mr. President, you could break this Medal in half and give the other half to the young man [Tom Norris] standing behind me because he saved my life too.'"

After three days of unauthorized leave, Mike returned Tom to the Bethesda Naval Hospital. Of the ceremony, Tom said, "I was truly very, very honored to be there. It was quite a privilege to witness a Medal of Honor presentation. I was happy for Mike and happy that I could be there with him. His family was proud of him, and I was proud of him. The event was simply overwhelming. I think Mike was overwhelmed by it all as well, but he handled it like it was just another gathering of his friends. Yet there he was with that blue ribbon around his neck and that coveted Medal hanging at his throat. It was really something."

At the time, Tom Norris hadn't a clue that two and a half years later, he would be standing before the president of the United States to receive his own Medal. And that a smiling and proud Mike Thornton would be standing close by.

TOM NORRIS AND THE MEDAL OF HONOR

It was sometime in early 1974 that Tom and your narrator were sitting around my kitchen table in Alexandria, Virginia, on a Saturday morning. We were having a cup of coffee and getting ready to hang some drywall, and we got to talking about our time in Vietnam—our platoon tours and Tom's advisory tour. Mike had received his Medal, and Tom was recounting some other anecdotes about Mike's preceremony exploits on the town. As they came to him, he shared some recollections about their stand among the dunes that last day in October of 1972, just south of the mouth of the Ben Hai River. At the time, there were two SEAL recipients of the Medal—Bob Kerrey and Mike Thornton. And it seemed that there would be no more. The war was over, at least for us in America, and the nation was anxious to move on. Richard Nixon was still president, but the Watergate scandal that was to force him from office was in full swing. All the SEALs were home, and no one was sure what might come next. Since their inception in 1962, the Navy SEALs had done little but fight in Vietnam.

As for his part in going behind enemy lines in the spring of 1972 to recover the two airmen, Tom treated it like it was just another operation. It was well known among all of us in the SEAL teams, and to those in the Air Force who were involved in the recovery, but to few others. Darrel Whitcomb had yet to publish *The Rescue of Bat 21,* and the movie, *Bat 21,* would not be out until 1988. I asked Tom if he ever heard from the two aviators he brought out, and he said he hadn't. I think he still felt a little guilty that he hadn't been able to save Bruce Walker, Covey 282 Alpha, the pilot who had perished at the hands of the Viet Cong.

"But, you know," he recalled, "those nights we spent moving along the Cam Lo River were kind of surreal. We saw columns of

NVA soldiers four abreast marching south. Tanks rolled by us not fifteen feet away. That last night, when it was just Kiet and me, was special. He was so loyal and such a good man. I knew what he was thinking, and he knew what I was thinking. We moved well together. He had my back and I had his. I keep thinking that if Bruce Walker was just a little farther south, we might have had a chance to get him. It would have been wonderful if we could have brought back all three."

This was how Tom Norris thought—and still thinks. What could I have done better? Was there something more I could have done to accomplish my mission? Tom had already been decorated for his recovery of First Lieutenant Mark Clark and Lieutenant Colonel Iceal Hambleton. Captain Robert F. Stanton, then Commander, Naval Special Warfare Group One, in Coronado, had presented Tom with the Silver Star Medal on one of his trips to Vietnam. Although he never said as much, I think Tom felt he had been duly recognized for his rescue of the two airmen. More than once I've heard Tommy say, "I simply did my job; any other SEAL assigned to the mission would have done the same thing." In my opinion, there were two things that delayed Tom's consideration for the Medal of Honor.

First of all, there were issues of classification. Some of the tactics, techniques, and procedures that relate to the recovery of downed airmen in Vietnam were not declassified until 1975. These issues could be glossed over with an award like the Silver Star, but not with the investigation and close scrutiny that accompanies the awarding of the Medal of Honor. Second, this was an Air Force operation that revolved around recovery of downed airmen. Five aircraft were shot down, numerous other aircraft rendered unflyable, and eleven airmen perished in the recovery effort. Courage and self-sacrifice by a great many brave flyers accompanied these efforts. In Tom's own words, "The real heroes in the rescue of Clark and Hambleton were those air crews who died trying to recover their brothers on the ground." In my research of the events of April 1972, I found a great deal of information about Air Force operations and sorties flown in support of the recovery operations, but not a great deal about the Navy SEAL lieutenant and his Sea Commandos who went in on the ground to make the recovery. Much has been written about the shoot-downs, the activity of the forward air controllers and support aircraft, and the movement of the airmen on the ground. But not so much about Tom, Kiet, and the others who worked their way along the Cam Lo River to find the airmen and bring them out.

When I attended SEAL cadre training at SEAL Team Two in 1969, a SEAL chief petty officer took me aside and said, "Sir, see all these guys around here with all those ribbons on their chests? You know how most of them got them? They got them because someone screwed up and they got in trouble, and someone else had to go and get them out of trouble." I never forgot that. In the reading of many citations for the Medal of Honor in Vietnam for ground combat, a great many of those awards were made, per the criteria for the Medal, when one warrior acted to save another—at "risk of his life above and beyond the call of duty." They went back. That's certainly what Mike Thornton did. He decided to go back, above and beyond, at the risk of his own life. And he made that decision in a split second and in the heat of combat.

The courage of Tom Norris was of a different sort, but no less worthy. He made no quick decision in the heat of battle; he had time to think about it. Yet he went back again and again, at great risk and knowing full well he might not return. He did this to save the life of another—not once, but repeatedly. Tom's courage is very much like the bravery of helicopter pilots like Major Pat Brady, Major Bruce Crandall, and Captain Ed "Too Tall" Freeman—all Medal of Honor recipients. These airmen flew into danger multiple times to bring in supplies to beleaguered men on the ground and to evacuate wounded. The danger was so great that they did not *have* to do this. Again, their risk was above and beyond the call of duty. But they did it. So on reflection and in light of declassification, Navy officials began to review Tom's role in the rescue of the two flyers. And they rightly concluded that what Tom Norris did between 10 and 13 April 1972 was conduct well in keeping with the criteria for the Medal.

After a quiet dinner with his parents and two brothers in the nation's capital prior to the event, Tom's family joined him at the White House on 6 March 1976 and watched President Gerald Ford award Tom the Medal of Honor. The citation reads:

> For conspicuous gallantry and intrepidity in action at the risk of his life above and beyond the call of duty while serving as a SEAL Advisor with the Strategic Technical Directorate Assistance Team, Headquarters, U.S. Military Assistance Command, Vietnam. During the period 10 to 13 April 1972, Lieutenant Norris completed an unprecedented ground rescue of two downed pilots deep within heavily controlled enemy territory in Quang Tri Province. Lieutenant Norris, on the night of 10 April, led a five-man patrol through 2,000 meters of heavily controlled enemy territory, located one of the downed pilots at daybreak, and returned to the Forward Operating Base (FOB). On 11 April, after a devastating mortar and rocket

attack on the small FOB, Lieutenant Norris led a three-man team on two unsuccessful rescue attempts for the second pilot. On the afternoon of the 12th, a Forward Air Controller located the pilot and notified Lieutenant Norris. Dressed in fishermen disguises and using a sampan, Lieutenant Norris and one Vietnamese traveled throughout that night and found the injured pilot at dawn. Covering the pilot with bamboo and vegetation, they began the return journey, successfully evading a North Vietnamese patrol. Approaching the FOB, they came under heavy machine gun fire. Lieutenant Norris called in an air strike which provided suppression fire and a smoke screen, allowing the rescue party to reach the FOB. By his outstanding display of decisive leadership, undaunted courage, and selfless dedication in the face of extreme danger, Lieutenant Norris enhanced the highest traditions of the United States Naval Service.

Standing nearby, wearing his own Medal and an ear-to-ear grin, was Petty Officer First Class Mike Thornton.

MIKE THORNTON—AFTER VIETNAM

Mike returned to Coronado and SEAL Team One in late November 1972, ahead of the other LDNN advisors. Like all returning SEALs, he was given end-of-tour leave and was able to spend Christmas with his wife and his young son, Mickey, who was now a year old and remembered nothing of his father. Not long after Mike's departure, Ryan McCombie, Bill Woodruff, and the other SEAL LDNN advisors left Vietnam as well. The American mission to that nation was all but done. Unlike Tom, Mike had no lengthy medical treatment ahead of him. The medics on board the *Newport News* were able to dig the bullet from his calf and put him on a regime of antibiotics. With a little follow-up, he was fine. After the holiday, he checked back into Team One and was immediately assigned duties with the team training cell. The training now was no longer predeployment training to prepare SEALs for combat in Vietnam. In fact, there was a great deal of discussion of just what SEALs should be doing or if there was still a need for Navy SEALs. The war—or at least American involvement in the war—was over, and no one knew what was in store for these naval commandos and their brother frogmen. The Underwater Demolition and SEAL teams knew that they, along with the rest of the Navy and the military, were sure to experience some downsizing. At both SEAL Team One on Coronado and SEAL Team Two at Little Creek, Virginia, it was back to basics. A great many skills like diving, parachuting, underwater demolition, harbor penetration, and over-the-beach operations had been neglected, as the focus of the active deployments had been direct-action combat in the jungles, rice paddies, and mangrove swamps of Vietnam.

"It was good to get back to the team routine, and go home to my family at night," Mike said of the period after his return. "It was almost a surreal experience. All the guys felt this way about coming off deployment. In Vietnam, there was the close camaraderie of the team guys between combat missions and in the loose barracks routine. When not in the field, we lived in swim trunks, T-shirts, and shower shoes. We commuted to work in armed helicopters and boats. And our lives revolved around operations—training our LDNNs and going out on combat operations. Back-home life was clean sheets, hot showers, Bermuda shorts, paved roads, and non-rice dishes. And the variety of food—even fast food! You could eat what you wanted, when you wanted. There were things like indoor plumbing, television, pro sports, all if it. It was not like you missed those things overseas, but it was strange to have them back again. There was getting to know my kid, who thought I was some stranger, which I was, to getting reacquainted with my wife. I'd been gone more than I was at home since we were married. And there was the absence of combat—both the worry of having to go into the field and, in some ways, missing the anticipation of getting ready to go on an operation. And the rush that comes from combat. I looked at all this as normal for any SEAL coming home, but it was still an adjustment.

"Coming back to the team this time was different from my first Vietnam tour, when you were labeled a one-tour wonder, or even from my Thailand tour. At SEAL Team One, you were not a made man until after your second combat rotation. It was not so much respect from the team veterans, as many of them had been on four or five combat rotations. It had more to do with acceptance. I was now one of them. When guys like Gary Gallagher and Walt Gustavel and Doc Sell came up to you and said, 'Nice job over there,' or 'Good work in getting your lieutenant off that beach,' it really meant something. And I even enjoyed the kidding. When one of the old hands came up and said, 'Christ, Thornton, I always knew you'd be the one to get lost and not be able to find the right insertion point,' well, you knew you were now one of them. But it was not all joy and congratulations at Team One. Up the chain of command, it was decided that the teams were overmanned, and thirty SEALs from Team One were sent back to the fleet. After making it through training and making a combat deployment or two, they were rewarded with shipboard duty. It wasn't right, but that was the way it was. Some of them worked their way back to the teams and others finished their enlistments and got out.

"That summer of 1973," Mike recalls, "I kind of knew a decoration was in the works, but I didn't pay much attention to it. I knew a lot of guys who did a lot more and went unrecognized, so any medal was just a passing thought. Then that summer I bumped into Bill Woodruff in the SEAL Team One compound and he said, 'Hey, Mike, word has it that you're in for the Big Blue, and I think that's great.' My reaction was, 'Yeah, right.' 'Well,' Woody said, 'they took a lengthy statement from me, and they don't do that for some Bronze or Silver Star. I think you're in for the big one.'

"Well, as it turned out, he was right. I was notified in September that I would receive the Medal of Honor. A lot goes through your mind when you think something like that is going to happen to you. You try to play it down in your mind, that it's is no big deal, but it really is a big deal. Everyone in uniform knows it's a big deal. I felt humbled and undeserving. And I swore that it was not going to change things—to change me. But no one, including me, can know what a difference it can make on a lot of different levels. So I tried not to think about it. And I didn't really believe it would happen until the next month when I was at the White House and President Nixon was behind me, snapping that blue ribbon around my neck. That's when it really set in. Tommy had to wear his Medal as a civilian, which meant he didn't wear it when he went to work. I planned to stay in the Navy. Every morning when I put on my uniform, at least my blues or a white dress uniform, sitting atop the ribbons on my left breast was this little baby-blue ribbon with the five stars on it. Every time I looked in the mirror I thought, *wow*!

"I'd like to say it didn't change things back at the team, but it did. I caught the new guys sneaking a sidelong look at me. And some of the officers treated me differently. Not all, but some, like they didn't know how to address me. And I think they were thinking that I might do something to embarrass the team or the Medal. And they were probably right to think that way. I like a night out with the boys now and then, and we could certainly do a little drinking and hell-raising. And I had to think about that as well. I was now a recipient. As much as you'd like to think things don't change—that I hadn't changed—they do. But the old hands treated me no differently. I heard a lot of 'Well done' and 'Congratulations,' but they treated me the same, and I really appreciated that. For the remainder of my time at Team One, I worked at the team training cell, again teaching tactics and special demolitions up in our mountain training facility at Cuyamaca. I also got involved with the cold-weather training in Alaska. After all that time we'd spent in the jungle, this was a real change of pace for us at Team One.

"I also got involved with the new men coming from BUD/S training to Team One. Back then, when they came to the team from the training unit, there was a six-month probationary period before they were awarded their SEAL pin—the Trident. During that time, they had a course of instruction to complete and practical factors that had to be signed off. And there was an oral board they had to pass. The board consisted of the team chief petty officers—'the goat locker,' we called it—and with the blessing of the team chiefs, they were awarded their Tridents. I'd made first class petty officer at the team, and as a cadre instructor it was a part of my job to help the new men with their coursework and to prepare for the chiefs' board. This kind of set me up for my next tour of duty. In the fall of 1974, I got orders to report to the Naval Special Warfare

Center. Even though the center was less than a hundred yards from the Team One compound, it was a whole different world."

The Naval Special Warfare Center on Coronado is the schoolhouse for Navy SEALs. The center conducts training in special demolitions, combat shooting, sniper training, advanced combat swimmer training, submarine lock-in/lock-out training, and outboard motor repair, to name just a few. Yet the center is best known for the basic SEAL qualification course, Basic Underwater Demolition/SEAL training, or BUD/S. Currently the center has grown in size, complexity, and facility footprint, but it is still the place where young men are assessed, tested, and trained in the basics of what it is to be a Navy SEAL. The center trains men for both East and West Coast teams. And it is still a rendering place to see if young men have the talent, intelligence, spirit, and grit to be Navy SEALs. Back in Tommy's, Mike's, and my day, only about one in five survived BUD/S. It was the same during Mike's tour as a BUD/S instructor, and it is much the same today. Today, perhaps more is required to get into SEAL training and there are elevated standards to graduate from the basic course, but the attrition still hovers around 80 percent—sometimes more.

Then as now, BUD/S is a six-month course divided into three phases. Phase One is the conditioning phase; Phase Two is the diving phase; and Phase Three is the land warfare phase. They have been called other things over the years and even conducted in different order. Yet this was how it was in our day and much as it is now. Phases One and Two are conducted at the center on Coronado, and Phase Three is conducted on Coronado and offshore at San Clemente Island. Hell Week, when most of the attrition occurs, is typically scheduled midway through Phase One.

"I was glad to get orders to the center—the training unit, as we called it. I began as a Phase One instructor. Most new instructors begin their tour at the training unit in Phase One. We instructors either led physical training or did PT with the trainees, so it was a chance to get back into top physical condition. Since the water was my thing, I was able to help some of the weaker trainees with their swimming. But we were not there to be nice to these guys. And having been put through training by Vince Olivera, I tried to pass a little of Olivera along to the men I put through training. And with the war over, there was not the need for new guys in the UDT and SEAL teams, so we made sure the ones we sent to the teams were the right guys.

"It was good duty at the training unit, but the hours were long. Days often began at 0500 with PT and we didn't knock off until late afternoon or early evening, unless there was a night evening evolution. During Hell Week, we worked the trainees in shifts, just like our instructors did to us—twenty-four hours on and twenty-four off. When I was going through training, I thought the instructors had it easy. Now that I was an instructor, I found that this was not necessarily the case. And it gave me a new respect for Olivera, Dick Allen, and Mother Moy. Those instructors had expectations of themselves and their trainees, and I had to live up to those expectations. I still do."

"Mike had the reputation of being something of a hard-ass," said then Lieutenant Commander Dick Flanagan—Mike's platoon officer from the Thailand deployment. He was then the assistant director of the Naval Special Warfare Center. "And more than once I had to rein him in, because he could really come down on the trainees. The trainees respected him, but they also feared him. But Mike could also be a great source of inspiration. They all knew his story and what he had done. I think his best work at the center took place when we made him a class proctor. Each class is assigned an instructor who is the class proctor. He serves as their counselor and mentor during all three phases of the training for that class. The class proctor served as the trainees' link in the chain of command, and it was the proctor's job to oversee their well-being and attend to any personal problems during the course. When he shed his hard-ass-instructor role for one of a mentor, no one was more effective than Mike."

"I was the proctor for Class 83 and Class 87. You work some long hours as a class proctor, but it was very rewarding. As proctor it was my job to see that they pulled together as a class—that they learned teamwork and how to help each other. I was there to mentor them, but I still came down on a trainee when he failed to take care of his swim buddy or didn't take time to look out for a classmate. I also made sure the officers looked after men in their boat crews and that they always kept track of enlisted trainees assigned to them. That's an officer's job. During their diving phase, I came in to supervise nighttime study hours and to ensure that the officers were helping the enlisted men prepare for their written diving exams.

"Partway through my tour at the center, I was moved to Phase Three. Phase Three was all about land warfare, handling weapons and weapons safety. This was also when these sailors were introduced to basic infantry tactics. We still kept the pressure on the trainees, but Phase Three was more about teaching SEAL skill sets than physical harassment. The training class and the Phase Three instructors moved out to San Clemente Island for the last half of the phase. On San Clemente there were no distractions; we trained every day, starting with PT before sunup and working into the night. There were day and night swims and day and night work on the shooting ranges. The trainees were assigned full-mission-profile combat problems and had to work them up, just like we did in Vietnam. They'd work up the training mission during the morning, brief the mission early afternoon, conduct rehearsals late afternoon, and conduct the mission at night. Then following the training mission, when the trainees were cold, wet, and beat tired, they had to conduct a debriefing and tend to their equipment. By the end of their time on San Clemente, those who were left in the class were now learning what it was like to be a Navy SEAL—long hours and hard work.

"I spent three years at the training unit. I was proud of the guys I put through training, especially the men in Class 83 and Class 87, the classes I proctored. I hope I did for them what my instructors did for me. In August 1977, I left the training unit and the West Coast. I had orders for SEAL Team Two in Little Creek, Virginia."

"I was at Team Two for only a year, but it was a great year. Again, I was assigned to the team training cell with a great bunch of East Coast SEALs. I worked for a guy named Bob Gallagher. We conducted cadre training and special operations training at the team on the Naval Amphibious Base at Little Creek and at Camp A.P. Hill down in central Virginia. Camp A.P. Hill served the East Coast teams much like Cuyamaca served the West Coast teams. In those days there was a bit of rivalry between two SEAL teams, Team One and Team Two. But most of us who had been around for a while knew each other from our tours in Vietnam or by reputation. Then as now, reputation was everything. At Team Two, I finally made chief petty officer. Putting on chief, for me, was a bigger deal than putting on the Medal. You have to do a career in the Navy to fully appreciate what it is to make chief. It was a goal of mine. It seemed unreachable for so long, and now I'd made it. Making it was one thing, but the informal initiation ceremony that goes with making chief was another story. Back then, the chief petty officer initiation that was conducted at the chief's club on base was a little abusive— and then some. It was a hazing, and the Team Two chiefs didn't hold back. That's when some of that East Coast–West Coast rivalry came into play. At SEAL Team Two, I worked for two team executive officers. One of those XOs was Gary Stubblefield."

"I was a teammate of Mike's at Team One," Gary Stubblefield recalled, "and as a young ensign, I felt he was the epitome of a Navy SEAL—big, tough, and walking around the compound with a serious scowl. But always ready with a grin or a helping hand. And here we were at Team Two. I was a new lieutenant and he was a new chief petty officer. As the team executive officer, I was responsible for issues that related to conduct of the men in the command. Mike was like a lot of good SEAL operators in that he never seemed to get into trouble when he was working—only when he didn't have enough to do. So I tried to keep guys like Mike busy. But on the job, they got it done, and Mike was better than most at getting the job done. He was simply a very capable and inspirational Navy SEAL. He was bigger than life back then, and he's still bigger than life today.

"I recently ran into him at the fiftieth anniversary of SEAL Team One on Coronado. My new wife was with me and she'd never met Mike. But she'd certainly heard me talk about him. When I introduced him to her, he leaned over and in a conspiratorial manner, but so I could hear as well, said, 'I know Gary travels on business a lot. Next time he leaves on a trip, you give me a call.' She was totally charmed."

"Also while at Team Two," Mike recalled, "my commanding officer for a short period was a fellow named Dick Marcinko. Our paths were to cross again a few years down the road.

"In September of 1977 I continued my Navy journey in an easterly direction. I received orders to a British Special Boat Service—an allied special operations unit that I've been asked not to discuss in detail for security considerations. This unit trained much like our own SEAL teams with advanced training much like SEAL Qualification Training is today. Fortunately I was able to validate much of their training requirements and standards—some of it, but not all of it. Here I was, a SEAL chief petty officer, and now I was back in training. But it was okay and the Brits treated me well—but they sure didn't cut me any slack. I had to show them I could do the work. But I like a challenge, and I was sort of duty bound to put on a good show. Actually, my SEAL training and experience, and my tour at the training unit, had me well prepared for their version of predeployment training they called Employment Training.

"One thing I had going for me, and that not many of them had, was combat experience. Some of them had been on operational missions, but none of them had the extended time on combat rotation that was so common with the veterans at the two U.S. SEAL teams. Back then and much like today, few allied special operators had as much trigger time as a Navy SEAL. When it came to weapons, I could shoot with the best of them. They were a thoroughly professional force and I was proud to serve with them. They kept me on my toes, and I wanted to make sure I held up the honor of the Yank special operators."

I made it a point to ask Mike about how they treated him as a recipient. "Oh, they knew about the Medal and what it meant. It was similar to their Victoria Cross—similar but not the same. The

VC has been around about as long as the Medal of Honor but with only about half the number of recipients when compared with our Medal. And by comparison, a much greater percentage of VC awards have been posthumous. I don't know how many living Victoria Cross recipients there were when I was with the SBS, but there weren't many. Today there are nine, compared with seventy-nine of us today who wear the Medal of Honor. The Brits like to drink beer as much as I do, and I did do some beer drinking with my Brit mates. But being a recipient, I had to be careful. I was still Mike Thornton, but being a recipient was always in the back of my mind.

"After I completed my Employment Training and did well, they made me an instructor. This was okay for a while, but I'd been in a training billet of one form or another for most of the last five years. I wanted to get back into the operational side of the business. As an E7 or chief petty officer, I was in line for a slot as platoon or operational team sergeant major in one of their platoons. So I volunteered for the job. They said okay, but first I had to plan and lead a training operation to qualify as a team sergeant major. It was a nighttime raid on a ship at anchor in a nearby coastal harbor. This was like a SEAL takedown of a ship at sea, something that I was very familiar with. I did well enough and was posted to a team as the sergeant major—the senior enlisted man on the team and a role that was similar to the platoon chief in a SEAL platoon. It was a good team and a great experience for me. We worked hard and we had a solid operational team. I finished my tour in September of 1980, so I was not there when it really counted. In the spring of 1982, the team was deployed with the British expeditionary force to recover the Falkland Islands in the South Atlantic. The team took casualties in the Falklands fighting, and two operators from another team were killed by friendly fire. I'd like to think that my work and training with my British teammates helped to get some of them through that crisis and safely back to England.

"With my tour in England completed, I headed back to the West Coast. I had orders to Underwater Demolition Team 11. The commanding officer of UDT 11 was Dick Flanagan, and I was looking forward to serving with him again. He was a great officer. I was also anxious to get my family back to the West Coast. The tour with the SBS was an accompanied tour, so my family was with me in England. But to be honest, I was having some problems at home. This was nothing new for SEALs with families, or anyone else in the military, for that matter. Even when we were home, we were gone for a few days here or a week there on training evolutions. We were home but not necessarily at home every night. Yet, now I had two kids. I loved them, and I missed them terribly when I was away. Looking back, I might have handled it better, but balancing family needs with the demands of a special operator was never easy. I did the best I could, and we'll leave it there. I'm sure the SEALs today deal with these same issues. Nonetheless, I thought getting back to San Diego and a tour at UDT 11 might improve things at home. But that did not happen. We divorced a few years later. Yet Gladys was a good Navy wife to me. She raised my children, Mikey and Gina, and was there for them when I was away. My children are the stars of my life, and I'm so proud of the people they've become today.

"There were changes ahead as I came back from England and we moved into the 1980s, and not just for me. There were forces in play that would create change for the entire SEAL community."

In the fall of 1980, the United States military was wrestling with two issues that would color much of the Reagan military buildup that was to take place during the 1980s and carry forward into the threat environment today. The first of these fell under the broad topic of terrorism. Just as our military developed a more robust unconventional warfare capability during and following the Kennedy years, there developed a need to meet the growing threat posed by terrorists—both the state-sponsored variety and those that were emerging from radical Islamic factions. The second problem was the U.S. military's apparent inability to respond quickly to a rapidly emerging crisis—especially if the response required joint-service cooperation. This deficiency was underscored by the failed *Operation Eagle Claw*, our unsuccessful attempt to free the imprisoned American embassy hostages taken by the new revolutionary government in Iran in April 1980. There was simply no integrated, multiservice capability to quickly plan, coordinate, and execute a small-scale engagement—a special operation.

This led to the creation of a joint command structure to deal with rapid, small-unit, expeditionary operations. The Army had one such special missions unit in place for these kinds of operations. Now it was the Navy's turn. Working this issue was a small task unit assigned to the Joint Chiefs of Staff known as the Terrorist Action Team. Assigned to this staff element was a charismatic and mercurial SEAL officer named Richard Marcinko. A Navy special missions unit needed to be put in place. That job was handed to Lieutenant Commander Marcinko with broad latitude and ample funding to create such a unit.

"It wasn't like we didn't see this coming," said then Lieutenant Norm Carley, who at the time was the operations officer at SEAL Team Two. "In early 1980, we had established MOB-6 at Team Two— Mobilization Platoon 6. There were twenty SEALs assigned to the platoon and we were allowed to allot 50 percent of their time training for the counterterror mission. We were given a free hand in this, and we went to other nations' militaries that had expertise in this area. Several European special missions units had some excellent capabilities in this area and we learned a great deal from them."

"I was given a lot of latitude and power," Marcinko recalled of his new unit, "and I can tell you that I was not the most popular guy around Coronado or Little Creek. The new unit was to begin with fifteen support personnel and eighty shooters, and I could take my pick of operational and support personnel from the existing teams. While the commanding officers of the SEAL teams and UDTs had to stand by and watch, I interviewed their people and took the ones I wanted. It didn't make them all that happy, but I had a job to do. One of those I chose was Mike Thornton. I knew about the Medal, of course, but I selected him for his combat experience, and I knew that he was talented, capable, and a little cocky. Well, maybe 'confident' was a better word for Mike, but he was just what I was looking for."

"Mike didn't really want to come to the new unit," said Carley, who became the executive officer for the new team and helped with the selection, "but Dick Marcinko can be very persuasive. And he wanted Mike. Overall, I think we did a pretty good job of selecting experience, leadership, and special skills. We took most of those SEALs at Team Two assigned to MOB-6 platoon and some of the Echo Platoon SEALs at Team One. It was a mix of talent and, candidly, some of the best operators in the two SEAL and four UDT teams then in place. But it did little for our popularity in the community."

"When I got back east with the new team, it was a whole new experience," Mike recalled. "We had to build new facilities and develop new tactics and procedures for this new counterterrorist mission. There were the normal SEAL skills like diving, parachuting, and marksmanship that we had to refine and keep current. There was also new equipment that had to be acquired and put into service. A great deal of what we did at the new team was original, outside the box, and classified, so I can't say much more about it. We were a select group of Navy SEALs doing things that had never been done before. I'm very proud today to have been one of the plank holders of this new unit.

"Life in the teams is hard and dangerous in the best of times. BUD/S was hard, predeployment training prior to going to Vietnam was hard, and the daily grind of staying in shape and keeping your skills and qualifications up to standard was hard. But I've never worked harder than those first six months at the new team. It was eighteen hours a day, seven days a week. When we did take time off from the work, it was usually to go out and have a few beers with the skipper. And with Dick Marcinko, it could sometimes be more than just a few beers. But we accomplished some amazing things in a very short period of time. At the time there were two teams or squadrons within the unit with forty men in each team. I was the team chief for one operational element and Bob Schamberger was the team chief for our sister element. Bob was a great operator and a great friend. He was killed in the Grenada operation."

"We were able to pass our operational certification in the spring of 1981," said Dick Marcinko of his new unit. "Yet there were still a lot of issues that needed to be addressed, including our command relationships. Operationally, we reported to one chain of command, but we were still part of the Navy and assigned to Atlantic Surface Force Commander for administrative support. We had a lot of non-standard equipment and we conducted nonstandard training, like traveling to third-world countries with irregular documentation. And we were not bound by the grooming standards that applied to the rest of the Navy. Yet, we were all still sailors, still in the United States Navy. We lived on or near Navy bases, used the Navy exchange, and our pay, benefits, and family services all came through the Navy. But my guys had beards and long hair. We got the reputation of looking like a bunch of hippies, and I guess we did. It's what we wanted to look like, but it flew in the face of the regular Navy. We were controversial and probably more than a little cocky."

"Complaints about our appearance and conduct finally worked their way up to our Navy boss at SURFLANT [Commander, Surface Force, Atlantic Fleet]," recalled Norm Carley. "He called our operational boss, an Army two-star general, and told him that a personnel inspection of his Navy guys might be in order. So a unit inspection was scheduled. When the general arrived, the team was paraded in choker whites (formal white dress uniform). It was actually a comical site; all these tall, fit SEALs in formal attire with beards and long hair. When the general emerged from his car, Commander Marcinko, thinking ahead, had arranged for him to be met by Mike. Mike was to be his escort for the inspection. Well, the first thing the general noticed about Mike was the Medal of Honor that hung from his neck. He, of course, saluted Mike and Mike returned the gesture with a parade-ground salute of his own. This sort of set the tone for the general's visit and the inspection proceeded from there."

"There are a great many stories that have been told about this special team," Mike says with a chuckle, "and some of them are even true. Yet a good many of them are classified, and those are the ones you'll not read about in this book. But when some of the old hands get together, we do talk about the way it was back then and you know, it seems like it was only yesterday.

"Throughout my Navy career," Mike continues, "I've always been blessed with great role models and mentors who helped me along and who looked out for me. When I was getting close to the end of my rotation at the new team, one of them suggested I consider becoming an officer and take my service career in another direction. I had just been advanced to senior chief petty officer, and my next move would have been back to one of the UDT or SEAL teams or off to recruiting duty. I was also looking for a change. For a guy like me who had no college degree there was but one choice if I was to join the officer ranks—limited-duty officer or LDO. The term 'limited-duty' can be misleading. It just means that as a commissioned officer, your duties are assigned within a designated specialty, like administration or logistics or engineering. So I put my papers in for the LDO program. There were no LDO billets in the SEAL Teams, but there were in the diving and salvage Navy. And as a salvage officer, it was a chance to do something different *and* a chance to get back into the water on more of a full-time basis. I was accepted into the program and in September of 1983, I got orders to 'knife and fork school.'

"Knife and fork school, or Limited-Duty Officer Training, was a five-week course at Pensacola, Florida, designed to help senior enlisted personnel make the transition from the enlisted ranks to the officer corps. It was mostly an administrative exercise with some classes on naval history, writing reports, procedures associated with officer duties, and writing enlisted evaluations. It was a good school, and I met a lot of other 'mustangs,' guys like me coming from the ranks and wanting to finish their Navy career as officers. At the end of the course, I was a brand-new ensign—an officer and a gentleman, so to speak—but I was still Mike Thornton. From there I went another sixty miles or so east along the Florida Panhandle to the Diving and Salvage Center in Panama City.

"I was back in training—again. Diving and Salvage Officers School was a hard six-month school that was challenging and a lot of fun. I knew a lot of the master divers who were instructors there. Most of those in my class were new college graduates, fresh out of Officer Candidate School. All were naval officers, with one coast guard officer and one Army officer. The Navy trains salvage officers for all services. The only old goats in the class were myself and another mustang, an explosive ordnance disposal warrant officer. Since I was a SEAL and I'd had diving training during my basic SEAL training, the initial pool work and the physical training were not a problem for me. I helped the young officers in the pool and with PT, and they helped me when we got into the more advanced work with diving and treatment tables and the written work. There was one young female Navy ensign in the class, and she was my swim buddy. We worked well together and I helped her learn how to be a Navy diver.

"I began the diving and salvage portion of my career back in Little Creek, Virginia, with orders to the Commander, Service Squadron Eight in the fall of 1984. This was the beginning of eight rewarding years as a Navy diving and salvage officer. Sure, I missed the SEAL teams and the rough camaraderie of the other SEAL operators, but this was a whole new challenge. The diving and salvage Navy is blue-collar work. Each job is a challenge, often an engineering challenge. Every day there was something new. Sometimes they'd call for divers for routine hull maintenance, but usually it's because something is wrong—something got broken underwater and we'd get called in to assess the damage and figure out a way to fix it. It was great. And as an LDO, I was usually put in charge of the operation; I was not told how to do the job—just to get the job done. Those were orders I could follow: get the job done. There's not a lot of posturing or bravado in the diving and salvage Navy, although there's an esprit de corps in the Navy diving community. But for the most part, it's a get-wet, get-dirty, and get-the-job-done business.

"My first posting was as the officer-in-charge of the Second Class Dive School. Second class divers are basically open-circuit scuba divers trained to help with basic underwater ship husbandry and hull inspections. It's the entry point for Navy divers and a starting place for more advanced Navy diving work. It was a lieutenant-commanders billet, and I filled it as a brand-new junior grade lieutenant. It was a good tour and I had some great instructors working for me. I did get into a little scrape when two of my students came in late one morning and were too hungover for morning physical training. When I told them to get changed and get ready for PT, one of them spit on me. So I grabbed one in each hand, cracked their heads together, and knocked them out. I thought my lead instructor was going to have a heart attack. This put an end to my students not showing up in the morning ready for PT, but it did earn me an office call with the Commander, Surface Force, Atlantic. He was understanding, but he also said I better never do that again.

"In January 1986, I received orders to the USS *Edenton* (ATS-1). The *Edenton* was a British-built, 282-foot rescue and salvage tug. I had just made full lieutenant and was assigned as the ship's first lieutenant and salvage officer. It was the first time I'd really been to sea since I was a young sailor aboard the USS *Brister*. Now I was an officer, had my own stateroom, and took my meals in the wardroom.

I also had a lot of responsibility, as I had the deck force under me as well as the diving and salvage crew. The ship was home-ported in Norfolk. Shortly after I came aboard, we made a short cruise to the Caribbean for refresher training. Then a few weeks later, we left for a deployment cruise to the Mediterranean—all this within a month after I reported aboard. We were tasked with a lot of routine diving and underwater hull maintenance duties, but the one I remember best was an emergency diving job on the USS *Mahan*."

In the spring of 1986, tensions between the United States and Libya seemed to be coming to a head. June 1985 saw the hijacking of TWA Flight 847 by Libyan-sponsored terrorists. Then there was military confrontation between units of the Sixth Fleet in the Gulf of Sidra in March 1986. That incident resulted in the sinking of a Libyan corvette and a Libyan patrol boat, and the downing of two Libyan fighter jets. Several other Libyan surface craft were damaged along with shore-based missile batteries. Then a nightclub attack in West Berlin on 5 April that killed three and wounded 229 was found to have been carried out by Libyan agents. President Reagan ordered air strikes on Tripoli that targeted Libyan military infrastructure and Libyan leader Muammar Gaddafi himself. These air strikes, from aircraft flown from land bases in England and from U.S. aircraft carriers, were scheduled for 15 April. With this in mind, units of the Sixth Fleet steamed south toward the North African coast.

One of the screening destroyers was the USS *Mahan* (DDG-42). The *Mahan* had just been equipped with the Terrier New Threat Upgrade Combat System and the extended-range RIM-67 Standard Missile. This made *Mahan* the most capable fleet air defense guided-missile destroyer in the U.S. Navy. Given the Libyan Air Force's strike capability with their Soviet-equipped MiG-23s, the fleet commander wanted

Mahan to be a part of his screening force. But the destroyer had just been damaged and was questionable for the planned attack on Libya.

"It seems that the *Mahan* was making her way into a Mediterranean port," Mike recalled, "and had scraped bottom, damaging both of her sonar domes. It was just a grounding in silt, but when we dove on her, we found both Mk 33 sonar domes were cracked. There was nothing wrong with her ability to shoot missiles, but she could not hunt submarines nor make more than a few knots without risking further damage to her sonars and her hull. So we went to work. I had only two days to get the destroyer ready for sea. We fabricated two bras of wire mesh and used come-alongs to hold them and the sonar domes in place while we moved the *Mahan* to another anchorage where we had crane services. Then I worked two crews of divers twenty-four hours a day to unbolt and remove the two domes. We then rigged them to the crane and swung them out and away from the hull. The sonar transducers were now exposed, but the ship was capable of making flank speed. She may not have been able to hunt subs, but she was able to rejoin the fleet in the Gulf of Sidra and provide fleet air defense for the attack on Lybia.

"Without the *Edenton* and my salvage crews, the USS *Mahan* would not have made it in time to help protect the fleet. And that was just one job. We did a lot of others, but perhaps none as important as that one. Working aboard a Navy ship and managing my salvage crew was a distinct privilege for me. I learned a great deal, and it was challenging work. Every job was different and involved assessing the damage or the job and figuring out how to solve the problem with the resources at hand. It was highly rewarding. And the *Edenton*'s skipper and crew afforded me a singular honor, perhaps one unique in the U.S. Navy. When a senior officer boards a

Navy ship, he is accorded the honor of being 'bonged' aboard when he arrives and again when he departs. The commanding officer of a ship, in this case the *Edenton,* a commander, was treated likewise. When he came aboard, his arrival was announced over the 1-MC [the ship's loudspeaker system], 'BONG-BONG—BONG-BONG, *Edenton* arriving,' or 'BONG-BONG—BONG-BONG, *Edenton* departing.' When I came and went it was 'BONG-BONG (just two bongs, as I was only a lieutenant), Medal of Honor arriving,' or 'BONG-BONG, Medal of Honor departing.'"

"In early 1989 I left *Edenton* for a Navy Construction Battalion in Norfolk—the renowned Navy Seabees. With the Seabees, I was assigned as the Bravo Company Commander, which meant I was responsible for all the barges, causeways, divers, and boats. I was also responsible for about four hundred sailors. To help with this, I had some very dedicated and talented Seabee chief petty officers. Their abilities called to mind the old Seabee saying from World War II in the Pacific: 'We've done so much with so little for so long, we can now do anything with nothing.' That applied to my senior enlisted leaders. It was good work and it was hard work—especially with the causeways. There were a lot of moving parts—literally—to maneuver causeways into place to move vehicles and supplies from ships offshore onto and across a landing beach. Again, this was not combat, but the troops ashore can do little without the supplies coming across the beach. So I got to the battalion and learned my job in time for the Gulf War, which began in August 1990 when Iraq invaded Kuwait. Oddly enough, my most challenging assignment with the Seabees was not getting supplies or material across the beach but another salvage operation."

On 2 August 1990, the Iraqis invaded Kuwait, and on 8 August, Saddam Hussein pronounced the annexation of Kuwait. The stage was set for the Gulf War. A U.S.-led coalition began combat operations with an air-warfare campaign on 17 January 1991, with the ground forces crossing the Saudi Arabia–Kuwait border on 24 February. The liberation of Kuwait soon followed. During the preceding six months, a massive buildup of forces took place. It was unknown early on in the crisis whether men and materials were to be administratively disembarked in friendly Persian Gulf ports in Saudi Arabia, Bahrain, or Qatar, or if there was to be an opposed landing in Kuwait proper. It was a logistics exercise unprecedented since the Korean War. And it was the presence of American troops on Saudi soil, in the same region as the holy sites of Mecca and Medina, that prompted a Saudi expatriate named Osama bin-Laden to begin planning attacks on U.S. soil.

Mike and a portion of his Seabee company were embarked in the USS *Saginaw* (LST-1188). It was part of a forty-plus-ship amphibious ready group making its way through the Suez Canal, to the Gulf of Aden and the northern Arabian Sea, up into the Persian Gulf. The *Saginaw* was one of a newer class of landing ships designed to handle causeways for the efficient unloading of troops and vehicles across the beach. One of the ships assisting in this flow of materials up through the Strait of Hormuz was the NSTS vessel the USNS *Andrew J. Higgins* (T-AO-190). The *Higgins* was a naval sea transport ship with a mixed crew of U.S. Navy sailors and merchant seamen. Named in honor of Andrew Higgins, whose landing crafts were key to the amphibious campaigns of World War II, the *Higgins* was a 677-foot fast fleet oiler carrying fuel oil, JP-5 aviation fuel, and refrigerated stores—material needed for the coming invasion and repatriation of Kuwait. En route, the big ship struck a reef off Oman, and was hard aground and leaking oil. The ready group commander, Rear Admiral John LaPlante, canvassed his scattered ships looking for a salvage officer and he found only one. It was Mike Thornton aboard the USS *Saginaw*.

"Admiral LaPlante called on me personally to see if I could do something to get the *Higgins* off the reef and refloated without further damage. Myself and a master diver from one of the other ships dove on the *Higgins* and found two long gashes in the hull several hundred feet long. It was a double-hulled vessel. That, and the compartmentization in the ship's design, prevented the ship from going down. We made some calculations and offloaded some of its fuel oil and JP-5 to lighten her up. Then I sent a message back to SUPSAL [the Navy's superintendent of diving and salvage] regarding how much air pressure we could put in the void between the inner and outer hulls without causing further damage. Then we rigged air compressors on the deck of the *Higgins* and ran air lines down into the flooded spaces along the hull. Just before the next high tide, we began putting compressed air into the hull. At high tide, she began to float free and we managed to pull her off the reef."

One of the vessels assisting in getting the *Higgins* off the reef was the USS *Portland* (LSD-37). "We were on our way with everyone else to the Persian Gulf," said Commander Mark Falkey, the captain of the *Portland,* "when we stopped to assist with the salvage of the *Higgins*. She was hard aground on an uncharted reef. There was a lieutenant diving and salvage officer, going from ship to ship borrowing boats and boatswain mates to get the *Higgins* off the reef. I saw him briefly and noticed that he wore a baby blue ribbon with five tiny stars on it, and thought, *could it be*? I later confirmed that the lieutenant was Mike Thornton. Small world? You bet. Close to twenty years ago in Vietnam, on 31 October 1972 to be exact, I was the junior officer of the deck on the USS *Morton* when we shot a naval gunfire support mission for some SEALs in hot water just south of the mouth of the Ben Hai River."

"Getting the *Higgins* off that reef was probably the highlight of my diving and salvage career," Mike recalled. "And I wasn't even in a salvage billet at the time. When we got her into Bahrain for repairs, Admiral LaPlante sought me out and personally thanked me for the job. The fuel and the stores aboard the *Higgins* got off-loaded and made it to the troops staging along the Saudi Arabia–Kuwait border a little late, but they got there. On board the USS *Saginaw,* we were standing offshore when the air war started and later on while the Army and Marines liberated Kuwait. I knew there were SEALs involved in the combat operations ashore, but I had no idea what they might be doing. So I waited out this war in the safety and comfort of an air-conditioned Navy LST. But if I'd had a choice, I'd have been ashore—a little overweight and a little out of shape, but I'd have still liked to have been a part of it. Later that summer, we began the long transit back home to Norfolk."

"In 1992, I had a decision to make. For more than ten years, I'd been an operational Navy SEAL. And while I'd enjoyed great tours of duty as a diving and salvage officer, I'd been away from the teams now for close to ten years. The Navy doctor who gave me my annual diving physical just before I left the *Saginaw* said that I was cleared for shipboard duty but that he would not certify me for diving or parachuting. This made a return to the SEALs problematic, and a diving and salvage officer who couldn't dive was a nonstarter, at least for me. And I had a terrific offer from a civilian company in

Pittsburgh. So after some consideration, I decided that it was time to go. After more than twenty-three years in uniform, I put in my papers to retire from the United States Navy."

On 31 May 1992, Mike Thornton was retired from active duty at the Naval Amphibious Base at Little Creek, Virginia, in a ceremony that was unprecedented for a Navy lieutenant. Many of Mike's former commanding officers were there, including Dick Marcinko. Also attending were thirteen Medal of Honor recipients. Tom Norris was not among them. Tom, then a special agent with the FBI, was on a case and couldn't break away. But Mike understood; the operational always takes precedence over the ceremonial. Vice Admiral Jim Stockdale, also a recipient, was the featured speaker. In such proceedings, the individual retiring is piped aboard the dais by his rank, "Lieutenant, United States Navy, arriving." At the completion of the ceremony and speeches, he is piped off, "Civilian, departing." During these comings and goings, the honoree is attended by side boys, a naval tradition from the days of sail. There were eight of them who lined up in two files to help get Mike "over the side." Among the side boys of senior naval officers, master chief petty officers, and master divers were Captain Dick Flanagan and Captain Ryan McCombie.

"I was astounded at the turnout," said Mike of his final day in uniform. "There were 150 invited guests, but at least three times that many showed up—from the base, from the East Coast teams, from my last SEAL team. There was a contingent of sailors from the Seabees and from the USS *Edenton*. I was honored, I was blessed, and I was very humbled. In my mind's eye, I can remember every detail of that day. It was truly overwhelming."

**At the time, Mike Thornton was the only Medal of Honor recipient on
active duty.**

TOM NORRIS—AFTER VIETNAM

"From the time I got back in late 1972 through 1977, I was either in
the hospital, just out of the hospital, or getting ready to go back into
the hospital for another operation. It was not a lot of fun, and it was
very frustrating. I'm a doer, and I wanted to get on with my life. But
about every six months, I'd be back to the Bethesda Naval Hospital
for another operation. Toward the end of that period, in 1975
and 1976, they were minor, reconstructive-type operations, but still
time in the hospital. And there were the headaches. They would
come and go, but sometimes when they came, they could bring me
down to my knees. I've known some pain in my life, but nothing
prepared me for those headaches. It took several years for them to
recede to the point that I could deal with them. I still get them now
and then, but they're manageable. But those first couple of years, it
was a struggle.

"My memory was not all that great at first. The doctors said it
may or may not get better with time. Fortunately, it did. It took
about a year and a half for it to fully return, or as near as I could
perceive that it was fully returned. And there was the issue of the
eye. I had to get used to the depth perception issues of having only
one eye, and then there was the getting used to the prosthetic eye. It
was a period of adjustment and it took time. To get physically stron-
ger, I could go to the gym and work out—I could be proactive in my
recovery. But with the injury and the eye, it just took time. And
through much of all this, I still hoped to be allowed to stay in the
Navy—and to remain with the SEAL teams.

"The concern was just how much I could recover physically and get past the headaches. For duty in the teams, I needed to be able to dive and to perform other tasks, like shooting and parachuting. It seemed that after each operation, I'd get a little better, but recovering from the brain and reconstructive surgeries was a challenge unto itself. In the end, it just wasn't in the cards. I'd lost a portion of the left side of my brain, and the Navy found that unacceptable for continued military service. I really did want to stay in uniform, but this was during the drawdown after Vietnam, and the separation boards were looking for ways to reduce the size of the military. So I was medically retired in April 1975. I was no longer on active duty, but the reconstruction on my head and around my eye continued. I really didn't want to leave the Navy, but I had no choice. I had to move on. The Navy put my disability at 80 percent and the Veterans Administration at 90 percent. I was retired with 75 percent pay."

A good many of us who spent time with Tommy during this in-and-out-of-the-hospital period knew little of his ordeal. Maybe a little of his frustration, but none of his pain. He kept that to himself. During much of this time, he seemed to be on a pilgrimage to help others. When not at home with his parents in Silver Spring, Maryland, he made extended visits with friends.

"Tommy spent several two- or three-month stays with us," Ryan McCombie said. "My wife and I were living in Virginia Beach, and we had a new baby. Tommy was the perfect house guest. But he was like a gun dog or a herding dog in that you had to keep him busy. He was always looking for projects around the house. And he was very precise about things. One weekend, he was helping me to install some chair railing in our dining room. The rule is that you measure twice and cut once. With Tommy, you measure twice, talk about it, measure again, recheck the level, talk some more, measure a final time, then cut and install. I remember when he built a deck at his folks' home in Silver Spring. He laid and nailed the whole deck, but was then dissatisfied with the nail heads showing. So he took up the deck, took out the nails, and relaid boards with countersunk screws. He didn't care about the time involved; he just wanted it right."

Many of us have our Tom Norris carpentry stories. He was helping me with a remodel project and we were framing in a wall. I noticed that he was bending more than his share of nails and occasionally banging his fingers. Half his fingernails had blood under them. When I kidded him about it, he said, "You try pounding a nail with one eye." So I did and the kidding stopped.

"When I was finally medically retired from the Navy I had to think about what I wanted to do and what I would be allowed to do. If I couldn't be a naval officer or a SEAL, then I'd try to be a federal agent. So I began the application process with those agencies—FBI, CIA, the Drug Enforcement Agency [DEA], Secret Service, and so on. But they all seemed to have physical restrictions that left me out. Of course, there were waiver processes, but none of that seemed to get me very far. My first choice was the DEA, as I had this thing about illegal drugs and wanted to join the fight against them. But the DEA, more than the other agencies, was pretty cool to any kind of a waiver for what they thought of as my disabilities. Heck, with the exception of the headaches, which I knew I could manage, I thought I was good to go. By this time I had been presented with the Medal, but that didn't seem to matter. Then I got an idea and called an old SEAL buddy—Sandy Prouty."

"I'd first met Tommy back in 1970," said Charles "Sandy" Prouty. In the teams and at the Naval Academy, he was known as Sandy (he and your narrator were classmates at Annapolis). At the FBI, he became Charles or Charlie. "We were both platoon officers and we both happened to be at Subic Bay in the Philippines, taking a break from combat operations in Vietnam. We were at a bar out in town when this fight broke out between some of my SEALs and some sailors from of one of the ships in port. Well, one of my guys, who hadn't a clue who Tommy was, grabbed him and was getting ready to punch him out. I stopped my guy and told him who it was he was about to hit. He said, 'Sorry about that, sir,' and returned to the fight. After that, the next time I saw Tommy was when he relieved me at MACVSOG in Saigon.

"I saw Tommy again briefly while he was undergoing treatment at Bethesda Naval Hospital. I was then with Underwater Demolition Team 21 in Little Creek, just before I left active service. I joined the FBI in 1973 and was assigned to the Alexandria field office when Tommy called and said he was thinking about becoming a federal agent."

"Sandy was really great to me," said Tom. "He had me come down to his office and introduced me around to all the other agents. This was in 1977. He took the time to show me what he did and how a bureau agent goes about his job. He even let me ride with him when he went out on interviews and to follow leads. It really whet my appetite to become an agent, but there was still the issue of me with the one eye and the brain damage. There just seemed to be no way for me to pass the bureau's physical examination—or anyone else's, for that matter. And the FBI's physical requirements were the most stringent of all of the federal agencies."

"I took Tommy down to Quantico with me to shoot on the

FBI range there," Prouty recalls, "and he could shoot pretty well. And he immediately bonded with the other agents there. Tom's a likeable fellow and the guys really took to him. He'd already been turned down by the bureau for failing to pass the physical, but several other agents and I encouraged him to put in for a waiver. I remember saying, 'You got nothing to lose. What are they going to do, send you back to Vietnam?'"

"So I wrote a personal letter to FBI Director William Webster and told him of my background, my disabilities, and my desire to become a bureau agent," continued Tom. "To my surprise, he gave me a waiver on the physical requirements for my agent application. I later learned that he was advised against granting this waiver, as his bureau advisors did not want to set a precedent. But he told them, 'I'm going give this guy a chance. He's earned the opportunity to try. If he can meet the same standards as anybody else applying for this position, then I'm going to let him give it a try.' Then a few days later, I got a call from the Baltimore field office, as that was the office closest to my home of record in Silver Spring. I went in for testing and, later, an interview. As it turned out, it wasn't like they wanted me to come in next month; they wanted me there right now. This was a good thing, as I was approaching thirty-five and there was an age limit for new agents; I didn't want to have to get another waiver. All this took place in January 1979. I passed all the other tests and early that spring I was accepted for training as an agent. It was not until many years later that I met Judge Webster and was able to thank him for affording me the opportunity to be an FBI special agent.

"My training class first met at the Hoover Building in Washington, where we were introduced to our instructors and proctors. Then it was off to Quantico for the agent training course. There were a few veterans like me, and most of those in the class had law degrees. The training was pretty intense, but if you paid attention in class, it wasn't a problem. And the physical conditioning, the running and push-ups and all, was a piece of cake. The only problem I had with shooting was shooting behind a barricade. You had to shoot with either hand and with either eye. Since I had only my right eye to work with, I had to lean out a little farther when shooting around the left side of a barricade, but it was really no problem. It was just a knack and I had to adjust with it. Fortunately, I have very good vision in my right eye. I had some great future agents in my class. One of them was Ed Mireles, who was involved in the epic FBI gun battle in Miami in April 1986 against two bank robbers. The FBI lost two agents in that shooting before Mireles, himself wounded, shot both of the robbers. After training, I was posted to the Washington field office. So finally, in late 1979, I was a special agent with the Federal Bureau of Investigation. At last, I was a bona fide federal agent.

"Like all new agents on their first posting, I was assigned routine duties that involved doing background investigations and interviews that related to people applying for jobs with the federal government. But I was blessed with some great mentors at the Washington field office, including my break-in agent, a guy named Henry Ragle. He was an agent who came up within the bureau ranks, having worked in a support capacity before qualifying as a special agent. Henry was on the bank robbery squad, and he saw to it that I could have as much work as I wanted, so I got to see it all. I would do most of my background interviews in the evening hours, so I had the days to work on bank robberies. On the weekends I got to work on bank robberies, kidnapping, extortion cases, gambling, and the like. I had no other distractions in my life, so I could work eighteen hours a day and put in time on the weekends. After so much hospital time and recovery time and down time, it was great to have work—and I really enjoyed the work. I even got to do some foreign counterintelligence surveillance and to work on some organized crime cases. Right from the beginning, I got to experience a broad range of FBI casework.

"You're supposed to be in the bureau for two years before you can do undercover work," Tom said, "and it was work that was usually reserved for senior agents. Back then, there was very little to prepare you for undercover assignments other than a short, three-day course conducted at Quantico. We had an undercover squad at the Washington field office, a group of agents who just worked undercover cases. But there were no vacancies on the squad. They knew I was interested in this kind of work, but the only way to get on this squad was to already be an undercover agent or develop an undercover case. My first assignment came on a stolen property/fencing operation involving pawn shops in the District. My job was to bring in alleged stolen property to the shops. Then we would get statements from the shop owners that they knew they were receiving stolen property. It was a minor role, but it got me started. After that, I was officially cleared for undercover work.

"There was a process for undercover work, or more specifically, how the field offices requested agents for undercover support. You were put into a pool of agents cleared for undercover assignment, along with a file that detailed your background, experience, and capabilities. If some field office across the country needed an outside undercover agent, they went to this pool of agents to match the undercover agent with the requirements of their case. Usually, this led to a meeting with the case agent, his supervisor, and possibly the special agent in charge to see if the undercover agent was right for the job. If they thought you could do the job, you were then detailed to help with that case. This could last for a few days to a few years, depending on the case. It wasn't too long after I got put into the undercover pool that I got a call from the resident agent at the Coeur d'Alene office in Idaho."

"By 1984, we had pretty much rolled up Richard Butler and his neo-Nazi Aryan Nations organization," recalled Wayne Manis, a veteran agent and former Marine Corps officer, "but there were several splinter groups we were very much concerned with. One of them was the Order, a radical right-wing group bent on killing Jews and blacks. They were pretty far out there. They wanted to use acts of terror to force the United States to cede the five northwest states to the Order. To do this, they were into robberies, assassinations, and counterfeiting, and they were very well armed. Their founder and leader, Robert Matthews, was killed in a shoot-out and house fire on Whidbey Island, Washington, in late 1984. But his organization was still active in northern Idaho. We had a former member of the Order who was willing to testify against a number of individuals in the Order, and we were building a case against them. We also had an informant inside the Order who told us that group's security chief, Elden 'Bud' Cutler, was hatching a plan to kill our witness. In fact, he was looking for a professional hit man to do the job. Enter Tommy Norris.

"I told the bureau what I was looking for in the way of an undercover operative, and they sent me Tommy. He was perfect. The Order was a hardened bunch, and they were wary of undercover federal agents, so this was a dangerous assignment. In scruffy street clothes and that injury to the left side of his head, Tommy looked nothing like a fed. Our inside informant surfaced Tommy as a killer for hire, and he met with Cutler. Cutler not only wanted him to kill our witness, but he wanted his head, literally, so he could use the severed head as a tool to intimidate others who might want to testify against the Order. Tommy took the job, but obviously he couldn't deliver the head of our witness. So with some applied makeup and air-brushed doctoring of a photo, we created an image of the 'dead' witness—decapitated. Tommy met with Cutler in a motel room, showed him the photo, and demanded payment. Cutler paid him for the hit, and we video-recorded the payoff. Case closed. Again, it was a dangerous piece of work, but Tommy brought it off perfectly. Cutler didn't have a clue who he was dealing with."

Tom was only in northern Idaho and Coeur d'Alene a few times on short, in-and-out trips, but he fell in love with the country. While completing work in support of the trial of Cutler and members of the Order, he returned to Idaho and purchased a small ranch on Hayden Lake—not far from a ranch owned by Wayne Manis, the case agent for the Cutler operation. And with the takedown of the Order, stories began to circulate within the bureau of this one-eyed former Navy SEAL who worked undercover.

In addition to his investigative work and his undercover work while assigned to the Washington field office, Tom took on additional duties as a member of the office's SWAT element and later on as one of the founding members of the FBI's Hostage Rescue Team—the HRT. At the time of its formation in 1982, the FBI had a well-developed Special Weapons and Tactics Team (SWAT) capability in most of its larger field offices. And most major cities had a SWAT component within their law enforcement organizations. The HRT was founded under the guidance of the legendary special agent and deputy assistant director Danny Coulson. As its name would suggest, the HRT was brought in when there was a confrontation that involved hostages.

The HRT was a national response element with expertise in hostage negotiation and armed assault when hostages were at risk. The organization was formally certified in the fall of 1983 and was placed on standby for the 1984 summer Olympic Games in Los Angeles.

"There were two hundred applicants for the fifty operational billets," recalled Sandy Prouty, who also arrived at the HRT in 1982. "That first year there were four of us who were former Navy SEALs, a few Army veterans, and a whole bunch of Marines. It was a competitive undertaking for those first fifty billets with a challenging obstacle course, running, and shooting. And you had to have a good bureau record. Tom made the cut on his own merit with no problems during the selection process. He was made one of the first assault-team leaders. There was a six-month initial training period that was part training and part setting up the organization, as well as establishing hostage-rescue protocols and procedures. Then we went to work."

"From the beginning, the HRT duty was a part-time venture for us," Tom said of the start-up operation. "Since most of us were from the Washington field office, we were allowed to spend only half of our time with the HRT. The rest of the time we were in the office with our case loads. So it was not an altogether ideal setup. And we started from scratch with nothing. Under Danny's direction we built the training facilities and shoot houses, and set up training and certification procedures. Other than that, a lot of us were combat veterans with combat experience in Vietnam. The terrorism/counterterrorism business was pretty new to everyone, so we went to the military for guidance and expertise, and they were very helpful. By then both the Army and the Navy had dedicated special missions units that focused on the terrorist target. And both of them were very willing to share their knowledge with us. Neither had the evidentiary or the investigative constraints that we worked under, nor did they do much negotiating with bad guys with guns. But they did know how to conduct combat assault. The HRT supervisor knew the commander of the Army unit, and I knew the commanding officer and many of operators in the Navy unit.

"At first the military special missions units were a little standoffish," Tom recalls with a grin. "Their attitude was, 'This is something we can do. Just give us a call and we'll storm the building for you.' When we told them about the precautionary and measured restrictions of a law enforcement confrontation and engagement, they became a little less interested. And when we told them that after every shooting where there are wounded or fatalities, we turn in our guns for forensic examination, they really stepped back. 'We'll stick to pure combat,' they said, 'and you can have the domestic law enforcement–related operations.' Of course, there was the issue of the Posse Comitatus Act that prohibits the military from being used to enforce state laws, but that was another issue. They wanted no part of our restrictions. But we had a good working relationship with both Army and Navy special missions units, and we enjoyed ongoing cross-training with them. We came to know, like, and respect them, and they felt much the same about us. We had similar mission requirements but different rules of engagement and different areas of responsibilities. So it was a good fit."

"The first time I was with Tommy on a serious confrontation," Prouty recalled, "we were after a group of violent Puerto Rican separatists in San Juan. These were some seriously bad guys called Los Macheteros. They had killed a guard in a bank robbery and now they were holed up in a building, and we thought they had hostages. I was outside the building, and Tommy was inside the front door near a staircase with another HRT member. The leader of the Macheteros,

Filberto Ojeda Rios, and his wife were up on the second floor. Tommy and his teammate rounded the staircase and began to climb the stairs when they ran into a hail of machine gun fire. The shooting resulted in Tommy's teammate taking some cement fragments in the leg. Tommy grabbed him off the stairway. Then we went into a long period of negotiations. Finally, Rios's wife came down and surrendered, but Rios would not surrender. As Tommy stepped outside to call for tear gas, Rios came down the stairs with his submachine gun slung. Suddenly, he raised a concealed handgun. One of the agents inside shot the gun from his hand. It was a lucky shot for sure, but we were doing everything possible to take him alive. Tommy reacted instantly. With only a pistol, he raced back into the building and took Rios into custody. I'd heard from SEAL buddies that Tommy had no fear, and this incident confirmed it for me. He was going back in to take on a guy with an automatic weapon with just his pistol.

"Another issue with Tommy was his use of bureau vehicles," Sandy continued, shaking his head with a grin. "The exact number is not known, and he wrecked just one while I was his supervisor. With only one eye, he had problems with depth perception. He even wrecked a car in a car wash, or got it so tangled with the car-wash equipment that they had to call a wrecker. He was a brave and very capable agent, but when he got behind the wheel, look out. After he left the HRT and was working for Wayne Manis in Idaho, he was chasing a bad guy and drove a car into Lake Coeur d'Alene. Going into a cold, deep lake with a car is serious business; the water pressure won't allow you to open the doors. But Tommy just waited for the car to settle and the water level to rise to the roof, then rolled down the window and swam out. But you had to love the guy. He put a lot of bad guys in jail."

Following his time in the Navy, Charles "Sandy" Prouty enjoyed a long and active career. He earned his law degree at George Mason at night while working at the Washington field office. He was one of the early supervisory agents at the FBI's Hostage Rescue Team, leaving the HRT for FBI headquarters in Washington, D.C. Prouty was the special agent in charge of the Boston field office at the time of 9/11. He retired as the executive assistant director for Law Enforcement Services at the FBI.

Perhaps Tom's most important and notable undercover operation was the Sikh sting, an operation that ultimately thwarted an attempt on the life of Indian Prime Minister Rajiv Gandhi. The operation started in late 1984 when a man named Frank Camper contacted the Birmingham office of the FBI. Camper later met with Cecil Moses, the special agent in charge of the Birmingham, Alabama, field office. Camper ran a mercenary-type shooting school of sorts that trained military wannabes and amateur soldiers of fortune—those who wanted to think of themselves as mercenaries. He also sold them guns, ammunition, and field gear. Camper was something of a character and a good old southern boy who had an inborn dislike of federal agents.

"When we met with him, Frank Camper told us this amazing story," Moses recalled. "He stated right off that he didn't like me or any other federal agent, but that this was maybe something I ought to know about. A group of four Sikhs from India who were part of a radical Sikh separatist organization based in New Jersey were enrolled in Camper's school for mercenary training. They apparently were very well funded and they seemed to trust Camper. They had just come to him and asked him if he knew anyone with expertise constructing bombs—improvised explosive devices. They further told Camper that they were preparing to target and assassinate the prime minister of India. They wanted someone to help them with this and to teach them bomb-making skills so they could take that knowledge back to the Punjab area of India and conduct terrorist operations there. Camper told them he would see what he could do. Now this guy had come to us with this."

"We needed an undercover agent who could pose as a disaffected, ex-military type who knew about demolitions," said case agent Bob Sligh. "And one that didn't look like an FBI agent sheep-dipped to appear like some radical bomb maker. I'd met Tommy briefly while I was assigned to the Washington field office and I knew he worked undercover. We asked for Tommy, and they sent him down to us for an interview and a briefing of what we were up against. When Cecil met him he agreed with me; Tommy was perfect for the job. I knew he was a decorated Navy SEAL, and since he was with the HRT, we figured he could handle himself. Camper made the introductions, and Tommy fell right in with these Sikhs. They liked him and they immediately trusted him. They also wanted to know if he could get them C-4 explosives, automatic weapons, and false passports. Tommy told them 'no problem,' that he could do it all.

"The Sikhs had a compound on some land in Delaware County, Pennsylvania," Sligh continued, "near the Pennsylvania–New Jersey state line. They wanted Tommy up there to work with them. In addition to bomb-making skills and documents, they wanted him to train them in urban warfare and urban assassinations. There were some thirty to forty active members of this Sikh separatist organization. Most of them were here on student visas. Their leader was a New York–based Sikh named Lal Singh. Their primary objective was to assassinate Prime Minister Rajiv Gandhi when he arrived in New York in June 1985 for a state visit.

"The government of Prime Minister Gandhi [Rajiv Gandhi was the prime minister of India from 1984 through 1989] was very unpopular among the Sikhs in India. Sikh bodyguards who were supposed to be protecting his mother and predecessor, Indira Gandhi, were the ones who had killed *her*. Rajiv Gandhi had initiated a campaign of repression against the Sikh community in India, and now they were out to get him—while he was on American soil. With Tommy on the inside, the FBI was going to let the plan mature and arrest them prior to the PM's scheduled visit. But the Sikhs had other ideas."

"Bhajan Lal, a senior Indian official, was scheduled to be in New Orleans for a medical procedure ahead of the Gandhi visit," said Cecil Moses, picking up the story, "so the Sikhs decided to target him as well. Through connections to Frank Camper and confirmed by Tommy, the FBI learned that four armed Sikhs were on their way to New Orleans to kill Lal. Bureau agents, working with local law enforcement, intercepted the four armed assassins moments before they would have killed Bhajan Lal. With this plot thwarted, the bureau had to quickly decide what to do. Did this action to save Lal jeopardize the plan to take down the Sikh compound in Pennsylvania? Was Tom Norris blown and now at risk? They decided to move. A host of bureau agents descended on the compound, but the Sikhs were gone. They had scattered, but their plot to assassinate Rajiv Gandhi was foiled."

"Without Tommy's undercover work," reported Bob Sligh, "the prime minister of India, the world's largest democracy, might have been assassinated in the United States."

"The work of the bureau and Tommy's role in the case had national implications," recalled Cecil Moses. "At the time, we weren't on all that good of terms with the Indian government. Thwarting plans to kill Bhajan Lal and Prime Minister Gandhi gave President Reagan a chance to bolster our relations with the Indians. As for Frank Camper, that was another story. He was later arrested for his involvement in a firebombing out in California, and did prison time as a result of the conviction. It was after I retired that he came up for parole. I was happy to testify at his parole hearing and see him released. He was a crook, but he was also a patriot. I still get a Christmas card from him each year."

"We managed to convict Lal Singh in New York and the four would-be assassins in New Orleans," Sligh said. "All did time. Following the arrests, myself and two other agents were with Tommy in New Orleans preparing for the trial. We were at Pat O'Brien's in the French Quarter having dinner the night before our scheduled court appearances. One of the agents who was having a beer excused himself to use the restroom. While the rest of us were talking, the waiter cleared the table and also took the guy's beer. Well, he came back and said, 'Hey, where's my beer?' We explained our oversight, and he ordered another beer. We talked for a while longer and the same guy said, 'I'm going to make another head call. This time, keep an eye on my beer.' When he returned, he reached for his beer and jerked his hand back. 'What th' hell!' he shouts. Sitting on top of his beer glass, on a coaster, is Tommy's glass eye. 'Well,' Tommy says with a wry smile, 'you said you wanted us to keep an eye on your beer.' Tommy was not without a sense of humor."

"It was a busy time for me at the bureau during the mid- and late 1980s," Tom recalled. "I was busy with the HRT, and I still had a caseload at the Washington field office. And these undercover assignments, which I really liked, kept coming up. I'd settle in to work on my caseload, then I'd have to zip across the country for a hostage-taking or an undercover assignment. I liked working in the Washington office and I liked being with the HRT down in Quantico. There were great people to work with in both places. But I was looking for a chance to move out west and get closer to my property in Idaho. That came about when a long-term undercover assignment came up at the Salt Lake City field office. It meant I'd have to leave the HRT and relocate to Salt Lake. Even so, I was ready to return to more of the investigative work and full-time law enforcement.

"I was also looking to settle down and be in one place for a while. I'd been in the bureau for close to ten years and I loved the work, but that work involved working a lot of overtime and it came with a lot of travel. I was dating then, but I didn't have a steady girlfriend or one I was seeing for any extended period of time—not with my schedule. It was in the back of my mind that if I were ever to get married or start a family, maybe I ought to be in one place. But it seemed that the job always came first.

"The Salt Lake City office was working on a big case that involved the theft of government property on a large scale. Some of the theft was taking place on nearby Hill Air Force Base, but it was going on at other bases across the country too. The case strategy was to set up a seemingly legal entity that would serve as a fence for stolen military property. Then the bad guys would come to us, and we could let them build the case against themselves. Investigating theft on a military base is not as easy as it sounds. It's a closed world, and while there are procedures for custody and disposition of government property, there are also ways around the system for those on the inside. At Hill, they were stealing property that ranged from gas masks and body armor to surplus jet engines.

"We set up this pawn-shop-slash-fencing operation, and let it be known that we didn't ask a lot of questions regarding items brought in for sale. We set up a storefront and took in a lot of legal and routine merchandise that was resold to other legitimate outlets at a taxpayer's discount. For about six months, another agent and I were living the life of borderline-legal used-goods brokers. Pretty soon we were getting in pilfered military equipment and consumables. All of the transactions were carefully documented by hidden video and audio surveillance monitors. From time to time we'd travel to gun shows, where we would set up a booth and buy military equipment. This gave us a chance to mingle with the other buyers to determine if they had or purchased stolen government property.

"It was a great operation. We'd make a buy and document the transaction for use later in court. The operation proved to net a good many government-property theft rings, and ended up convicting and putting a lot of people in jail. It was very satisfying.

"While all this was going on, the special agent in charge of the Salt Lake City office asked me what I'd like to do after we wrapped this thing up. I said that I'd like a transfer up to the Coeur d'Alene office. I knew there was an opening up there in the office with Wayne Manis. He was responsible for the federal investigations across northern Idaho. He told me he thought I would be happier in Salt Lake, but he agreed to the Coeur d'Alene transfer. Shortly after the prosecution and trial work associated with the government thefts, I was on my way to the panhandle of Idaho. Coeur d'Alene is the Kootenai County seat and, with a population then of about 25,000, it was an Idaho metropolis. The office was only a half-hour drive from my ranch on Hayden Lake. After all the traveling, the moving, the undercover work, and all, I was finally home—home in the mountains of Idaho."

After a twenty-year career in the FBI, Tom Norris officially retired from the bureau and the Coeur d'Alene office in 1999. Tom's duties included the full range of federal investigative work, but he became best known in the FBI for his undercover work. Moving among criminals while posing as one of them takes a special kind of person—sort of like moving behind the lines through enemy territory in Vietnam. Here again, Tom seemed to have a knack for it. He saw duty as one of the first assault team leaders with the newly formed Hostage Rescue Team. Today, active and retired FBI agents tell stories of Tom Norris and his exploits in the bureau, just as Navy SEALs reminisce of his combat exploits in Vietnam. When asked about all this, Tom will often demur or try to change the subject. I know he's proud to have been a Navy SEAL and very proud to have earned the right to wear the Medal of Honor. But if you press him on the subject or ask him about the sum of his life, he will tell you, "I was very lucky to have had some great work both in the Navy and in the bureau, and some great people to work with."

At his retirement ceremony in Coeur d'Alene in late 1999, there was a large gathering. Representing the many present from the bureau were Wayne Manis, Sandy Prouty, and other former SEALs who became bureau agents. Several SEAL team commanding officers and command master chiefs were there in full-dress whites. Medal of Honor recipients Vice Admiral Jim Stockdale, Drew Dix, and Mike Thornton were there. Among the former SEALs, there was Ryan McCombie and Dick Couch. His brothers, Kenny and Jim, were present as well. There was a lot of good fun and gag gifts presented to Tom.

The one I like best came from a contingent of current and former members of the HRT. It seems that when Tom left the team and they were cleaning out his desk, they found one of his extra glass eyeballs that he left behind. The HRT agents had it painted, replacing the iris with the crest of the HRT. When they presented it to him, to much applause and no few shrieks from the ladies present, Tommy promptly popped out his prosthetic eye and popped in the HRT adorned replacement. He wore it for the rest of the evening.

AN EXCLUSIVE CLUB

In receiving the Medal of Honor, Tom Norris and Mike Thornton qualified to join an exclusive club, perhaps the most exclusive club in America—the Congressional Medal of Honor Society. The society was created on 14 August 1958 by legislation signed by President Dwight Eisenhower. The purpose of the organization, as spelled out in Chapter 33, Title 36, of the U.S. Code, is:

1. Creation of a bond of brotherhood and comradeship among all living recipients of the Medal of Honor.
2. Maintaining the memory and respect for those who had died receiving the Medal of Honor, as well as those living recipients who had since died.
3. Protection and preservation of the dignity and honor of the Medal of Honor at all times and on all occasions.
4. Protecting the name of the Medal of Honor as well as individual Medal of Honor recipients from exploitation.
5. Providing assistance and aid to needy Medal of Honor recipients, their spouses or widows, and their children.
6. Promoting patriotism and allegiance to the Government and Constitution of the United States.

7. To serve the United States in peace or war.

8. To promote and perpetuate the principles upon which
   our nation is founded.

9. To foster patriotism and inspire and stimulate our youth
   to become worthy citizens of our country.

At the invitation of Mike and Tommy, your narrator recently attended a Congressional Medal of Honor Foundation function in
Dallas, Texas, and it was indeed a privilege to be among warriors of
this caliber. But theirs is an organization of limited numbers, and that
number grows smaller each year. Attending this function were twenty-
one recipients. Since this same function a year ago, eight recipients
had passed on. At the time of this event, there were but a total of
seventy-nine still living. I spent the better part of an afternoon with
former Army Specialist Fourth Class Bob Patterson. The action for
which Bob received his award took place in December 1967, and he
was decorated by President Nixon in October 1969. Shortly there-
after, he attended his first Congressional Medal of Honor Society
gathering. "There were 305 of us there—mostly from World War II
but also a lot of guys from World War I—guys I thought old back
then, but who are my age now. Every year there are fewer of us, and
we view that as a good thing."

Regarding their numbers and their history, the society has a
realistic vision of itself; they see themselves in a depictive manner.
Their organization (from their own history) "is certainly one of the
most unique. Its small membership includes men of all races, social
classes and economic levels. They range in stature from five foot two
to six foot seven, in age from twenty-six to ninety-four, and they live
in all areas of our country. Among them are scholars and ordinary
men, successful entrepreneurs and struggling laborers, ministers and

misfits, the very rich to the very poor. No amount of money, power or influence can buy one's rite of passage to this exclusive circle, and unlike almost any other organization, this group's members hope that there will be NO MORE INDUCTEES. Beyond this attitude toward recruitment, about all they have in common is a passionate love for the United States of America and the distinct honor of wearing our Nation's highest award for military valor, The Medal of Honor."

"When I attended my first society meeting in the late 1970s," said Tom, "there were 185 of us present that day, mostly World War II guys. Now there are less than a hundred of us. It's a sad day when we lose a recipient, although there may come a day when there are none of us left."

"Twenty or thirty years from now, there will probably be only five or six," said Mike of the society's dwindling numbers. "But the few new guys who have just recently received their award are outstanding men—true warriors. I wish there were more of them, but I'm glad there are not. And the new inductees have a tougher go than we ever did. Unlike in our day, the pressure from the media, Hollywood, and other commercial interests to exploit these new recipients is unbelievable. They get calls every day from someone wanting to pay them to do this or show up at that corporate function wearing their medal. That's another thing that we here at the society are able to do for the new guys—help them with this sudden and newfound notoriety. God knows they earned it; now we old guys have to help them learn how to wear it."

Regarding these new recipients, the global war on terror and its attendant insurgent conflicts have now replaced the Korean War as having the highest percentage of medals presented posthumously. Again, this makes for fewer living recipients.

One particular aspect of the society that I found especially compelling is that this shrinking band of brothers, who have already given so much, are continuing to look for more and better ways to give back. The theme that I heard repeatedly from these genuine heroes is that the lessons of heroism in combat can be applied to all aspects of life— that being a good citizen and serving one's community is a heroic and noble enterprise. This extension of their physical courage to our daily lives is reflected in the stated values of their Congressional Medal of Honor Foundation. They are:

> COURAGE. We embrace the indomitable courage demonstrated by the recipients of America's highest military honor for valor as an ideal that should endure in all ways of life.

> SACRIFICE. We support sacrifice and service above self as principles that all Americans should strive for as citizens of a free and prosperous nation.

> PATRIOTISM. We promote love of country and are committed to support and defend the freedoms we enjoy as Americans.

> CITIZENSHIP. We believe that America's destiny lies in its youth and are committed to helping them become worthy citizens of our country in the belief that ordinary Americans have the potential to challenge fate and change the course of history.

INTEGRITY. We believe that the mark of a true hero is to have the moral courage to do what needs to be done because it is the right thing to do.

COMMITMENT. We steadfastly support the valiant men and women who serve their country in the same spirit of commitment and sacrifice as those who preceded them.

For additional information and for ways to become involved and to support the Congressional Medal of Honor Foundation, go to their Web site: www.cmohfoundation.org.

BURDENS AND BENEFITS OF CLUB MEMBERSHIP

"You know, it really is harder to wear the Medal than to earn the Medal," says Tom. "To begin with, you earn it by doing your job, and I really thought it was no more than that. I still do. But all of a sudden, you become an example to others. People—really fine people— look up to you. You become a representative of the highest award this country can give for a courageous action in combat. Suddenly you're on this pedestal and you have to realize that there are responsibilities that go with this honor—that you represent this award and all it stands for. And you have to realize that what you say and what you do are going to be closely judged. Most of us feel we wear the Medal for others—teammates and others in the military who have performed bravely or who have died in combat—people whose sacrifice has gone unrecognized or underrecognized. But that does not let you off the hook, because you personally are the guy who wears the Medal. Sometimes it's tough to wear it, it really is.

"We get asked to do a lot of things—more things than most of us really have time for. And sometimes we're asked to attend an event and made to feel—and this is unintentional—like we're being put on exhibit. It can be uncomfortable, at least for me. Or we're asked to speak about the action for which we received the Medal. I personally don't like to talk about the operation for which I was recognized, because I don't think it was anything special. It was a mission—the job for which I was trained for. I'd like to think I did a good job, but it was a job that any SEAL could have done." Tom pauses, looking for the right words. "I'm really just an average guy. But I was recognized for an action that I performed, and I have to live with that. On the positive side, being a recipient opens a lot of doors for you. One such door was that it permitted me to become a federal agent. And it allows you to have access to things and people that I never would have otherwise. Yet, I'm not any different from the guys I served with who didn't get the Medal.

"For me, an important benefit of being a recipient is that I get to meet and talk to a lot of schoolkids—grade school and high school kids. The same with veterans groups. I'd like to think that some of my experiences will help or inspire them to be a better student or a better citizen or to serve their country in some way. Sometimes years later, I get a letter from a parent saying, hey, my son or daughter listened to you and as a result, this is what they've done or this is how they succeeded. And I can tell you, there's no better feeling than to know you've made a difference in a young life."

For Mike, the Medal seems to have rested on his shoulders a little easier, but then Mike has much broader shoulders than Tommy. "I never thought much of medals and I don't think many of us did. We did our job, and when we fought, we fought for each other—the guys in your unit or on your team. What I was able to do for Tommy was the same as Tommy or any other SEAL would have done for me. Past that, I was blessed to serve with some great people, both in the teams as an enlisted sailor and as an officer after that. And I had some great mentors who helped me and guided me. I'd like to say they kept me out of trouble, but I've always been pretty good at getting into trouble. They kept me out of deeper trouble. It seems I've always had great people around me, looking out for me.

"But Tommy's right when he says it's easier to earn the Medal than to wear it. I'm still Mike Thornton and I'm a rowdy guy. I like to have fun, and I've been called on the carpet a few times for it. At Bob Kerrey's retirement ceremony from the U.S. Senate, the speaker was Admiral Elmo Zumwalt. Steve Frisk and Barry Enoch and some other SEALs who served with Bob in Vietnam were there as well. The admiral pointed to me and said, 'And then there's Mike Thornton, the only recipient who was called to admiral's mast [non-judicial review] five times and still received an honorable discharge from the Navy.' Well, Admiral Zumwalt should know; he was one of those admirals.

"To me, the Navy was about the fellowship and the love we feel for each other. That was very important to me. It still is. As for the Medal, we wear it for those who served with us who are no longer with us, or whose sacrifice and service went unnoticed. We wear it for all Americans who served with honor. And at times, it can be a burden, but that's the nature of receiving this distinguished award. None of us like being held up as an example for others. I sure don't, but it comes with the Medal. You not only have to live up to it, you have to grow into it.

"But with the Medal, you know you're in the company of greatness. I remember General Doolittle saying to me, 'Mike, welcome to the greatest organization and fraternity in the world,' and he was right. I met men like Jack Lucas, who joined the Marine Corps at the age of thirteen under his brother's name and became a recipient on Iwo Jima. There are generals and corporals, college graduates with Ph.D.s and high school dropouts, rich and poor. I'm truly honored to be in such company. I want to be worthy of their company. And I want to make my children, my stepson, and my grandchildren proud of me."

EPILOGUE

When I began this project with Tommy and Mike, I thought I knew these two guys reasonably well. I can certainly say that I know a lot more *about* them now—about their service to their nation and to their Navy, their exploits in combat, and their lives as they live them today. Yet I'm not sure I can say that I really *know* these men—what motivates them, what makes them tick. American heroes, for sure. They don't regard themselves as anything out of the ordinary, but, with respect to what they often say, they truly are heroes. One question that has been with me throughout this venture is: just how are they different from the rest of us?

Regarding their operational lives, back in the day as combat Navy SEALs, I've always known they were two very special men. I'd read the citations and we'd talked on occasion over the years about the two events that led to their awards. And their actions have been detailed in articles and in other books. Yet as I spent more time with Mike and Tommy, and we worked our way into the details of their operational SEAL tours, two things became apparent. The first is that what I'd previously known about the specific actions for which they were decorated did not do justice to their actual deeds. Clearly, both had performed "above and beyond" and at "great personal risk" on those occasions for which they received our nation's highest award. Not only were they incredibly heroic during those events, but they were almost superhuman—even by Navy SEAL metrics. My personal knowledge and combat experience only served as a prism for me to fully appreciate just how bravely they had conducted themselves. And while these two stand-alone actions were simply incredible, they were part of a pattern; they were consistent with how these two Navy SEALs approached extreme danger and their duty—how they saw that duty and how they responded.

The second issue is one of perception, and this is a topic on which a great many other SEALs and I have had numerous conversations. Bravery and courage under fire are often described as overcoming fear to complete the mission. So, are Tommy and Mike brave, or are they just two guys who were born without the fear gene? Both feel and have said on many occasions that any Navy SEAL put in that situation would have reacted in the same way—done the same thing. As a former Navy SEAL, I find that flattering. But when they say *any* SEAL would have done what they did, I have to pause. Certainly we all would like to think that had we been in their shoes we would have acted as courageously as they did. When it counted, Mike and Tommy came through—not once but many times. The rest of us will never know for sure—and never want to be put to such a test. So, are these two heroes brave men who faced down danger and physical risk to do what they did? Were they given the gift of valor? Or were they simply born fearless? That's one I've yet to answer to my own satisfaction.

•   •   •

My wife, Julia, always reads behind my writing and offers valuable perspective. After finishing the text, she offered: "There's no question that Mike and Tommy are very different men and that both are courageous. But I'd sure like to know more about their personal lives and their relationships." My answer to her is: so would I. I know more about these two guys than has gone into these pages, yet both are very closed when it comes to their personal lives. Both are semipublic figures and both are willing to share their past experiences and their current beliefs and value sets. Both are capable of inspiring others. When they are asked to address an audience of veterans or a group of wounded warriors, they can be compassionate and compelling. Tommy is a forceful presence in his modest, shy, straightforward manner. And Mike—well, Mike can be bigger than life and can more than fill up a room. Yet each in his own way connects with those around him, and each exudes sincerity and confidence. I've heard them speak many times, and each time, I'm moved. On the surface Mike is outgoing, gregarious, eloquent, and physically imposing. Tommy is quiet and understated. Yet both are powerful.

Mike has been married three times and has three ex-wives to show for it. Tommy has never married, although he has, by his admission, a wonderful woman whom he admires and with whom he shares his life. Mike lives large and believes that money is to be spent. Tom drives old pickup trucks and buys secondhand. Yet both are generous to a fault when it comes to the needs of others. If I were to pick up the phone and call either one and say I'm in trouble, they would be on the next plane. And not just for me but for others as well. Both are givers—to friends and to veteran-support organizations. But both are protective of their inner selves.

Sybil Stockdale, a truly heroic woman herself, is no stranger to heroes or Medal of Honor recipients. Yet she and her late husband, Vice Admiral Jim Stockdale, had a very special place in their hearts for Tom Norris and Mike Thornton. I once asked her about Tommy and Mike. "I've never known a more humble, polite, and nicer person than Tommy Norris," she said. "He's so easy to be around. There can be more than a little bluster about when we attend a Medal of Honor function. But there is little of that with Tommy. Mike can be a little rough and rowdy, but he can also be very considerate. One morning I came out for the paper and found him sleeping on my front porch swing. He's always welcome, but I had no idea what he was doing there or that he was even in town. 'I got in late last night,' he said. 'I didn't want to wake you or the admiral, so I slept out here.'"

"Tom Norris is a legend among Navy SEALs," says Gary Bonelli. Gary is the only SEAL to rise from seaman recruit through the ranks to rear admiral and served as the 9th Force Commander of Naval Special Warfare. Now retired, he chairs the board of the Navy SEAL Foundation. "Tommy epitomizes our SEAL ethos as fierce and relentless warrior, yet always humble and willing to help a teammate." Mike Thornton is perhaps best captured in a comment from Tom Boyhan, Mike's first platoon officer. Taking a quote from *The Emerald Mile* by Kevin Fedarko, he says of Mike, "His personality is large enough to generate its own weather."

Today both Mike and Tommy are very busy. Both are involved in the work of the Congressional Medal of Honor Society and Congressional Medal of Honor Foundation and their fund-raising events. Both actively support the Navy SEAL Foundation (www .Navysealfoundation.org) and make appearances for both. Mike serves on the board of the Naval Special Warfare Family Foundation (www.nswff.org). And they both find time to spend with wounded veterans of our recent conflicts.

Mike is active in charity work in and around the Houston area. He is active on the speakers circuit and can be found at www.mike -thornton.com. If an organization is looking for a powerful keynote address, Mike Thornton is your man. Tom is a rancher in northern Idaho. When not traveling in support of one worthy cause or another, he can be found fixing a tractor, putting up hay, or helping a mare with her foal. So in many ways they *are* like the rest of us— just two old guys looking to fill their days with meaningful work. Yet back in the day, when courage above and beyond was called for, they were not like the rest of us—they were so very much more. Today, just as that last day in October 1972 when they went into combat together, they remain two very different men. Yet in a great many ways, they are brothers of a rare and unique breed that sets them apart from all of us. They both know the Gift of Valor.

—Dick Couch
Ketchum, Idaho

INDEX